DATE DUE

T. WYATT WATKINS

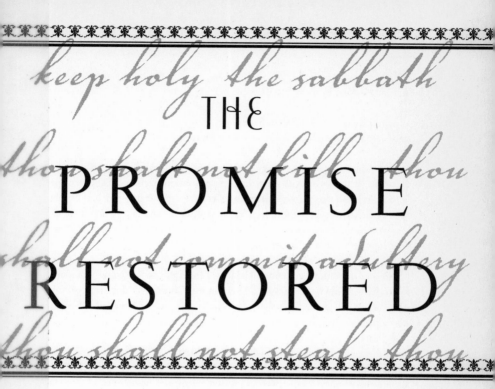

THE PROMISE RESTORED

REDISCOVERING THE TEN COMMANDMENTS IN AN UNCERTAIN WORLD

NEW WORLD LIBRARY
NOVATO, CALIFORNIA

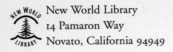
New World Library
14 Pamaron Way
Novato, California 94949

Copyright © 2002 by T. Wyatt Watkins

Front cover design by Mary Beth Salmon
Text design and typography by Tona Pearce Myers

Library of Congress Cataloging-in-Publication Data
Watkins, T. Wyatt.
 The promise restored : rediscovering the Ten Commandments in an
uncertain world / T. Wyatt Watkins.
     p.   cm.
Includes index.
 ISBN 1-57731-204-x (pbk. : alk. paper)
1. Ten commandments. I. Title.
BV4655 .W36 2002
241.5´2—dc21   2001008125

First Printing, March 2002
ISBN 1-57731-204-x
Printed in Canada on acid-free, partially recylced paper
Distributed to the trade by Publishers Group West

10 9 8 7 6 5 4 3 2 1

*To my children, Rachael, Rebecca, Sarah,
and Seth Watkins — grist for the writer's mill;
honey in their father's heart.
May the Ten Words dwell in you richly!*

Take comfort! What perishes not
is the everlasting law, by which
Flourish and bloom the lily and the rose.

— GOETHE

CONTENTS

ACKNOWLEDGMENTS

I have many to thank for much along the journey of this book. First, I am grateful to my wife, Donna, and my parents, Bedford and Eugenia Watkins, always the first to review my writing. Without the lengthy phone conversations with the latter, and the tolerance of my many fretful days and late nights of writing by the former, this manuscript would never have reached completion.

I am likewise indebted to my literary agent, Barbara Neighbors Deal, who believed in this project from its early stages and revived the flame of hope in me for its potential, and to George H. Tooze, colleague in ministry, who extended to me the grace of an introduction to Ms. Deal. Where would any of us be in life without such kindness? To Georgia A. Hughes, my superb editor and friend, and to the tremendous team of tireless book enthusiasts at New World Library, I offer deeply felt thanks.

To all who have shaped my understanding of the Ten Commandments, the Scriptures that contain them, and the message of divine grace they help bring to light, especially J. Gerald Janzen, I am eternally grateful. I am particularly indebted to D. Newell Williams, professor and friend, who reviewed the manuscript as it evolved and whose thought and example have spurred along my own view that the love and enjoyment of God are the end of life. Also, to my friend, the violinist Lawrence Shapiro, who was "instrumental" in shaping some of my connections between Sabbath rest and violin pedagogy, I express thanks.

Finally, I am grateful to the many members of my extended family who were unwittingly dragged into my narrative reflections on the contemporary meanings of these commands. Last, I say "thank you" to my four children, Rachael, Rebecca, Sarah, and Seth. Their wondrous lives are a daily source of both fascination and inspiration along my road to clarity about these Ten Words and their enduring power to lead us into loving relations with God and one another.

INTRODUCTION

THE GRACE OF LAW

You shall not lick an iron porch rail in subzero temperatures. If you do, your tongue will stick to it and freeze. Your mother will panic. She will boil water, and the punishment will exceed the crime. Once at liberty, you will be unable to talk about this to anyone for days. The silent suffering of it will drive you insane.

Our lives are fixed in limits, both descriptive and prescriptive. Some of these limits are as intractable as the past, shaping fundamentally life as we know it. Indeed, they are life, for without them we would surely die. We have a name for these limits. We call them natural law.

Natural laws are descriptive. They tell us how things are, quite apart from how we might wish them to be. My bones are law. They govern the limits of my bodily movement. Take them away and I am a jellyfish out of water, a heap of flesh with no get up and go. The law of bones is this: I need structure to leverage freedom. Without the imposition of limits, there is no real self-determination.

The law of gravity, on the other hand, adds weight to my decisions of movement. It also limits where my skeleton may get up and safely take me. If I manage to scale a mountain or tall building — but then slip — gravity will ask me to pay dearly. But without gravity, I am told, everything around me would be hopelessly hurled into space. Natural laws like these are tedious but good for me. In the bid to stay alive, such laws, it turns out, are actually grace defined!

Other laws are prescriptive. They tell how things ought to be. In particular, they prescribe behavioral limits in order to foster favorable relations not only among us humans, but between us and our world, even between us and our God. As to whether any one of these laws is human or God-given, views will differ. Either way, we follow them by choice, and they are subject to constant change and reinterpretation. A law considered good in one place and time may be wholly disagreeable in another. Unlike natural laws, these laws do not always require that we pay an immediate price when we break them. Thieves do not always get caught; murderers may go unpunished; lies are not always exposed. Yet their violation does have consequences. If these laws have been established for the sake of a collective trust, then with their every infraction that trust is broken. Relations with God, neighbor, and world suffer. Everyone pays. Life is diminished.

Almost from their first breath, children begin to knock heads with laws of all types. For instance, only once has a child of mine slipped on our spiral staircase. Eldest daughter Rachael caught herself only on the fifth step of her descent. She chipped a tooth but suffered no other long-term consequences. Yet she learned a life lesson of real gravity. Now she holds onto the banister and sees that her younger siblings do the same!

From the moment they can sit up and spy out upon their world, children begin as well the long and painful education in that other kind of law. They wrestle with expectations, choices, and consequences. They enter the lifelong battle of wills with other human beings. They struggle with questions of fairness and equality, and of mercy, grace, and forgiveness. Who they are becomes intimately connected with what they choose to do. Little wonder the human family takes its laws seriously.

> I am the Lord your God. . . . You will have
> no other gods before me.
>
> — EXODUS 20:2A, 3

In the history of the West, no code of conduct has been as pivotal and binding as the Ten Commandments. Though they stand alongside 600 other laws in the Jewish Book of the Covenant handed down at Sinai, they have always held first place among them. And although these Ten Words differ within the various traditions — Jewish, Catholic, Protestant — together they form one defining word for all who claim them. Surely this is due in part to the prominent place of God among them. Indeed, the whole covenantal code is predicated on a single notion: there is one God who alone is worthy of our trust and obedience. The first four commands (in their Protestant expression) concern exclusively Israel's relationship with God and, by extension, our own. The laws that follow, called neighbor laws, have no meaning independent of this basic premise: there is one God, one people, one covenant. For the Hebrew nomads wandering across the Sinai Peninsula, the giving of this law, too, was a grace and a blessing. In a place of chaos, it ordered their relations with God and one another. It girded them with hope.

The place of these laws in modern life is being hotly debated. Copies of the Ten Commandments are turning up in courtrooms and on the walls of county councils. Those responsible cite a growing secularism that only the principles associated with these commands can guard against. These same acts spark outcries from church-state separationists, who view each posting of the commands as one more tear in the fabric of the First Amendment's Establishment Clause and another (or a further) example of the politicizing of religion. Yet the United States House of Representatives itself voted recently to give the states the right to display the Decalogue in schools. Congress and the courts continue a long jurisdictional battle over the legal status of the Ten Commandments in American life.

Meanwhile, some of us are hoping to raise in these days of uncertainty children who are both morally grounded and intellectually independent. Like the Hebrews at Sinai, we want to know if these laws still offer an affirmative grace — or if they have become an irrelevant burden — to the challenge of faithful living. How can the Ten Commandments speak both again and afresh to our peculiar time? How may they continue to reveal the gracious presence of the God of all life who stands behind them? These are the questions that guide this book.

I

ULTIMATE ALLEGIANCE
YOU SHALL HAVE NO OTHER
GODS BEFORE ME

BEGINNINGS

Israel is a people made from nothing, ex nihilo in the Latin. They cross the Red Sea a mixed multitude of ex-slaves, bound only by their broken bonds. Yahweh says of them, I found you "like grapes in the wilderness. You were not a people, but I made you a people. . . ."

A newborn babe, to be exact. Crossing the sea is like a birth: the water breaks in two and a neonate passes into being. Once on dry land, the infant toddles through a forty-year desert to adulthood. Growing up here will be no cakewalk. But this child is chosen. She will set out in the sight of holiness. "I will have no other child before me," says God. It is a great given thing. No decision Israel can make will even come close.

It is an aloha morning on Oahu. Wakea, the Hawaiian Sky Father, has painted the heavens blue, throwing in a gentle bay breeze for good measure. Pele, volcanic goddess of fire and destruction, has been off on a neighboring island now for decades and more. Here, in the arm of the sea, all is the picture of peace.

It is also a Sunday, the Christian Sabbath. My family gathers to acknowledge the one our faith names True God. We will do so on the forecastle of a United States Navy guided missile cruiser, docked at Pearl Harbor. She is the USS *Port Royal,* our floating sanctuary. The *Port Royal* is swift, stalwart, and state-of-the-art. She boasts two combat helicopters whose mission is to engage and prosecute enemy submarines. My cousin, Lt. Comdr. John McLain, flies one of these. This is his ship, and we are proud of him.

But our real satisfaction this day lies elsewhere. While away at sea, Cousin John has become the father of a baby boy, Finn Lockerby McLain. Now safely ashore, John celebrates, and we with him. All gifts should be acknowledged — newborn babies themselves no less than rattles, bibs, and crib sheets. So we gather in gratitude to God for this unspeakable grace, and we add to that of Finn's parents our own pledge to guard this little one's welfare. I think of Moses, who floated among the bulrushes, cradled in a basket, safe from harm. He was a child of destiny, the hope of his people. Finn is likewise a child of promise. He, too, is cradled — on the deck of a navy warship, high above the waters of chaos and death.

The *Port Royal* is docked along the southeast loch of Pearl Harbor. We enter the naval reservation by way of the Admiral Nimitz Gate and head to the water. It is a proud approach. Naval vessels tower about us and dot the horizon. Our Pacific Fleet is a picture of readiness — a fact not to be taken lightly.

Indeed, all is as it was on a Sunday in December 1941. Out from our loch and across the harbor toward Ford Island lies the

USS *Arizona* Memorial. Just out of sight from us, it is a palpable presence at any distance. There, fifty-nine years ago, 1,177 crewmen went down in a heap of burning, twisted metal. Pearl Harbor ceased to be merely a place that day and became an event, one forever enshrined in the American psyche. "Remember Pearl Harbor!" And we do. We must. For all its calm, this is just one more dangerous day in a dangerous world.

TERRIBLE BENEFICENCE

They went three days in the wilderness and found
no water. When they came to Marah, they could
not drink the water of Marah because it was bitter.
That is why it was called Marah.... [Moses] cried
out to the LORD; and the LORD showed him a
piece of wood; he threw it into the water, and the
water became sweet.

— EXODUS 15:22B–23, 25A

Then the Lord said to Moses, "I am going to rain
bread from heaven for you, and each day people
shall go out and gather enough for that day."
... The house of Israel called it manna; it was like
coriander seed, white, and the taste of it was like
wafers made with honey.

— EXODUS 16:4A, 31

Israel's wilderness journey is racked by conflict and doubt. The desert is a harsh teacher. Enemies abound. Amalek wishes not to share the wilderness with a sea of hungry Hebrews, so the Amalekites choose war. And they suffer the consequences. "Write it in a book," God says. "There will be war with Amalek from generation to generation." "The Lord is my banner," Moses declares. Meanwhile, a more wary Israel roves on.

Sustenance is scarce. In Egypt, life was bitter — but the water wasn't. In Egypt there were fish and cucumbers, onions and garlic. "We sat by the fleshpots and ate our fill of bread," the people complain. "Did you bring us out of Egypt to kill us with thirst?" they ask. God and Moses agree: this is a stiff-necked people. "I should destroy them all," says God. Instead, they get manna and quails.

The Hebrews' dilemma is this: they seek God's face, for without it, they will surely die; yet Israel does not encounter the God of the Exodus on a sunny verandah, sipping lemonade. In the midst of perfect holiness, they may be smitten at any instant. In a wicked wilderness, life comes with this paradox — or not at all.

Moses said, "Show me your glory, I pray." And [God] said, "I will make all my goodness pass before you, and will proclaim before you the name, 'The Lord'; and I will be gracious to whom I will be gracious, and will show mercy on whom I will show mercy. But," he said, "you cannot see my face; for no one shall see me and live."

— EXODUS 33:18–20

We climb the gangplank and board the missile cruiser. Standing at ease on the gangway to greet us is my cousin John. He has abandoned his regimentals for the occasion. Today, he is all father and looks the part. He leads us up the vessel's starboard side to the forecastle. We pass the ship's refueling station, where thousands of gallons of oil are pumped into the ship's tanks, enough fuel to keep her cruising for weeks at a time. It takes the better part of a day just to fill them, for she is a hungry hulk, a city on the sea. At last we reach the open deck, where already the equatorial heat has come into play. A harbor breeze provides periodic relief, while the waters below us appear cool and inviting.

Now we pause to get our bearings. The forecastle is spacious, roughly the size of a large sanctuary. Deck rails frame our open-air cathedral, converging in the distance at the ship's stem. Occupying mid-deck is a single 5-inch gun, its barrel pointing into the sky. Facing aft, I glimpse the ship's giant superstructure. Against a sheer wall of metal, a low table has been draped with a white cloth. On it are a silver bowl and a leather-bound Bible. The bowl holds holy water, the Bible, holy words. This is our chancel. No screen demarcates the spot. No stained glass or altarpiece is in view. Only a large octagonal panel breaks the monotony of bare wall. This panel houses the sophisticated radar system, dubbed AN/SPY, lethal at our distance when activated. Turn it on, and we die. I can almost imagine we are the Hebrews in the tabernacle, hovering near the most holy place of God's presence, courting holiness and risking death at every instant.

Padded chairs have been placed in a long row across the front, but no one sits here. Instead, we stand starboard and port. Our nave is spoken for. It holds the missile bays of a vertical launching system. Each bay is itself a separate perch, ideal for cross-legged sitting. The children begin to climb on these, the best seats in the house. They move freely from bay to bay, peering at the pastor and priest who prepare our ceremony. The pastor is my Uncle Joe, a Presbyterian, retired. He has presided over many a sacred family rite. As an infant, I was baptized by his hand. Years later, he spoke words of union at my wedding. We recognize in his clear, strong voice the nearness of God. The priest serves the *Port Royal*. He is dressed in summer khakis and dons a billed cap with ship insignia. He defers graciously to my uncle, as to an elder. On this day, the traditions of Catholicism and Protestantism shake hands.

Intoxicated by the freedom of open-air worship, my son Seth bounds about the missile bays like a hop toad. Soon, atop missiles aimed heavenward, he will witness heaven itself swooping down to bless his baby cousin. Both are oblivious to the presence of unspeakable power. There is enough deadly force on this ship to sink a soul in terror. And yet, we feel strangely comforted. Here is a jeopardy we embrace. Benevolent peril, call it. Courted danger. It is the price of life apart from tyranny, a price we have agreed to pay. And it is not cheap.

> Then the cloud covered the tent of meeting, and
> the glory of the Lord filled the tabernacle. . . . The
> cloud of the Lord was on the tabernacle by day, and
> fire was in the cloud by night, before the eyes of all
> the house of Israel at each stage of their journey.
>
> — EXODUS 40:34, 38

ARIZONA

> By the rivers of Babylon — there we sat down
> and there we wept when we remembered Zion.
>
> — PSALM 137:1

"Is Yahweh among us or not?" This is the Hebrews' consistent cry. It is difficult to believe in God in the midst of an endless

desert. Their vexed question rings down through history, min-
gling with unanswered pleas of our own. It touches us here,
where once an endless sea of burning debris and death taxed
belief to the point of final denial.

The Israelites offered Yahweh a careful accounting of their
every woe. Even in their disillusionment, they kept in touch. We
prefer to barricade bad memories, to hold the pain at bay. Little
hurt gets out — but little help gets in. Now and then, some
great excellence runs the blockade. On a good day, we recognize
it as God.

❦   ❦   ❦

The congregation quiets as the priest brings words of welcome and invocation. But I scarcely hear them. My mind has
wandered a mile up the shore from the *Port Royal,* where the
North Halawa River fingers down into the harbor. Here, a
memorial visitors' center serves as the sole gateway to the
final resting place of a national monument: the USS *Arizona.*
We had toured this memorial, run by the National Park
Service, on the previous day, and it had marked me indelibly.
After viewing a short documentary about that fateful event,
pilgrims ferry across the harbor on a navy shuttle. By the end
of the film, I was struggling to hold back tears.

This is the response calculated by the Park Service. They
wish to educate my generation and all who did not experience that fearsome event and its aftermath. So they whip up
strong feeling, delivering us to the brink of despair — and I
am grateful. Somehow, this exercise helps to placate my guilt
for having lived out almost my entire adulthood in peace-
time. Sometimes raw sentiment alone can conjure an appreciation for the sacrifice of war.

From the visitors' center, we were shuttled to the memorial, lying along Battleship Row on the northeast tip of Ford Island. Directly across the island lies the USS *Utah*. It capsized near the legendary home of the goddess Kaahupahau, famed protector of residents of Oahu — from sharks, at least. She had no sway that day over Japanese bombers and torpedo planes. Single-purpose gods are as hit-and-miss as deck guns.

The memorial spans the midsection of the sunken *Arizona*. As our shuttle slowed on approach to a landing platform, our guide cautioned us to avoid loud speech or any hint of irreverence. The ship was a shrine, she informed us, a resting place of the dead. The building is itself like a vessel, a long, narrow, open-aired structure. It sags in the middle but "stands strong and vigorous at the ends," we were told, a symbol of "initial defeat and ultimate victory." But I had to strain to see victory here. I sensed only infamy, loss.

We stepped from the entry area into the memorial's sparsely furnished main hall. About us were no sacred emblems to intercede in our sorrow. No altars or crosses, candles or sepulchres. No eternal lights burning to infinity. We were left to assign our own symbols to the sadness of this place. But with each step I seemed to journey more deeply into the presence of holiness. "Remove your sandals, Moses, for you are treading on holy ground."

Yet, the openness of the place also provided room to run. Soon our children were darting from porthole to porthole, peering out at the rusted metal where it juts from the deep, as it has for half a century. They pointed and gawked at its sad disfigurement. We covered our eyes, soon abandoning all hope of conjuring from them a reverence beyond their knowing. And yet, perhaps they were the best symbols on site — a living, breathing vindication of the senseless robbery of a thousand futures. The winsome whirring of children above the ghost of a naval titan — what under heaven to better please the dead?

At length we found our way to the shrine room. Here, on a great marble tablet, were etched the names of all who lost their lives on the *Arizona*. With nowhere else to go, the pattering of feet stopped. A hush fell over us. Even our children grew strangely silent. Staring at the names, I became aware of breathing — that of those around me and my own. I could almost make out the beating of the hearts I love most. Yet soon, through the stillness, I began to hear the echo of battle — sirens, explosions, screams, the terrible din of dying. It had seemed somehow as if that noise were made for this silence, this silence for that noise.

Among the named, entombed below us, was my father's hometown friend, C. E. Hardin, Seaman, First Class — or Gene, as he was known. He was only nineteen when he left the little town of Monette, Arkansas, to make his mark in the navy. He had probably barely awakened when the armor-piercing bomb exploded over the forward ammunition magazine. Likely, he had been dreaming, perhaps of a love back home, the Monette girl he would make his bride. They would settle down, raise a family, grow gracefully old together. But a bomb blasted his dreams. In nine short minutes, all fond hopes sank to the bottom of the bay. Gene went down with them at nineteen, and nineteen he remains. My father shed an aged tear for him. He was a proud, only slightly embarrassed grandfather that day, while Gene will stay a teenager for eternity.

Our tour ended as the next wave of visitors pulled up to the dock. Climbing aboard the pontoon ferry, we glanced back at Battleship Row and took up a roll call of the states:

Nevada, West Virginia, Tennessee, Oklahoma, Maryland, California. One proud December day, these warships were the hope of the Pacific. All have long since been decommissioned, their great hulls as still as the placid waters that wash over Bombarded Battleship 39, the *Arizona.*

Meanwhile, we had worshipped. No words were spoken or rituals performed. There had been no divine evocations of any kind. Neither had we extolled the virtues of valor, strength, or shallow victory. But God was near, in the sheer pity of it.

Some have viewed Pearl Harbor as a lamentable yet glorious spark that ignited a nation's rise to world supremacy. I see it instead as a testament to the relentless march of time. Wars, nations, their idolized fallen — all are swept away, hurled from memory. They are false gods. Yet here, as in all places of ignominious end, the holy is at hand. It is above all in defeat that God comes to us, and in defeat that we flee home to God.

OF GRACE AND GRATITUDE

And when your children ask you, "What do you
mean by this observance?" you shall say, "It is the
passover sacrifice to the Lord, for he passed over
the houses of the Israelites in Egypt, when he
struck down the Egyptians but spared our houses."
And the people bowed down and worshipped.

— EXODUS 12:26–27

Back on the deck of the USS *Port Royal,* worship proper commences. We sing and pray and share a litany of thanksgiving. And we have much for which to be thankful. Rarely are a biological family and a worshipping congregation one and the same. Yet, assemblage for worship of God is a natural act for this family. It is a birthright. Failure to gather would be failure to be ourselves, a forfeiture of our identity as a community of memory. None of us pauses to think these things. We name them true in the doing of them. Baby Finn, already front and center, is now the chief attestation to this fact. On another day, in a not so far-off future, he will add to ours his formal profession of it. Yet by then, we imagine, his very life will already have long embraced the truth of this. As the child Israel early discovered, favor courts faithfulness, chosenness kindles choice.

For now, Finn is caught in the mystery of grace, in a showering of unbidden love. My uncle takes him into his sure arms. Together, pastor and priest pour living water over his unsuspecting head. Below us flows an endless sea of chaos, ancient place of unbeing, but here above, numbered droplets claim Finn for immortality.

My daughter Rachael, our first born, is watching these proceedings with wide-eyed interest. She was the first of my children to be baptized. Unlike Finn's, hers was a ritual of believer's immersion, the accepted mode of my chosen tradition. Here is the other side of things — not God's choice of us, but our choice of God. Having "no other gods" is our earnest response to God's undivided grace. Faith is gratitude seeking its source. Creeds aside, our Rachael appears to me as a window into the likely journey of baby Finn.

I flip the pages back several years to the time of Rachael's own baptism. Gone are the sultry sun and scorching heat. It is a frigid February day back in Indiana, far removed from any thoughts of tropical paradise. It has all begun with a question, interjected between sentences of a chapter I have been reading in a book about questions.

"When am I old enough to be baptized?"

The book, a systematic theology, has just posited that there are good and not so good questions, as well as very good and very bad questions, that we may ask of God and the world. The impertinent asker of this question is daughter Rachael. Hers is at once a very good and a very bad question, I decide. I close the book with my thumb in the page and look up to study her eyes. She is in earnest.

"Dad, I *do* want to be baptized!" She grows emphatic. "I'm ready!"

It would be simpler if she were inquiring along with other nine year olds about dating, wearing a bra, or babysitting for money. Instead, she is plunging into deeper waters than I care to tread. As a pastor, I have led discipleship classes into the mysteries of the Christian way, expounded upon the symbolism of Christian baptism, and celebrated the public faith professions of countless initiates. But I know Rachael through and through — the good and the bad, the greatly hopeful and deeply troubling. She and I are practically one person, it seems. To baptize my own daughter is nearly to baptize myself!

Now I dog-ear a page and lay the question book aside. We will talk this through without distraction. We will do it with her mother present. It is, after all, a question of Rachael's sense of ultimate belonging. If I foul this up, I'd like someone to help shoulder the blame. So we sit at the kitchen table, my wife Donna, Rachael, and I, sipping hot chocolate and emptying a box of Rachael's Girl Scout cookies.

"When did you decide you want to be baptized?" we ask. I already suspect the answer. The children of our church are always present at baptisms. We want them to see this ritual at work, because a tenet of our faith is that good news is catching. Indeed, they ogle over the act as if it were a spectator sport. Soon, they have signed up for their turn. Children have a natural fascination for water and a healthy craving for attention. At the sanctuary baptistery these twin attractions coincide.

Rachael confirms my suspicion outright. She has recently watched several older girls disappear into these mysterious waters. Their names were printed in the Sunday bulletin. Their parents lighted candles in the front of the sanctuary at the moment of plunging, to the rhapsodic swooning of the gathered. Once out of the water, the girls were helped into great terry cloth bathrobes, whisked away by an entourage of doting women, and adoringly primped for the close of worship, where they were awarded colorful certificates before the admiring throng, which rose to greet them at the final benediction. Like most of our rituals, Christian baptism thrives on pageantry. Why should our daughter be exempt from the pomp?

"So, what does baptism mean to you?" we continue. To you, ask Donna and I — children of the sixties, for whom personal experience is a prime category. We bequeath to Rachael this same freedom, that of an authentic response to an open-ended question. Rachael's will to work out the truth for herself, to interpret the categories and propositions being passed on to her daily as cold hard fact — this remains our first concern.

Rachael ponders for a moment, then begins to speak. She is a thoughtful child. We can quarrel with nothing we hear. To be baptized, she says, means "believing in God the way God believes in you, knowing Jesus loves you, saying you are sorry when you're wrong, and meaning it, caring for animals — yes, and people, too — knowing you belong, and (naturally) getting to share the bread and juice with your friends — yes, and other people, too."

The father's heart swells with pride. These are finer, more provocative answers than I can tease out of most adults.

"So, *why* do you believe in God, or believe that God loves you?"

Getting back to questions, this one is both a very good and a very bad one. It is unfair that I have asked it. It requires a level of reflection people from age nine to ninety struggle to attain. But Rachael has already accepted the question and is stirring it around like cold soup on the stove. At last she says, simply and decisively, "I guess I believe because you told me."

We take her point. We know much of what we know because someone has bothered to share it with us. Yet, some of what we are told is later proven false. Blacks are not inferior to whites, or women to men. Swearing is no worse for kids than for adults. And wars are not God's will. Just now, though, my mind settles on a subject more benign yet ubiquitous in the affairs of parenting, that great triumvirate of deception: Santa Claus, the Tooth Fairy, and the Easter Bunny.

Santa, of course, is the case in point on the whole matter of parental truth telling. What is the relationship, Donna and I ponder, between the baptism of faith in the living God and the great Santa myth? What is the price we pay for having nurtured these two systems of belief side by side? How can we expect children to give their lives to a God whose Son's best friend is a red-suited elf? What becomes of the Son when the elf is debunked as a fraud?

"There are some things we think you should know," we begin, "if you are serious about Christian baptism.... Things about, for instance, the Easter Bunny," we add, feeling deservedly silly.

"He's not *real?*" she asks.

"Well, we..."

"You're the Easter Bunny?" Rachael interrupts. "I *knew* it!"

"And, well, the Tooth Fairy..."

"What about the Tooth Fairy? She's not real *either? You're* the Tooth Fairy, too?"

We nod heads.

Rachael's mouth drops open. She is a sleuth, unraveling nine-year-old unsolved mysteries. She is thinking hard. These were secrets carefully guarded.

"But I know *Santa Claus* is real!" she utters at last. "I know *he* got me my American Girl doll. *No way* you would have paid for that!"

Yes, I recall having been a little miffed at Santa for hoarding all the gratitude for my daughter's most highly prized possession. After the expense of Samantha Doll, there was little left for Mom and Dad to lavish on their eldest child. Consumerism and Santa-ism have been in cahoots for decades. Our children are suffering from a malady once unheard of — the plague of plenitude. Many have more stuff than they have either time or brain power to channel appreciation for. The logical outcome is a gratitude deficit, a diminished capacity to feel or express thanks for life's blessings.

There is more at stake here than good manners. To lose interest in the Source of blessings is to be left with but the blessings themselves. It is a small step from here to the construction of gods out of things. Our children have grown expert at this, due in no small part to their many teachers. The promise of fulfillment through greedy acquisition is more than smart advertising; it is new religion. And in a day of unparalleled abundance, it is a small chink of silver away from inevitable.

Donna and I struggle to respond, but each passing second of silence is answer enough.

"You mean...?" Rachael controls the moment. By now she is wide-eyed, animated. The house of cards, elaborately built, is falling. What will be left standing when it crashes to the ground?

"Well, just *tell* me!" she pleads. "Was it you or was it Santa? I don't care. I just want to know who to thank!"

"Who to thank!" These are her very words. I savor them like sweet honey. *"Who to thank!"* Suddenly, my fears are allayed. Rachael's reliable framework of mythmaking is imploding around her, yet her chief concern lies not with the myth itself. Instead, she is taken up with the proper place to direct her gratitude. *"Who to thank!"* Our Rachael is no systematic theologian, but she reasons with a grateful heart. Thankfulness seeks a source of thanksgiving. It ultimately finds it, not in Samantha Dolls, or Santa Clauses, or even munificent moms and dads. Sooner or later, true thankfulness winds its way back home to God.

Satisfied, we rise to give Rachael an affectionate squeeze. I gaze wonderingly into her round, ripening eyes. We're finished here. But not quite.

"So, when *am* I old enough to be baptized?" Rachael asks once more.

"Last Christmas morning!" is my answer. The day we celebrated God's gift of love, and Rachael's old friend Santa brought Samantha Doll, and her heart beat in gratitude for both.

BUTTER AND GUNS

Israel casts a longing eye across the Jordan, into the land of Canaan. By the standards of the desert, it is verdant, inviting. There are cities that she did not build, houses filled with goods that she did not produce, vineyards and olive groves she did not plant. But this is her promised land. It is a pledge: the nations will be driven out of it, dispossessed.

Israel's power to possess this land is a terrible power. "The Lord your God is a great and awesome God," explains Moses, "a devouring fire." Might carries consequences. You shall walk in the ways of God, who loves the orphan, the widow, and the stranger. For you were a stranger in the land of Egypt. You shall fear the Lord your God; him alone shall you worship, for he is your praise. Israel learns early and well: loyalty to God and love of neighbor go hand in hand — but first she must have the land!

At last, our worship on deck draws to a close. Finn is again cradled in his mother's arms, his hallowed crown drying out on a soft towel. Soon, we will take a tour of the vessel and learn of its peerless power to repel destruction or, should the need arise, to deliver it.

Yet, we have still to share a tune of childhood, one with a text far removed from mortal combat: "Jesus loves me, this I know (and this we know by heart) for the Bible tells me so; little ones to him belong, they are weak but he is strong. . . ."

As children of God we sing it — here, where human might has reached its latest zenith. And we tippy-toe around these competing notions of power as around an unexploded shell.

After a final word of benediction, it is time to see the ship. Cousin John leads us along our way. He is a veritable

encyclopedia of facts, detailing the cruiser's heritage and
design, its engines and armaments. The *Port Royal*'s namesake
is the sound by that name along the South Carolina coast, celebrated site of various Revolutionary and Civil War campaigns. The original USS *Port Royal* was a wooden, side-wheel
gunboat that enjoyed a mere four-year existence. Stacking it up
against this vessel is like aiming a popgun at a ballistic missile.

We stop amidships to view the *Port Royal*'s crest and
shield. It reads like a catalogue of virtue: courage, sacrifice,
excellence, high ideals. But these are conveyed in symbol
only. The motto is just four words, blunt and to the point:
THE WILL TO WIN. And this, of course, is everything. In
war we play to win. In a summary of the ship's mission, the
verbiage of engagement is on display: "combat operations . . .
assault groups . . . engage the adversary . . . long-range attack."
At the heart of the shield, the tines of a trident represent
three theaters of battle in which the *Port Royal* is poised to
prevail: surface, subsurface, and air. In all earthly spheres,
she will "counter all current and projected threats."

"Counter," I repeat in my head. "To oppose, to check." This
vessel's posture is defensive. I find myself clinging to this: never
will our USS *Port Royal* launch an unprovoked attack on another
vessel. never will she engage in a dastardly first strike like Pearl
Harbor. It is a surprise to me how greatly I wish to draw out this
distinction. Our American military stance is nonaggressive. Its
mission is the avoidance of war, not the waging of war. My
nation has not made military might into a god.

That things are rarely so simple is a thought that comes
grudgingly. While we don't maintain a military to topple governments, we will do so and have done so to protect so-called
vital strategic interests. And though we are not in the habit of
taking the possessions of others at gunpoint, we regularly

deploy our military might to safeguard the steady flow of the world's depleting resources to our doorstep. Butter and guns, guns and butter — regardless of the order, these occur together.

The Israelites in the desert were provoked into battle with Amalek and waged a war of survival. Later, they willingly stormed the land of Canaan, slaughtering every man, woman, and child in their path. Both campaigns were carried out with a perceived blessing, even mandate, from God. *Holy war.* God promised a land flowing with milk and honey, but the promise was fulfilled at the point of a sword. When does war or even the threat of it become idolatry, something carried out for dehumanizing ends, diminishing all parties? The answer turns on butter as well as guns.

Words of a dear friend, a veteran of World War II, come to mind. "Remember Pearl Harbor" remains his mantra. But to these he has added, "I'll never forgive the Japanese. Not for what they did. Not for the way they did it!" This, one imagines, the Canaanite elders told their children after Israel conquered the land. Never forgive. Hope that when the opportunity for vengeance appears, you have the stronger god — or at least the stronger weaponry.

God knows the nation currently in possession of the strongest weaponry! Isolated acts of terror notwithstanding, none on earth could hope to catch *this* fleet flat-footed. Our butter is secure. But God help us if we fail the widows and orphans and strangers. Even here, in the triumph seat of butter and guns, all souls remain subject to the mercy seat of God.

NOAH'S ARK WITHOUT THE ANIMALS

The flood continued forty days on the earth; and
the waters increased, and bore up the ark, and it

> rose high above the earth. . . . And the waters swelled
> on the earth for one hundred fifty days. . . . Then
> [Noah] sent out the dove from him, to see if the
> waters had subsided from the face of the ground.
>
> — GENESIS 7:17, 24; 8:8

Along a narrow corridor of the *Port Royal*'s upper deck, we
get a glimpse of John's cabin. Even a commander's quarters
are cramped, spartan. He shares the small space with
another officer. Their quarters boast a small desk and a computer, but it is too confining for serious work. Instead, they
spend their days in the officers' lounge, working on laptops.
John has the cabin's upper bunk. I haven't thought seriously
about bunk beds since grade school, but these I study. They
are custom metal frame units, equipped with drawers, curtains, and reading lamps. Taped to John's ceiling is child's
art, the work of his older son Jack. John lies awake off duty
and stares up at Jack's handiwork as if at the stars in the
heavens.

As John tells this, I am reminded of a monk who has
taken holy orders. The room is his cell, his oath to serve this
ship is a religious vow. The ship itself is a floating monastery,
set apart from the wider world's madness. Or is a life lived
apart from the world the real madness? John confesses it
could drive anyone crazy. In matters of war and religion, the
jury is always out on sanity.

There are over four hundred naval personnel assigned to
this vessel, including many sailors. We do not visit their
quarters below decks. Undoubtedly they contain bunk beds
and house more than two to a cabin! Noah warehoused animals in the bowels of the ark. Over lonely seas, he trusted in
God. This he did with high purpose, though undoubtedly it

stank to high heaven down below. But lives were saved, leaving Noah smelling pretty. We and all the other animals of earth are grateful to him still. And I am grateful to John.

Now we head to the ship's stern and up the companionway to the poop deck. We are staring into a hangar, home to two combat helicopters. Both birds have migrated to a marine base hangar while the ship is at port. The space seems inadequate to accommodate a pair of such sizable crafts, but John informs us otherwise. The very stillness here causes me anxiety, and I feel like Goldilocks before the bears come home. Sometimes might speaks loudest in its absence. I wonder whether, in this truth, the power of God is not excluded.

Noah himself awaited a bird, I muse. He had let it loose to test God's promise of a dry-landed future. When the dove flew back with an olive leaf, Noah knew God had made peace with the world. When John's helos return, it will not be as doves, nor will they bear olive branches. Yet, for all our sakes, may they be suffered to wage peace and not war.

Looking down onto the rear deck, I spy a second 5-inch gun and vertical launching system. We have walked the ship's entire length. From stem to stern, we have considered her soundness and found her a marvel. And yet, the *Port Royal* remains an inanimate thing, a mere means to tenuous ends in a world of ephemeral methodologies.

AT THE END, WHERE IT ALL BEGAN

Before disembarking, we pose for a family photo. All told, there are thirty-nine of us present. We line up behind the missile bays, which number even more. But we are flesh and blood, soul and spirit, from my mother Eugenia Bowles

Watkins, the family matriarch, down to little Finn Lockerby McLain. Again, he captures center stage, as we scrunch together beneath squinting-bright sun. I wonder to myself what besides a photo Finn will take away from this day. The answer of course hinges on memory. Like Israel, we are a people steeped in recollection. As long as this story is told, it will continue to shape our habits and stir our souls. As long as the story begins with the Author of blessings, then we will live freely and avoid the slavery of false gods.

"Say 'Finn!'" shouts the photographer. And we do. But it is barely audible, for just then, a jet fighter comes in for a landing at Hickam Air Force Base, immediately to our south. For all the racket of this Sabbath morning, that jet takes the prize.

"The sound of freedom," someone remarks. We nod our heads in agreement, for surely that is what it is.

But another noise murmurs down at the decibel of every beating heart. It is a sound clearer and truer still, singing the deliverance of the human soul: "Be still and know that I am God."

2

CHASING IMAGES
YOU SHALL NOT MAKE
FOR YOURSELF AN IDOL

Chase: To run after; follow; pursue;
to ornament by engraving, embossing.

— WEBSTER'S NEW WORLD DICTIONARY

THE GOD OF NO PLACE

Now the Lord said to Abram, "Go from your country and your kindred and your father's house to the
land that I will show you." ... So Abram went...

— GENESIS 12:1, 4A

Then Moses ordered Israel to set out from the
Red Sea, and they went into the wilderness...

— EXODUS 15:22

*By the time of the Exodus, Egypt had ruled the Valley of
the Nile for nearly two millennia. Its citizenry were sedentary,
nestled in the towns and cities of the Nile Delta. Divided into
districts, they worshipped the gods of their fathers, yoked to*

23

separate sacred places — Re, god of the sun, centered at Heliopolis, Amon, god of wind, at Thebes, Isis, god of nature, at Memphis.

Deities were each distinctly portrayed. Re had the head of a hawk atop a human body; Osiris, god of the underworld, was depicted as a mummy; Isis wore a cow horn crown and sun disk. Images of the gods of Egypt were big, ubiquitous, and as fixed as columns of stone. One might argue they were the stones themselves.

The God of the Exodus, by contrast, was a deity of nomads, tied to no image and bound to no place. When Abraham, father of Hebrew faith, wandered from his homeland in the east, he strayed as well from the religion of ancient Mesopotamia, forming a covenant relationship with this unseen, unbound God. Once in Canaan, Abraham and his offspring wandered further, driven by the promise of a land of their own in some unknown, far-off future. At last, the descendants of Abraham settled in Egypt, having joined other nomadic groups in a peaceful migration to the delta. Here they sojourned for four hundred years, falling victim over time to the oppressive conscription policies of the Egyptians, in need of cheap labor for their massive building projects.

In their bondage, the book of Exodus reports, the Hebrews cried out to the God of their ancestors. And "the God of Abraham, the God of Isaac, and the God of Jacob" heard their cries and set them free. Suddenly, a band of Egyptian slaves was back on the trail of its forebears. For the first time in generations, the children of Abraham traveled again in the dusty wilderness, led by the unseen God, the God of no place, on a journey to a land long ago promised.

I usher my children out-of-doors and into the mild morning air with a sense of excitement. They each step onto the patio a bit uncertainly, bringing to mind that split-second hesitation on Christmas morning just before the mad dash to their stockings. But on this day in June, they scan the scene with a lingering hesitation.

Laid out on the picnic table are sheets of paper, pencils, and books containing whimsical images of animals and other unnamed characters of fancy. On the ground nearby lie four blocks of redwood, cut from a long 4 x 4 inch fence post. Each block of wood is 18 inches in length. On a nearby table is amassed a collection of carving tools, including small chisels and gouges, files and rasps. An assortment of sandpaper in varying degrees of coarseness is also there, as well as a sharpening stone.

We will get to all of these in time, but first things first. It is "art day" at the Watkins home, and while I have hinted at the design of this day, my children remain in the dark as to the ultimate shape it will take. I am uncertain as well — indeed, the mystery of it is half the idea. My children sit at the picnic table as I hold up for them a single block of redwood, marked off in three 6-inch sections. Soon, it will be cut and coaxed into images of faith and fancy. "Today," I tell them, "we're carving totem poles!"

Not far from our home is one of the finest museums of the art of the American West in the country. Two years earlier, our family had visited the museum as it was commissioning some professional carvers to create a 30-foot totem pole to be added to its permanent collection. The pole carving had itself become a live exhibit. The sheer scope of the project had left a deep impression on me. Dominating one wing of the museum was the largest, straightest chunk of cedar wood I had ever seen. More affecting still were the images these sculptors were carving artfully into the wood: birds with enormous beaks and massive wing spans, a bear with a salmon in its claws, a frog in descending posture as if prepared to leap from the pole at any moment. My interest kindled, I then began to explore these and other Native tribal symbols, to learn of their meanings and of those who created them. I had also resolved secretly that in the not-too-distant future we would try our hand at this craft on a humbler scale ourselves.

It has come as a great surprise to me to learn that the Native tribes of the northwest coastal United States, British Columbia, and Alaska alone were responsible for the totem poles we so admire. No other North American Indian tribes carved them. Why were West Coast tribes the sole totem pole carvers of North America? Some point to the giant cedars for the answer, noting that their straight trunks and soft wood made the discovery of carving almost inevitable. Looking out across our fence at an Indiana beech tree, its bark busy with the initials of long-ago lovers, leaves me luke-warm to this suggestion. My neighbor's beech is a carving tree if anything is. It's practically a totem pole itself. Still, western cedar is universally acknowledged as the best totem-carving wood around, a fact my children and I will rue as we begin to hew our way through redwood. Other authorities have suggested that Polynesian totems were carried by sea, washing up eventually on West Coast shores where North American Natives copied them. This 1,000-pound-message-in-a-bottle hypothesis appeals to me, affirming once again the cross-pollination of cultures as universal and boundless. Art and life are always intertwined more than we think. Cultures are distinct but never separate. The authoritative images of our lives, whether captured on the artist's canvas or the canvas of our dreams, are shared, fungible realities.

But there is a yet more compelling theory about West Coast totem poles that turns on the crucial meaning of the poles themselves. Nature was kind to the coastal Natives, providing an abundant supply of food year-round. Fish, fowl, caribou, bear — these and more made for a life of great plenty. Thus, the West Coast tribes stayed put. Unlike more nomadic tribes in the interior of North America, they expressed their beliefs in gods and spirits through art of greater permanence. And given the great abundance of resources enjoyed by these coastal Indians, carvers were free to practice their craft supported by the tribe.

Beyond the practical aspect of this lies a philosophical one: the less disturbed a culture is by adversity or diversity, the more fixed and codified become its core values, beliefs, and symbols. This is true especially in the realm of religion, where faint glimmers of truth harden over time into self-assured dogmas. The gods get set in concrete. Likenesses, whether of ancient fertility gods, Native American warrior spirits, or Christian icons, eventually cease merely to point to a reality; they become it. This is how images become idols.

And yet, graven images carry value, meaning, history. They can teach and inspire. A totem pole is a message board, a vividly rendered catalogue of value and virtue, publishing the identity of a family or clan for all to regard. One carver has aptly compared these poles that reach skyward to a sort of tribal library.

Totems, also called *phratries,* are the individual images arranged vertically on such a pole. These images come from the realms of earth, sky, and water — even from the land of the dead. Indeed, the phratries on a pole, while symbolizing tribal values and beliefs, are thought to connect directly to the spirit world. Carvers have claimed that to hew into the wood is to uncover hidden spirits and gradually bring them to life. The Italian sculptor Michelangelo is said to have thought something not unlike this about a slab of marble — that a finished form resided there already, awaiting the sculptor's chisel to reveal it. To gaze upon his statue of David in Florence or the *Pietà* at the Vatican in Rome is somehow to agree that an image is more than the stone or wood from which it is fashioned. It is to begin to imagine that the grain of the marble or the wood runs in the direction of truth, that carved symbols somehow participate in, perhaps even shape, the reality to which they point.

These are unwieldy thoughts for young children and I spare my brood of them. The purpose of totem carving in the Watkins clan is of a more modest order. My children will capture in wood something of who they are and what they most value. This is how I explain it, at least, as they flip through the pages of tribal phratries I have supplied. Now I leave them alone on the patio to ponder. After a while, I will come back and see what decisions they have made.

ALL IN A CHILD'S MIND

You shall not make for yourself an idol, whether
in the form of anything that is in heaven above,
or that is on the earth beneath, or that is in
the water under the earth. You shall not bow
down to them or worship them.

— EXODUS 20:4–5A

Try to succor my dead pictures and my fame;
Since foul I fare and painting is my shame.

— MICHELANGELO

The first sign of trouble is the patter of feet up the stairs to Seth's room and down again. Back out to the patio he flies, bearing a book of his own. I had been thinking of the tribal phratries of eagles, ravens, and bears. But Seth's cursory glances at these captivating images have sparked instead a rush to judgment. While these totems hold interest, Seth can do better. When I arrive back at the patio, he is already flipping full throttle through the pages of his most treasured possession in life: the official Pokemon trading card collectors' album.

Seth, one of our five-year-old twins and our only boy, is a peewee with attitude. He likes to stand at my side and jump repeatedly into the air, measuring how high he can reach his up-stretched arm. He yearns to grow into his older cousin's hand-me-down jeans. At night, Seth prays that he will wake up a giant.

Because Seth draws Pokemon characters constantly, I should have known that his phratries would each be pulled from the pages of Pokemon lore. Still, when I see them, I am aghast. Pokemon figures come in many types, each based on a different source of power — water, electricity, fire, nature, even psychic energy. The Pokemon phenomenon turns on a fanciful harnessing of these powers in the ongoing battle between good and evil. Other than this, I know nothing about the Pokemon figures, except that they have made the shareholders of their parent toy company, Hasbro, exceedingly rich.

Seth's three picks represent three distinct types of Pokemon power: Rhydon is a rhinoceros-like, rock-type

Pokemon, Abra, a mousy psychic type, and Growlithe, a canine fire Pokemon that also barks and bites in self-defense. Each power type trumps another. Electricity takes water, water takes fire, fire takes nature, and psychic power takes them all. I ask Seth why these three particular Pokemon, but I already know the answer. "Because they are powerful Pokemon!" In Seth's world, power is the currency of consequence. And while according to both Seth and the Pokemon ideal, power is to be harnessed for good in order to defeat evil, coercive and uncompromising power is the ultimate means of achieving this goal. It is power that brings harmony and works peace.

Recalling the days of rock-paper-scissors, I muse that the world has grown madly complicated since I was a lad of five. But I choose to honor Seth's chosen totems. There are lessons here about the nature of power, including its limits. Through a clairvoyant mouse, a dog in flames, and a rhino on steroids, Seth will explore some of these before this day is out.

Seth's sisters, meanwhile, have rushed ahead to their own images of virtue and greatness. The totem books lie shut to the side, but pencils are in motion. Seth's twin Sarah has chosen characters of already long-standing significance to her, those of the A. A. Milne story, *Winnie the Pooh*. She can sit for hours in front of the video screen, mesmerized by the quaint adventures of a stuffed bear and his nursery companions on the loose in the Hundred-Acre Wood. "All right," I play along, "which characters, and why?" "Pooh Bear," she answers, "'cause he's nice, and Piglet 'cause she's little — just like me!"

"Wait a minute," I stop her, "Piglet's a girl?" I had always thought Piglet was a male pig. Indeed, I had been certain the whole Pooh gang was male except Kanga, the kangaroo mother. Could I have been mistaken about this all these years? Sarah says she isn't sure, but she thinks so. Either way, it is a curious thing: Disney's Milne characters are surely among the most asexual creatures on film, yet we ascribe to them a gender anyway, filling in details according to our own identities. We do this with all our icons, of course — making them after our own image until the only truth they tell us is one about ourselves.

Already, I have begun to suppose that before long we will be referring to Sarah's as the "Pooh Pole." But this still leaves Sarah's third choice, and I brace myself as it comes. "Daddy," she says in that coy way of hers, "can I also have...a Barbie?" It is inevitable. In a family with three daughters there will always be at least one future fashion plate. But while I've mustered a tolerance for Pokemon and Pooh Bear, I'd like to draw the line at Barbies. Besides, I doubt a Barbie could be carved from wood.

"It just wouldn't look right, Sarah," I am about to say. But I stop myself. Instead I tell her, "Sure, Sarah! A Barbie doll will be fine!" There is something good here, I have concluded: a Barbie cut from a slab of redwood — a wooden, blockish, Pinocchio-like Barbie to stand in opposition to the cookie-cutter perfect, impossibly proportioned fable being turned out by the hundreds of thousands at Mattel even as I write. This tyranny of an ideal, superimposed on every little girl's fragile bodily image, will not be easily defeated. But at least today, in my own backyard, Sarah herself will carve out a counterimage and christen it "Barbie."

My eldest, Rachael, on the other hand, has been thinking things through like a good tribal citizen. She has quickly chosen two representatives from her pantheon of animal favorites: the owl and the panda. "The panda is for peace," she informs me. "They are peaceful animals. Trusting, too. The owl," she continues, "is for watchfulness. The Indians say that the owl sees what others don't, sees what's in your soul. They see when you have lied, so you cannot forget it." This is why my eldest scares me. Not yet a teenager, she is already plumbing greater depths than many adults I know. At moments, she seems to peer like an owl into my own soul.

But she is still a child, seeking her own identity, and so Rachael's third choice is curious but understandable. She plans to carve a portrait of herself.

"Yourself?" I ask.

"Sure. Why not?" she says. "It's my totem pole, right?"

The last to choose is my middle child Rebecca, and true to form, her three phratries top all the rest in controversy. First, like Rachael she decides on the panda. Rebecca's habit of copying her big sister at every turn is long-standing. She wants to have what Rachael has and to do what Rachael does at the precise moment Rachael has it or does it. Rachael balks at this, as usual. "She can't have a panda," I am told. "The panda's mine!" But Rebecca is in earnest. She loves pandas, too. "One person can't own a kind of animal!" Rebecca cries, followed by her favorite mantra, "Rachael can't tell me what to do!"

"Wait a minute," I break in. "I thought the panda stood for *peace!*"

Rachael pauses. "Well, if she does get the panda, then she can't put it on the very top like mine."

Rebecca knits her brow but goes along. For once, compromise has prevailed. In a world prone to hierarchy, to clear winners and losers, true peace means accommodation. Rebecca's point seems a good one, that the things of the earth belong to us all. But for the most part, hierarchy predominates. When it comes to tribal totem poles, this fact is on visual display. By custom, phratries or totems were arranged on poles from higher to lower positions depending on their status in the tribe — hence the phrase, "high (low) on the totem pole." Moreover, individual totems of animals were thought to be related by blood to specific families or clans. Clans might have their own rank within a particular Indian nation, represented by the clan totem symbolizing a particular virtue or attribute, and these were passed down from generation to generation. On a family pole, the totem of the wife's clan was invariably relegated to a lower position than that of her husband. Once again, hierarchies prevail.

I reflect on these things carefully. Pure egalitarianism is certainly a myth. Distinctions of habit and history are unavoidable. Life is full of valuations and judgments. But when such valuations are set in stone, they close the future, oppress possibility. Emblems of truth become cast in falsehood. This is another way that images become idols.

The debate is settled. Two of my daughters will have pandas. And the panda each one carves will be, like Rachael and Rebecca, as different from the other as night is from day. As Native carvers learned long ago, no two totems ever come out alike.

Rebecca's second choice is the figure of a leprechaun, that fairy of Irish lore you can rarely see and almost never catch. But now Rebecca will tie him to a fence post! Why in the summer, four months after St. Patrick's Day, she has thought of this I cannot fathom at first. But then I recall the crock of gold it is fabled such a fairy will find for you once you catch it. Rebecca possesses a bit of a leprechaun's deviousness, I remind myself. This phratry will be a caught leprechaun if ever there was one. "He will have a tall hat and a pipe," she says, "and lots of gold!"

Yet it is Rebecca's third choice that catches me utterly off guard. I have already begun to think ahead to the technical aspects of drawing and carving — which tasks my children can do on their own and which they'll need my help carrying out — when she announces the one possibility I have least prepared for. In a tone of solemnity, Rebecca informs me that, at the top of her pole, in the position of highest honor, she will carve God!

GODS THAT WILL GO

When the people saw that Moses delayed to come
down from the mountain, the people gathered
around Aaron, and said to him, "Come, make gods
for us, who shall go before us; as for this Moses,
the man who brought us up out of the land of
Egypt, we do not know what has become of him."
So all the people took off the gold rings from their
ears, and brought them to Aaron. He took the gold
from them, formed it in a mold, and cast an image
of a calf; and they said, "These are your gods, O
Israel, who brought you out of the land of Egypt!"

— EXODUS 32:1, 3, 4

When Israel reaches Mount Sinai, God calls Moses up into a cloud for forty days and nights, while the people remain below. Moses waits for six days just for God to speak. On the seventh day, God breaks the silence and proceeds to talk for what seems like an eternity.

Back down in the valley, the Israelites grow anxious. Talk of Moses' demise comes to dominate every waking hour. Though this drama has left little doubt that their Deliverer has been the unseen God, Moses has been the constant, palpable presence of the holy in their midst. The Israelites have looked to him both for comfort and in complaint. Through his voice, his rod, his physical presence, the people have been sustained. By his guidance, they have found their way. Now, with his loss, they are lost.

And so they remove their gold earrings and bring them to Aaron, who melts them down into the shape of a bull calf. The bull might represent fertility or victory in battle. Either way, it will bring consolation to those battling a death by attrition in a merciless wasteland.

At last, Moses descends the mountain bearing the Ten Commandments on stone tablets, only to find a scene of raucous worship around the image of a bull. "I threw it into the fire," a sheepish Aaron explains, "and out came this calf!" The story is funny, to be sure — but its final outcome is not. Moses breaks the commandments into pieces and melts the calf down to dust. This he mixes with water and serves to the Israelites for breakfast. Next, the tribe of Levi is commanded to draw swords and go through the camp, slaying the guilty. Three thousand are killed on that day, butchered for the image of a golden bull, and for their trouble the Levites are christened the priestly tribe of Israel. Those left standing, meanwhile, strip off their remaining jewelry and ornaments and do not wear them again.

The rationale for such rewards and punishments is dim. Is it the image of the calf itself? But even God commanded that a bronze image of a snake be fashioned in the wilderness to prevent death by snakebite. Even God instructed that twin cherubim should be hammered out of gold for use in the tabernacle. Or is it, instead, Israel's failure of nerve and abandonment of trust? Her falling back on a slab of shiny metal that cannot save? Her bowing down to an image unworthy of the image of God that Israel is only now beginning to discover in herself?

We will never reconcile the sheer carnage of this punishment with a spirit of tolerance and decency. But the lesson against placing ultimate trust in any image or thing, as if these were salvation, is a lesson we ignore at our own peril.

My children have begun to draw on a guideline poster board laid out in half-inch grid squares. While carvers of real totems use whole logs, squared posts such as ours will make it easier to transfer drawings from paper to wood.

With pencils, they trace out their shapes in each section — front view first, then the profile. Bounded by the dictates of both shape and proportion, this proves more difficult than they have imagined. Totem carvers claim to carve with their eyes as well as their hands, but our eyes can deceive us. I volunteer to attempt a sample drawing on the grid myself. "What are you going to draw?" Rachael asks. I stop to think, but Rachael quickly supplies her own answer. "Draw yourself!" she says. Perhaps Rachael wants me to pioneer her intriguing choice of a self-portrait. Or maybe she simply wants to know how her dad might appear on a block of redwood. Either way, I comply with her suggestion.

Drawing the front view is not so difficult. The resulting face, neck, and shoulders look not unlike me, though they could also easily pass for any of a million other dads. The profile is more of a challenge. Making each curve and feature line up, front and side, is awkward enough. But drawing my silhouette is like sketching a perfect stranger — the angle from nose to forehead that seems all wrong, the distance from the base of the nose to its tip that seems too long. I am working from memory as well as from a basic distaste for my image in contour. I rarely see my profile, of course, but each time I do it produces a fresh shock. It is that image of me that others see and carry in their mind's eye, an image about which I know little. This is truer still, I suppose, of our backsides, which makes the phrase "watch your back!" as ludicrous as it is ominous. I find it strange to consider that before the invention of the looking glass, people went their whole lives without a single clear glimpse of themselves. They relied on the descriptions of others, I suppose, like a blind man "watching" a sunset through verbal testimony.

I complete the front- and side-view drawings of myself on the grid paper and lean back to examine them. The whole thing reminds me of a mug shot.

"You look funny, Dad!" my children all concur. It is the first real agreement of the day.

I have always wondered what notables through the centuries have thought of their own likenesses on display: the pharaohs captured in stone, portraits of kings and popes and wealthy men of finance, tribal chiefs as totems on their own poles, holding the speaker stick, the emblem of highest prestige in the clan. Indeed, prestige, a sense of greatness, must be the primary motivation for such images, with a bid for immortality not far behind.

Part of the beauty of art, though, is that it can alter our appearance to our own liking. Not so a photograph. The camera doesn't lie, as they say. Little wonder there is a nearly universal abhorrence of personal photos. "That doesn't look like me at all — does it?" we ask hopefully.

The Jewish Talmud discourages the making of monuments *(nefashot)* to the righteous, "for their words are their memorial." Looking at my image on paper, thinking of it sculpted in wood and set in concrete, exposed to eyes and elements alike, I can readily accept this as sage advice. It is a good thing that there is no piece of wood left over for me.

My children continue to draw, guided by the patterns of Mattel and Disney and their own imaginations. Some of their totems are faces only. Others sprout arms and legs, which I help to coax back into the field of each phratry. Rhydon has horns and clawed feet. Piglet's ears look like leaves, and he (or she) has a flat snout shaped like a soft-cornered triangle. Many of the lines have to be greatly simplified for purposes of carving. My children chastise me for every alteration of their own lines, but in each case we reach an accord. Wood and tools, of course, will be the ultimate arbiters of detail.

Rachael works quickly, dispensing with her panda and owl copied from books in order to get going with her would-be tour de force: the self-portrait. It is a neck-up affair, taken from a recent photograph. Only her eyeglasses are omitted. She, too, struggles with her profile until I assist her, sketching in her outlines as she poses.

Now only Rebecca's phratries remain unfinished, and she has stopped, frozen in time like a totem. It is not the panda or leprechaun that have her stymied. Rachael has actually ended up drawing for her a panda identical to her own, and Rebecca's leprechaun looks ready to come to life. Rather, it is Rebecca's attempts at drawing God that have led to frustration.

"I know he must have a white beard like Santa," she says, "and big eyes, because he can see everything." But she can't seem to get the nose to her liking, or the cheeks, or the mouth. "I'm sure he's handsome, but I don't think this is," she offers preemptively, lifting up the page for me to see. I glance down at an image that resembles more a fish with a beard than any rendering of God I have known. "Do you think God would like it?" she asks.

I stare into her soft, plaintive eyes that can't quite manage just now to look into mine. At least God has been on her mind this morning. In fact, our children's degree of familiarity with God is quite a source of comfort to us. My wife Donna and I are glad that talk of God stirs in them feelings of warmth and assurance rather than fear. I marvel especially at their curious habit of praying not only *to* God but also, in the same breath, *for* God and Jesus, as if God and Jesus were just two more important people in their lives to be concerned about.

At this moment, I am myself assuming an attitude of prayer for my Rebecca and her sweet, sensitive spirit. She is seeking an assurance I am not qualified to give. I recall reading that Leonardo da Vinci spent years perfecting the face of Christ in his famous Last Supper fresco, painted on the refectory wall of the Santa Maria delle Grazie Monastery in Milan. Even the great master was nonplussed by the challenge of imaging the divine.

"I think it's very nice, Rebecca," I tell her, gently squaring God's jaw and straightening God's nose a bit. "I'm sure God would be pleased." And I don't doubt my words for a minute.

"I hope so," she says.

And now we are done. Soon, we will transfer their images to wood. Then, the real provocative work will commence.

FORM AND SUBSTANCE

You shall not bow down to (idols)
or worship them...

—— EXODUS 20:5A

And these sepulchral stones, so old and brown,
That pave with level flags their burial place,
Seem like the tablets of the Law, thrown down
And broken by Moses at the mountain's base.

—— HENRY WADSWORTH LONGFELLOW

Across the centuries, Jewish interpretations of the Second Commandment have taken many directions. To the specific question of just what sort of object constitutes an image or an idol, there are two primary responses. One view holds that images are in and of themselves idolatrous and thus forbidden. Many variations of this tenet have been advanced. Some have labeled all sculpted images as blasphemous; others prohibit only "built-up" three-dimensional images. Some condemn all portraits outright; others draw a distinction between profiles and frontal portraits, only the latter being prohibited.

The other view maintains a far narrower definition of a forbidden image: that fashioned by a Jew for the purpose of worship by another Jew. Beyond such blatant engagement in idolatry, Jewish art and sculpture are permissible. This view has at times predominated.

However, as Western art through the centuries grew increasingly Christian in character and evangelistic in purpose, Jewish opposition toward it heightened. Stricter readings of the Second Commandment followed, and the first view of images prevailed. There was one exception.

I am flipping through the pages of a compact volume of art photos. Each page is filled with vivid images, mostly carved in stone. Lions, dragons, sea creatures, human skeletons, serpents, suns and moons and signs of the zodiac — these figures and more are sculpted in elaborate detail on moss-covered, weather-worn gravestones. Even a vintage 1940s sedan sits atop a memorial in one of hundreds of Jewish cemeteries across Europe, in the former strongholds of Jewry.

The old centers of Ashkenazic and Sephardic Judaism are now long gone, but memories of their days of strength and prosperity are preserved through, of all things, graven images. From England to Russia, Spain to the West Indies, memorials to the lives of Jews have survived the ravages of war, holocaust, and time. They are sculpted and incised, cast, fired, and molded into art objects of permanence.

Chaim Potok asks poignantly, "Did our forefathers avoid images in life only to accept them in death?"

A Sephardic gravestone in Ouderkerk, the Netherlands, depicts Moses descending the mountain and bearing the Ten Commandments. It is rendered in white marble in the baroque style. Written on the tablets is the Second Commandment, for many Jews a prohibition against this very image itself!

At last it is time to begin carving. We have cut out the drawings from the guide paper and traced their outlines onto the wood posts, filling in the details as we go. Each totem pole has been fastened onto a sawhorse, leaving plenty of room for each child to maneuver around. Post by post, I have made large cuts from the children's totems myself, using a small handsaw and a fantail gouge. Their task is to do the shaping

and finishing. I have wooden mallets for the younger children, to avoid smashed fingers. While the twins and even
Rebecca are too young to do much serious carving, they have
been practicing with the tools on other wood while I rough-
cut their poles. They know to chisel and carve away from
themselves and to protect their fingers. Now, with mallets
and small-diameter gouges, they get to work.

Almost immediately, Rachael hits a snag. At her request,
I have left some bigger cuts for her to make. With a fantail
gouge and hammer, she chips away at the image of her own
face, suddenly taking a sizable chunk out of one of her
own cheeks. "Owie!" she yells. At first I think she has
injured herself. Tears stream down her face, suggesting that
she thinks so, too. She has a pained look, as if a deep layer
of her own face has been peeled away, never to be restored.
It is an existential moment, to be sure.

A recent experience leaps to mind. For a school project
on myths and fairy tales, Rachael had chosen to reenact for
her class the Greek adventure myth, Jason and the
Argonauts. In it, Jason of Iolchus sets sail for Colchus in
search of the Golden Fleece, aided by the goddess Hera.
According to one adaptation of the story, Hera speaks to
Jason through the ship *Argo*'s figurehead, carved as a beauti-
ful maiden. Rachael had built a copy of the *Argo* out of
Popsicle sticks, but she needed a female figurehead to attach
at the ship's stern, facing into the boat. She had sought out
her mother's advice. The goddess Hera should be pretty,
Rachael informed her, and about the size of a Barbie doll.
That was all Donna had needed to hear. Next thing I knew,
I was in the shop sawing an old unwanted Barbie doll in half.
But as my hacksaw cut deeper and deeper into her torso,
clamped tightly in a vice, I was stricken with a gnawing

sensation of guilt. I looked down at my own hands and suddenly recognized there the hands of a serial killer, engaged in one of a stream of gruesome crimes. I had to stop several times before finishing the deed. All the while, the Barbie maintained her vapid smile, unaffected by her tragic fate, until half of her perfect body fell in a pleasant thud to the floor. Though I appreciated the silliness of my concern over a lump of molded plastic, I could not shake the perception that my hacksaw and I had participated in something unspeakable that would require the secret disposal of body parts.

Only later did I realize that the Barbie's human form had caused this sensation. It was not as if this Barbie doll resembled any specific human being of my experience. But Barbies are fashioned in the form of a human being and carry that unique configuration of torso, hips, legs, arms, neck, and head that distinguishes us from all other creatures. It is the outline shared by every soul we love, and it is ours as well. Add to this the weight of religious teaching that we are created in the *imago Dei*, the very image of God, and the impact of the human form on the psyche is enormous. There is a singular sanctity to our bodily form, unexplainable yet irrefutable. To violate this form is somehow to violate ourselves.

I move to reassure my daughter: "It's okay. We can glue the wood back on and file down what we need to after it dries. She'll be fine." I say "she" as if Rachael's totem image were alive, and to Rachael, at this moment, it surely is.

The balance of the morning unfolds around the sawhorses. Then at noon we break for lunch. As we sit around the kitchen table, my children show me their carving wounds — small blisters and cuts on the palms and fingers of their hands. They count them up as every child must and

Seth wins, as boys will. He has seven sores in all. I have a few myself. "The wood's too hard!" they complain, and I concur. I should have tracked down some western cedar after all. Back on the patio with Band-Aids and gloves, my children start again. Progress is slow in the afternoon. My kids are tiring. I begin to rotate from pole to pole, doing much of the carving, chipping, and rasping myself. Fashioning totems, even simple ones, is hard work.

It is also disappointing. While I had not contemplated perfection, I had hoped we would at least carve recognizable figures. Yet much of the detail from our original drawings has failed to materialize. It is there in the wood somewhere, I am certain, but we have not found it. Still, we continue on to the end. Rasps and rifflers will gradually replace gouges and knives as we smooth our shapes and prepare for sanding.

I have done much of Sarah's work myself, transforming her post into the Pooh pole, with Pooh on the top, followed by Piglet, and Barbie at the base. Bear and pig are faintly recognizable, while Barbie, just as I had imagined, is not. Sarah has been swinging on the swing set for the last half-hour. Now I call her to inspect the finished product. I follow the movement of her eyes from the top of the pole all the way down. As they settle on the totem at the bottom, Sarah's smile sags into a frown.

"That's Barbie?" she asks.

"Yep," I tell her. "That's Barbie!"

Silence.

I take pity. "Tomorrow we can paint her, Sarah! Give her lipstick and blonde hair..." These aren't words I want to hear emanating from my own lips — I, Sarah's anti-Barbie dad. They come, unbidden. I know I do not control my children's images of beauty, that they will form these for themselves over time. Yet I worry over the influence of all that masquerades as beauty but is only veneer over plastic, hollow facade. False images of beauty have long altered destinies and poisoned souls. In such a world as this, what I wish most for Sarah is that she carry a sense of her own inherent loveliness. Today, I will shepherd along that sense by valuing what she values, even her wish for a lovely Barbie.

"She'll be very pretty," I tell her, "very pretty!"

Sarah smiles and nods her head, then rushes back to the swing set. I watch her go, bright and buoyant, and am struck by the thought that beneath her own image resides the highest beauty that could ever be.

Seth, too, has tired of totems — but not of Pokemon. All the carving has made him wistful for battle, and so he has amassed on the grass his collection of Pokemon figures as well as some plastic dinosaurs and conscripted them in all-out war. His totem pole, meanwhile, remains a partially carved affair. I examine his three Pokemon phratries — Rhydon, whose horns need sharpening, Abra, whose large feet remain buried in wood, and Growlithe, whose splintered snout looks like roadkill. They seem far removed from the sources of power that had caused my son to choose them.

"Are you done here, Seth?" I ask, interrupting him in the pitch of battle. Seth comes to my side and takes a hard look at his handiwork. "Maybe I'll do more later," he says, but he won't, which is fine by me. I'm already getting used to his figures just as they are.

I think of Michelangelo's unfinished sculptures dubbed *The Prisoners,* a series of statues ordered by Pope Julius II for his own tomb. Julius had died before they could be finished, and the commission was canceled. Thus, the figures have remained in their unfinished state, trapped through the centuries in their own blocks of stone. Hewn in the muscular poses of the Italian Renaissance, they press against the rock but never burst free. They were intended to signify papal victory over the world. Now they stand as monuments to the strain and struggle of existence. I see in Seth's Pokemon phratries a similar message about the limits of all earthly power, ever both tenuous and temporary.

Taking a knife, I carve the eyes into all three figures, and they seem to awaken from sleep — even Abra, whose eyes are only slits, squint with a new awareness. Though inanimate objects, they now at least can look out upon the world of the living. And we'll look back at them and be glad that, though frail, we at least are alive.

In Rachael and Rebecca, I am producing two serious carvers, though their approaches to the wood are quite different. Rachael is meticulous, taking great care over every surface of wood. In the early afternoon, she discovered the wood rasp and hasn't looked back. Even the chunk of cheek chiseled from her own image has long since been glued and clamped fast, and she has slowly rounded it into shape.

Rebecca, on the other hand, is a free spirit in the possession of cutting tools who seems simply to enjoy pounding chisels into wood with mallets. She has discovered many ways to chip into the grain — wherever it is! I recall that as a young child she didn't enjoy coloring in the lines, either.

I take up a rasp and begin to smooth the surfaces on Rebecca's pole — the leprechaun's hat and big bag of gold, her giant panda's round ears, bearlike nose, and sad eyes. When I get to her totem of God, I pause. There is a face here somewhere, I think.

"So, how did it go with God, Rebecca?" I ask.

"Well, not like I thought," she says, "but I guess I don't really know what God looks like anyway."

I nod in agreement. "I guess no one does, Rebecca."

I recall those Jewish voices of opposition to the making of all images for whatever purpose, especially of God. I also reflect in a new light on the inherent difficulty in my own Christian tradition with the exclusive identification of God with one Hebrew man in first-century Palestine. Hasn't this identification fed the human hunger for absolute knowledge of God? Doesn't it explain in part the struggle of women in the church — this image of God as wholly, identifiably male? Or the struggle of those of African descent with the false presumption that Jesus (and hence God) is a light-skinned European? Or that of Native Americans over this God from half a world away who brought to these shores disinheritance and disease? Of course, all followers of Christ have freely recast this image into a counterimage of their liking — denying the Jewishness of Jesus, making him European, African, Asian, Latino, Aryan, or a revolutionary, or a Young Republican. And yet, Jesus remains a first-century Jewish rabbi. If God's image is bound up exclusively with Jesus, then all variant views are wishful thinking, self-portraits of deluded worshippers. Nothing more.

I look once again at Rebecca's image of God. It is inscrutable, arcane, a study in jagged unevenness. The longer I look, the more hints of recognizable features I think I see and the greater my confusion grows. Rarely in my experience has confusion spoken greater truth.

"Well, I like your sculpture of God, Rebecca!" I tell her. And I leave it just as it is — just as it has always been.

Now, for better or worse, we are finished. Some final

shaping and sanding is in order, but that can wait for tomorrow. Then, we will paint, nail the poles to firm bases, and celebrate.

IN A WORLD OF IMAGES

... for I the Lord your God am a jealous God,
punishing children for the iniquity of parents, to
the third and the fourth generation of those
who reject me, but showing steadfast love to the
thousandth generation of those who love me
and keep my commandments.

— EXODUS 20:5B–6

Perched high in the Hindu Kush Mountains west of Kabul is a giant alcove hewn into solid rock. It brings to mind a recessed crypt into which an Egyptian sarcophagus might be placed upright. Rubble fills the opening's base and spills out onto the path like the remains of an avalanche. This heap of rock is all that survives of a 175-foot Buddha in Bamian, Afghanistan. It was demolished by decree of the ruling Taliban regime, along with thousands of open-air statues and museum relics. Taliban leader Mullah Mohammed Omar, self-declared "king of the Muslims," had pronounced this tallest of Buddhas in the world an affront to Islam's absolute prohibition against idols. No depiction of the human form can be considered true art by the pious, he had claimed.

The Taliban action was almost universally condemned in the Muslim world. In the view of many Islamic scholars, the Taliban's extreme brand of fundamentalism takes holy teachings too literally — the same accusation leveled against fundamentalisms of every religious persuasion! When Muslims conquered Egypt shortly after Muhammad's lifetime, they point out, pre-Islamic statuary was for the most part spared. Hence, ancient tributes to the likes of Isis and Osiris still draw curious sightseers from all over the world. But no longer are there Buddhas in Afghanistan. Maybe the Taliban will crush and flatten the rocks into a road stretching back to civilization. But one wonders, just what order of civilization would that be?

A photograph of the same scene prior to the rise of the Taliban reveals a Buddha that is chipped and windblown but unmoved over centuries. This Buddha was carved at the time of Christ. Would it have stood so long in the Christian West?

Arnold Schwartzman writes that the ramparts of Furth, Germany, were built from Jewish tombstones after the expulsion of all Jews from the city.[1] Jews were walled out by the very memories of their ancestors — or were the Christians walled in by them?

Ironically, it is idolatry itself that makes it impossible for us to tolerate difference. The Taliban, like fundamentalists of every stripe, condemn the images of others while missing the corrupting power of their own. These may be visible to the eye or not. They may be nothing more than mental pictures of conquering glory or the vision of a pure, purged society. "Idolatry," meanwhile, becomes the charge idolaters level against others in order to justify themselves.

It is Sunday afternoon. Back on our patio, art class has again been in session, but this time Donna has been the instructor. Every project needs a saving grace, and in the case of our redwood totems this has been paint. With Donna's expert

---

[1] Arnold Schwartzman, *Graven Images: Graphic Motifs of the Jewish Gravestone* (New York: Abrams), 1993.

eye and words of encouragement, the children have brought their phratries to vivid, colorful life. The giant panda's black and white, the leprechaun's green and gold, Pooh's brown and Piglet's pink — all have conspired to create order out of our carving chaos.

I had risen early to file and sand things smoother and to affix each totem pole to an 8 x 8 inch base. After church, our children had changed hastily into painting clothes and set to work. Now they are finished and the paint is nearly dry. It is time to celebrate.

We sit on patio chairs in a semicircle, facing the picnic table where all four totem poles stretch in a line. We are holding our family version of the potlatch ceremony, a Native American tribal celebration marking the completion of an important totem pole. These are my children's poles. They qualify for a potlatch if any do!

The children come to the front one at a time, holding up their totem poles for us to examine and telling the story of each phratry. Seth leads off. He lifts his pole high in the air, a great grin across his face. "These are three powerful Pokemon," he begins. But then he sizes them up with greater care. Even freshly painted they look as if they've lost their last battle. "Well," he says, "they were *supposed* to be three powerful Pokemon. But I guess they got beat. Actually, though, they were brave Pokemon, and that's what matters. I like my totem pole because my Pokemon tried hard, and you should always try hard!" It occurs to me to mention that, in this project, Seth might have tried harder himself, but I don't. Seth's revised views of value and worth are ones I am heartened to hear. From now on, this will be known as the totem of brave Pokemon. Seth takes his seat.

Sarah stands before us next, proud as punch of her Pooh

and Piglet pair. Simple cartoon figures do well in wood, it turns out. Few lines, no fuss. Then Sarah comes to her beloved Barbie — blond hair, blue eyes, red lips, and all. "She's not so pretty for a Barbie," Sarah says, "but I made her, and I love her, and she's mine!" And once again, I'm delighted that Sarah is *mine*. Through her experience with this image, and without a word from us, she has put outward appearance in its place — outward! Lasting beauty, meanwhile, she has located elsewhere, deep in the heart. Sarah sits down, satisfied.

Now Rachael steps forward and holds her totem. She starts at the top and works her way down. The great panda and owl have gone well. Especially with paint, their shapes are unmistakable. And since we did not carve the owl's feathers as real artisans do, Donna has helped Rachael to paint them on instead, in row after row of horseshoe curves, resembling a knight's mail.

"And this is me," she says, pointing now to the bottom phratry, to the sculpture of herself. "Except, she doesn't really look like me, I guess — does she?" Rachael asks, then waits for an answer. Donna weighs in at last: "She's great — you're just much prettier!"

Rachael ponders. "Maybe it's good she looks different. If she looked too much like me, I think I'd freak out."

"You know, like she was real or something. But I know there's only one me," she continues, "and I like it that way."

It is so: Rachael's being, like every other, is unique and thereby infinitely precious, even irreplaceable. But her words betray our human habit of assigning a power to images and symbols, especially those closely associated with our own lives. By choosing to carve an image of herself, Rachael has looked this tendency literally in the face. She has drawn a distinction in value that many never manage. Symbols, however potent or vivid, have no meaning apart from that which we assign them. They may be pressed into the service of good or evil. They are mirrors of human action and intention — nothing more, nothing less.

Rebecca is the last to take her turn. Gently, she lifts her totem pole, then gazes out at us with her usual solemnity.

"Well, this is my panda," she begins. I regard an image that my middle daughter has painted with uncharacteristic care. "And it came out a lot like Rachael's," she adds. Rachael winces. But for Rebecca, this is a precious link with a big sister who often seems aloof and unapproachable. Now my two eldest daughters are connected by a visible symbol — a lovable animal that stands for peace and harmony, as Rachael has said herself.

Rebecca's leprechaun is a mass of green, although the eyes sparkle gold, thanks to metallic paint. This brings to its otherwise sorry countenance the aura of life and the hint of mischief. Rebecca points to his feet. "He's got gold," she says. "Lots of it."

Now her eyes settle on the top of the totem pole, on a stark figure of unpainted wood. No paintbrush has touched its perplexing form. "I didn't know how to paint this one," she explains. "Then, I decided God didn't need any paint. I decided just to let God be the color that God wants to be."

Here is grace and wisdom wrapped in innocence. Of course, God's name itself has said it: Yahweh — "I will be who I will be" — God as freedom, bound only by love. But coming from the lips of babes, such realizations strike an especially resonant chord.

Rebecca sits down, and our experiment with totem carving ends. At moments, I had questioned the wisdom of this endeavor, but now all misgivings are laid to rest. It is a wonder: my children have sculpted images while shunning idolatry in the process. By wrestling with the images of their own lives, they have learned lessons about themselves. They have also instructed their father, for I have wrestled through- out my life with these very idols: physical beauty, power, self-image, even the desire to pin down the holy, to make it into a thing possessed. Through their simple discoveries, I have come to comprehend with a new clarity that it is not images that make idols; idols take shape in our minds when- ever we confuse limited things with final truth.

In the Sinai wilderness, Israel hid her images in fear, but they were not forgotten. Idolatry in various forms would remain Israel's single greatest temptation. The Second Commandment ends with the ominous threat of punish- ment for idolatry, "to the third and fourth generation..." This is a heartless response on the part of a loving God, one is inclined to think. Yet in a world of mutual influence, we all experience the far-reaching consequences of the actions of others — the codependencies of substance abuse, the results of a violent upbringing, the tyrannies of religious fanaticism.

But better news follows. God is also a God of "steadfast love to the *thousandth* generation." To take seriously the interconnectedness of all things is to be not only discour- aged but heartened. I do not presume to have conquered my idols, yet neither have they conquered me. And in some small way, at least, our children's gift for discerning images reflects their parents' faith in the God unbounded by either name or place — Yahweh: "I will be who I will be."

Our four family totem poles are slated to perch in a garden by our back fence. Over time, they will undoubtedly suffer from both the elements and benign neglect. My children will abandon their current symbols of meaning and value in favor of new ones. Already, I read, Pokemon are on the wane in popularity. Hasbro has reported a sales slump in Pokemon trading cards. To me this is not unwelcome news, but it was at any rate inevitable. Every image is at best a partial, temporary embodiment of meaning. None can satisfy the final yearnings of our souls. These live down inside of us where "deep calls to deep," as the Psalmist says, and where God draws too near for mere eyes to behold.

Meanwhile, the holiest images I know are the lives of children like my own, steadily tracing the true shapes of beauty and goodness, awakening to their destinies as carved in the image of God.

For the cloud of the Lord was on the tabernacle
by day, and fire was in the cloud by night,
before the eyes of all the house of Israel
at each stage of their journey.

— EXODUS 40:38

3

PROPER NAMING

YOU SHALL NOT TAKE THE NAME
OF THE LORD YOUR GOD IN VAIN

NAME GAME

God called to [Moses] out of the bush,
"Moses, Moses! . . . I am the God of your father,
the God of Abraham, the God of Isaac,
and the God of Jacob." And Moses hid his face,
for he was afraid to look at God.

— EXODUS 3:4, 6

Let us speak plain: there is more force in names
than most men dream of.

— JAMES RUSSELL LOWELL

*Long before Moses meets Yahweh on the mountain in a bush
that does not burn (Exod. 3:1, 2), the Hebrews already knew
God by many names. When Abraham journeyed to Canaan
from Mesopotamia, he brought with him the divine name,
Shaddai, "the Mountain One" (Gen. 17:1, 23:3, 43:14). During
their sojourn there, the patriarchs Abraham, Isaac, and Jacob
became acquainted with the chief deity of Canaanite religion,
El, the "Mighty One." El was worshipped in holy places*

throughout Canaan — as El Bethel at Bethel, El Elyon at Jerusalem, and El Olam at Beersheba. In time, the patriarchs came to worship God as El Shaddai, "God Almighty" (Gen. 17:1; Exod. 6:2, 3). Names for God were mingled like streams merging into a mighty river.

Still, over time, the faith of Israel evolved into something novel. Rival deities ruled in the impersonal forces of nature, in storm and fire and fertility. The God of the Hebrews was a God of intimate relationship: a divine shepherd who leads the flock into plenitude and safety (Psalm 23); the hidden head of every household; a faithful partner in a binding covenant. In time these attributes issued in a new name — Yahweh, "I Am Who I Am." On the holy mountain, Moses hears this name for the first time and soon the world with him. The world has not been the same since.

We sink into the sofa for a ritual act. My wife Donna commands the couch, sprawling lengthwise, head propped up by a pillow, stomach just beginning to swell with the unnamed future. In a word, we're *expecting*.

We do not take on this naming exercise unarmed. I have purchased a baby-name book, one that claims to hold between its covers the names my children were destined to bear. It is thick, nearly five hundred pages, and divides nicely down the middle with names of girls, then of boys.

As I open the book, our eldest daughter skips onto the scene. "Rikki-Tikki-Tavi," Rachael crows, after Kipling — just as I have taught her. But she has her own way with words, and her own notions of proper sibling appellations. It is just as well. We'll need the brilliance of both a Rudyard and a Rachael today, for this will be a double naming. We're expecting twins!

Turning to the beginning of the girl names, I read aloud: "Aba, Abebi, Abelia, Abeda, Abigail..." "Abigail" is the first name I recognize, and even it comes with options — "Abagil," "Abbe," "Abbey," "Abbi" — nineteen in all! This is just the Ab's. The Ac's don't start until the next page. I flip once more to the front cover: "Updated with more than 10,000 names!" it boasts. This is going to be a long day.

Up until now, Donna and I have chosen for our children names of Hebrew origin: Rachael, "like a lamb," and Rebecca, "bound." Just now Rebecca is napping. What is the meaning of "bound?" "Bound to awaken soon from her nap" is the only answer at hand. So we set to work, running down the alphabet, aiming at perhaps another biblical name or two, though we are avowedly open to alternatives.

The solemn act of naming a child is tedious work, all the more so with twins. There are boy-boy, girl-girl, and boy-girl pairs to think about, middle names to consider, alliteration and numbers of syllables to take into account. It is daunting. What if one were expecting triplets, or quadruplets, or more? Of course, in those situations all is mayhem anyway, the trials of baby naming a mere prelude to madness. A few good names on the comfort of our couch should be child's play by comparison. I share this thought with Donna and she nods in doubtful agreement.

We christened our daughters Rachael and Rebecca because of the pleasant sound of these names in our ears. Lately, though, I have begun tracing them to their depths. Rachel was the favored wife of Jacob, grandson of Abraham, in a time when multiple wives and concubines were common. Rebekah was Jacob's mother. She, too, played favorites, preferring Jacob to his twin, Esau. Rebekah married Isaac, the son of Abraham. At the urging of a servant of Abraham, Rebekah had agreed to travel to distant Canaan and marry Isaac, sight unseen. The ultimate blind date. As a toddler at least, our Rebecca seems likewise impulsive by nature and perhaps overly trusting. She will be the kind, I fear, who acts in the moment and copes with the consequences sight unseen. Her teenage years are far away, but thoughts of them have already begun to keep me up nights.

Our elder daughter Rachael, on the other hand, is methodical, calculating. It has not taken us long to compare her to her namesake. Rachel, Jacob's wife, was the second daughter of Laban, Rebekah's brother. When Jacob fled from his uncle Laban to return to the land of his father Isaac, Rachel stole Laban's household gods and hid them beneath the straw on which she sat, in the monthly way of women. Laban searched her tent but dared not look there! Our Rachael is too young for straw and harbors no idols, but she has a hard time sharing her dolls. She has her own room, which, like Laban in his daughter's tent, I enter at my own risk.

It is tempting to make much of such parallels, to ascribe to mere names a power beyond our ken. My rational side dismisses the notion. Names are only names, empty vessels to fill with whatever meaning we choose. The rest is curious coincidence — or is it?

ROOTS

Then the Lord said, "I have observed the misery of
my people who are in Egypt; I have heard their cry on
account of their taskmasters. . . . So come, I will send

you to Pharaoh to bring my people, the Israelites, out
of Egypt." ... But Moses said to God, "If I come to
the Israelites and say to them, 'The God of your
ancestors has sent me to you,' and they ask me, 'What
is his name?' what shall I say to them?"

— EXODUS 3:7, 10, 13

What's in a name?

— ROMEO AND JULIET, 2.2.43

*After four hundred years in Egypt, the descendants of Jacob cry
out in agony. They have become slaves. But they are numerous,
a threat to the kingdom, and so Pharaoh commands that every
male born to a Hebrew should die. The mother of the infant
Moses hides him in a papyrus basket by the reeds of the Nile.
Pharaoh's daughter discovers him there and raises him as an
Egyptian.*

*Once grown, Moses beholds the misery of his fellow
Hebrews. He kills an Egyptian who is beating one of his kins-
men, then flees for his life to the land of Midian. There he marries and takes up the life of a shepherd.*

*While tending his father-in-law's flock, Moses wanders onto
the mountain of God, where he encounters the burning bush
and the voice of God, calling him to rescue his people. Moses
resists the summons, but the voice is unyielding. Moses must go.
The voice promises to be present in signs and wonders that will
sway Israelite and Egyptian alike. "I will be with your mouth
and teach you what you are to speak," it says. But even these
promises are not enough. Before Moses will do the bidding of
this mysterious voice, he must know its origin. Before the
Israelites dare embrace the promise of liberation, they will want*

its warrant. And before the Egyptians will heed this God of slaves and let the people go, they will insist on a source, a proof of pedigree — a name.

We have arrived at the Co's: "Cody, Coffee, Colanda, Colby…" Two of these can be purchased at the neighborhood grocery. Together, in fact, these names represent four distinct origins: Irish, African, Old English, and American. They range in meaning from "helpful" to "frightening," from "flower" to "coal black." Yet, all have been stirred into a common melting pot, our shared American ethos in the making — *commingled.*

Every name originated somewhere. To trace one's own to its roots is a special privilege. Genealogical Web sites have made such a search considerably easier than in the past. Some people do not have the option, of course: African American children of slaves who were dragged from their heritage, Asians, smuggled to these shores with only the shirts on their backs, orphans with no past at all. Their whole histories may be linked solely to the names they are known by. Where is the meaning in that? Or might it be that what we cannot learn of our past makes the names we bear all the more precious?

I have gone by different names in my life. As a child I was Tommy, and later Tom. Now and then, I flirted with "Thomas," thinking it would conjure out of me a new air of dignity and lend me greater respect. Briefly, as Thomas, I gave up my Tom Sawyer ways. I dressed in uncomfortable clothes, cleaned my room daily, and practiced the violin. These stints with sophistication usually lasted up to three days. After that, it was back to "Tom," wearing ragged jeans, and hunting crawdads at the local pond.

Much later, as I prepared for both marriage and Christian seminary life in a new city, I abandoned "Tom" again, this time for my middle name, Wyatt. I originally adopted "Wyatt" on the off chance I might someday become an author. T. Wyatt seemed to me a better pen name than Thomas W. But making a clean break from something as personal as a name is harder than one might imagine. Friends, family, anyone with whom I had former relations continued on with Tom. A dear childhood baby-sitter, up in years, still called me Tommy. I went along gladly — not that she asked. More, I feared this name schizophrenia might augment the confusion I already felt about the purpose of my life. Was I intended to be Tom, the musician, or Wyatt, the minister? Or neither? Or both?

Now, twenty years later, I still have no answer and I'm still known by two names. Perhaps over time these disparate names have divided me further between my twin worlds. Or maybe the worlds have fixed the names. The Bible itself introduces dozens of names for the God of the Hebrews with hardly an explanation. On the bright side, even today, when I answer the phone, I know immediately which of my lives is calling. Perhaps, in a world of too many religions to count, it is like this with God and prayer.

OLD AND NEW BLOOD, BORROWED, BLUE BLOOD

Increasingly, "Wyatt" has eclipsed "Tom" in terms of how I see myself. The meaning and etymology of "Wyatt" have become sources of endless fascination. Recently, I consulted a random set of baby-name books to see what they would yield. On this weighty matter there seems to be no end of confusion. One book defines "Wyatt" as "lively," another as "brave," a third, "hardy." The common thread running through them is the association of my name with war. Two books go so far as to dub me "little warrior." Though I'm nearly 6 feet tall, my Wyatt ancestors have traditionally been a short people. That definition certainly fuels any inclination of ours toward a Napoleon complex.

However, the most common thought on "Wyatt" and the one I favor by far is, "guide." I endorse it in part because of my years in pastoral ministry, where I have seen myself less as an "answer man" than one in possession of some of the right questions. As Wyatt, I have hoped to guide my community along its own search for meaning — to point toward, not presume to define, ultimate truth.

More recently, I have taken a keen interest in "Wyatt" as an old family name, specifically the maiden name of my father's mother. I am indebted to our family genealogist, Uncle Oscar Wyatt, whose diligence has put the shine back on our family lineage. It seems we are descended from noble stock. This has been welcome news — though we Wyatts had long suspected it!

The Wyatts shared the court of the Henrys of Tudor England and, naturally, paid the price for that association more than once. Henry Wyatt was thrown in the Tower of London for two years, surviving only on raw pigeon meat delivered by a cat. Mary Tudor beheaded Thomas Wyatt, the younger, for his part in a failed anti-Catholic insurrection. Nobility has its responsibilities, I've been learning.

Now we have managed to trace ourselves back even further into greatness, back to the famous Bayeux tapestry, a twelfth-century canvas of the Norman Conquest, still on display at the former Bishop's Palace at Bayeux, France. Prior to the Battle of Hastings, which brought Duke William to the English throne, Edward the Confessor had handpicked William as his successor. He sent his brother-in-law, Harold, a Saxon earl, to France to deliver the news. When Harold's ship was blown off course, he landed in the domain of Guy de Ponthieu, who promptly threw him in jail for ransom. This Guy looks to have been the ancestor of the Tudor Wyatts, including my namesake Sir Thomas Wyatt, the poet. Guy eventually bowed to William's pressure and released Harold, who later returned to England. Then, upon Edward's death, Harold violated his oath of allegiance to William and seized the throne for himself. The balance of the Bayeux narrative depicts William's decisive victory on the plain of Hastings and his ascendancy.

While it might at first appear that Guy made a fatal choice in obstructing the way for William by throwing Harold in the clink, twenty-twenty hindsight suggests he was not a bad judge of character. The tapestry further indicates that the son of Guy, or Guy-ot (later Wyatt), accompanied William on his conquest. Nothing like ending up on the winning side!

Of course, none of this has really much of anything to do with me. It is one-thousand-year-old history, recorded on a fading strip of cloth. While it all seems plausible enough, just what difference it makes to me personally is hard to fathom. For my wife Donna, it is at least worth a few laughs to hear me share my family lineage with pride. Even if she believed it, the notion that it somehow matters would still strike her as comical. The only Wyatt she cares about is the flesh and blood butt of her jokes. The rest might be fact or fable — it doesn't matter which. But for this one Wyatt, I've no doubt, she'd give her life — "or die trying!" as we noble Wyatts like to say.

When Moses encountered God in the burning bush, he learned immediately the connection to his own ancestry. Here was the God of old, of Abraham, Isaac, and Jacob. But Moses sought more: he sought the name for the hour at hand, sought to know how God would choose to be God for that present, unrepeatable moment in time — his own time. Do we seek anything less?

Perhaps the orphan, the alien, and the descendant of slaves, all with no roots, have been granted the greatest gift: the task of a new naming, of founding a future unshackled by the past. Perhaps this is God's gift to us all. Like the Israelites in the wilderness, we are to preserve what we can of the past, then journey into the future. And all along the way, the God of signs and wonders, of old names and new, will be with us.

"I know!" I offer at last. "If we have a boy we can just name him Wyatt!" Donna cracks a smile, then bursts into laughter. Faded greatness gets no respect.

SCRABBLE

God said to Moses, "I AM WHO I AM.... This is
my name forever, and this is my title for generations."

— EXODUS 3:14, 15B

The voice relents. God speaks the name to Moses: Yahweh, "I AM WHO I AM." All at once, Moses knows everything — and nothing.

In the ancient world, a name carried weight, participated in the power to which it pointed. Nowhere was this truer than in the case of divine names. A deity was present in its name the way an explosion resides in a stick of dynamite. Call on the name and light the fuse. Speak it, and harness its power. The name might confer the palliative power of healing, the generative force of fertility, or the destructive power of warfare. In any case, the power was in the god, and the god was in the name. Utter it, and rock the future.

Except for the name of Yahweh. This name, spoken to Moses, is inscrutable. Does it really mean "Who I am"? Or might it mean "That I am"? Or should the verb, as many scholars suggest, be rendered in the future tense: "That I will be," or "Who I will be"? These questions are long-standing.

The spelling itself is indeterminate. The Hebrew language was written with consonants only, no vowels. The transmission through time of correct vowel sounds in words was a function of speech. In the Christian era, when vowels were added, the correct rendering of "YHWH" was not indicated. The name of God had traditionally been deemed too holy to utter. Thus, the original vowels that accompanied the Hebrew name "YHWH" have been lost. The name remains shrouded in mystery.

It is poetic to ascribe to this concealment a divine intent. The God who will not be imaged refuses as well to be pinned down by a name. God is who God is, will be who God will be. The power in this name is God's alone to wield. It is always a gift, never a possession, delivered on wings of grace.

❧ ❧ ❧

"Kasey" — also "Kacey," "Kaci," "Kacie," "Kacy," "Kaycee" — and "K.C."!

A new trend has crept into the lexicon of naming: initials

only. J. R. of *Dallas* fame may be responsible. Rap stars may have shepherded it along. This is certainly no Jewish trend, yet there may be an affinity here with the Hebrew, consonant-only name of God: YHWH. The God of the Hebrews resists name clarification as well. We can all attest to the same tendency among the young. Parents name their children after their own parents or grandparents, aunts or uncles, even themselves. They do so often with the expectation that children will come, in character and appearance, to resemble their namesakes.

This is naming done in vain. Each child is a unique individual. Personalities fill names, not the other way around. Often, in an assertion of independence, children reject their names altogether. Deborah shortens her name to "Deb"; Robert finds "Rob" more appealing, later settling on "Bob"; Guillermo, seeking to fit into an adoptive culture, discovers "Bill." According to polling data, a full third of Americans wish at one time or another that they had been given another name. Every year, fifty thousand Americans legally change their names to suit themselves.

Perhaps the trend of using initials as names is a healthy one. "K. C." might become Kitty Carlisle, or Kevin Costner, or Kwame Clyngenpeel. He or she might also remain simply K. C. and let the world wonder. The child will be who the child will be. The God of the Hebrews would understand.

Yet a child is not a god. A child is a vulnerable being, winding his or her tenuous way in the world. As children develop and grow, they try on many names for size. Names like "pliable" and "stubborn," "kind" and "cruel," "forgiving" and "vengeful," "tolerant" and "quick-tempered." They fly these names like kites to see where the wind will blow them. They are busily unraveling the mystery inside themselves and all around them.

It is mystery wound on an endless spool of string.

"HOLLOWED" BE THY NAME?

The naming book has been laid aside. A friend of Donna's has come by to visit and fill us in on her latest skirmish on the battlefield of dating. She is plump and in her mid-thirties. At dinner the night before, she had eaten her entire meal with mascara rolling down both cheeks from a coughing spell during the appetizer. Her date had not said a word. She had only discovered the streaks of black in the women's room on the way out.

"Oh God, was that embarrassing or what?" she says. "God, did I ever feel silly! I'll never forgive myself," she laughs. "I'll never forgive *him!* God!" And we talk, she, Donna, and I — and God. Except God is not really on our minds. Not the God who knows us as we know ourselves and then some. Not the God who loves us anyway. The God who forgives what others cannot. The God who wipes tears clean away, mascara and all. Not that God.

"God, the bastard!" she says, and I get that familiar twinge of discomfort, that unease long programmed into my psyche at the sound of "God" recruited into such a sentence. It is there presumably for special emphasis — though there is nothing special about it, stuck like a ripe olive on a cheap hors d'oeuvre. But just what, I ask myself, is the harm in it? There is no malice at work here, no intent to malign or degrade.

"I could never go out with him again," our friend concludes. "How could I? Why would I trust him with squat? I hate dating, and I hate *men!* . . . Oh, no offense!" she adds, looking my way.

"He was probably just too embarrassed himself to say anything." Donna has already suggested, but our friend wasn't listening. In her world, every date is the last date, every bid for intimacy an unmitigated failure.

And with that my question is answered. The problem with loose talk of God is not one of commission, but omission. It is not a bad door opened, but a good door closed. Our friend has it down like a game of solitaire: occasional bad dates are her way of skirting intimacy; careless God talk is a strategy for skirting ultimacy. The more she invokes the name, the more eviscerated of meaning it becomes. She can remain safe and alone, an island.

"Besides, I like being by myself," she offers on her way out the door, and the words hang hollow in the air. "Oh, God, what a pity," I say once she has gone. I say it to Donna and to myself, and I say it to God.

THE NURTURE OF GOD

How precious is your steadfast love, O God!
All people may take refuge in the shadow of your
wings.
They feast on the abundance of your house, and
you give them drink from the river of your
delights.
For with you is the fountain of life; in your light
we see light.

— PSALMS 36:7–9

We have barely closed the front door when the sound of life cries out from the nursery. Our daughter Rebecca has awakened. The commotion has stirred her from her dreams. I climb the stairs to her crib and lift her into my arms. Donna follows with Rachael at a slower pace and returns to our bedroom couch.

"Daddy, Daddy, Daddy," Rebecca intones. These words were her very first, I recall proudly. Even now they are first on her lips after sleep. Yet they are not intended for me. As I carry her into our bedroom, her bright blue eyes eagerly seek out another, the source of her sustenance — mother's milk. Rebecca has not wanted to wean.

Indeed, it is no longer about sustenance at all. Baby food and cereal have been in her diet for over a year. But to be at breast is to be at home. There seems no substitute for the primal impulse of sucking.

I lower her to her mother and she coos anew: "Daddy, Daddy... Mommy!" Then she latches on.

I pick up the book and we resume: "Marina, Martiza, Maru, Mary..."

With over one hundred variations, "Mary" is one of the most popular names in the world. Its Hebrew form is "Miriam," the name of Moses' sister, who convinced the pharaoh's daughter to give the infant Moses a Hebrew nurse-maid. She summoned Jochebed, his own mother, doubtless lessening her anguish. Later in the desert, upon her rebuke of Moses' leadership, Miriam contracted leprosy. She was later cured.

Of the six Marys in the New Testament, Mary the mother of Jesus stands out. According to the Gospels, she bore the Son of God, only to see him suffer on a cross. Other Marys joined her there. It is fitting that arguably the most popular name of all means "bitter."

At least a portion of the meaning of "bitter," I suspect,

is tied to gender itself. For all its seeming importance in our world, "Mary" plays a surprisingly inconsequential role in the Scriptures, gaining mention barely fifty times in the entire New Testament. The Bible, after all, is a male-oriented work, penned in patriarchy over millennia. God language, too, is decidedly masculine. Even in modern translations where male-oriented language in references to men and women has been eliminated, the masculine third person singular pronoun for God remains. God is *he* and *him,* and that which is God's is *his.*

And yet the biblical indeterminacy of "Yahweh" extends to gender. Yahweh is not a man. God is altogether beyond gender. This is good news for many, since talk of God as "Father" is not universally attractive. In the ongoing struggle of women to gain equality with men, whether in home, workplace, or house of worship, the assumption of God's maleness still constitutes more a barrier than a blessing.

Moreover, the very word "father" carries an onus in many settings, some of them unexpected. A friend of mine, once a chaplain in Chicago's Cook County Jail, discovered a great distaste among the residents there for descriptions of God as Father. For many of them, "father" was synonymous with "abuse" and "neglect." Call God Father and open the floodgates of unresolved anger and bad feeling, drive one more wedge between the inmate and deity. You might address the divine by any name, but don't confuse the God of loving faithfulness with, of all things, a father.

Mothers, however, were another story. Inmates revered their mothers. Despite the failings of their lives, beyond all hardness and despair, their hearts still beat for the women who bore them, nurtured them, and who, after everything, would carry their names to the grave. At least a God known as "Mother" would love you anyway. At least a God you called "Mom" would never walk away.

On with the M's: "Maureen, Mausi, May, Maya..."

"Maya" refers to the divine power to create life — a power that Hindu faith ascribes to men and women alike. Good for the Hindus. Good for Christians who recognize something of God's generative power in both male and female. Good for preachers who acknowledge the feminine names for God in Hebrew scripture: *shekkinah,* the all-present one, *ruach,* the spirit of God, *chokman,* woman wisdom. God is neither male nor female, but that fact is obscured when we speak of God from only one gender per-spective. No matter how we try, assumptions of gender creep into our God consciousness. In this way, too, God's name is taken in vain.

Father, Son and Holy Spirit, one God,
mother of us all.

— WILLIAM C. PLACHER

Or is God the God of Jews only? Is he not the
God of Gentiles also? Yes, of Gentiles also, since
God is one; and he will justify the circumcised on
the ground of faith and the uncircumcised through
that same faith. Do we then overthrow the law
by this faith? By no means! On the contrary,
we uphold the law.

— ROMANS 3:29–31

The name "Yahweh" then, is mystery itself. It resists etymological classification. God's holiness is God's unbridgeable "otherness."

Language falls short of describing such a reality. Symbols fly apart in the presence of the Unknowable. The God who could be fully known would cease to be God altogether. Nor is the name Yahweh tied to a single time and place or even a single people. The apostle Paul, writing fourteen centuries after Moses, resisted a growing factionalism within the early Christian church. He insisted that God is not a God of Jew only or Gentile only. God is God to any with faith.

Might God even be God to those with no faith at all? Perhaps the answer lies in the name — I will be who I will be.

They come to us unexpectedly, like the plot of a dream long after waking. We have been stuck in a patch of seductive N names — "Nadia," "Natalia," "Natania," "Natasha" — when two Hebrew names claw their way to consciousness. Perhaps they were triggered by the endings of these N names, their relaxed, low-back vowel sounds. The names we have found, or which have found us, share similar endings. They are pleasant, potent names. They are "Sarah" and "Hannah."

Sarah means, on the one hand, "princess," and on the other, "one who laughs." As Abraham's aging wife, Sarah laughed at God's promise of a son. She bore one anyway and at God's behest named him Isaac — "laughter."

We have a personal inducement for choosing this name. A jaunt through Donna's and my family trees yields no fewer than fifteen sightings of "Sarah." Especially among the Wyatts in America, the name Sarah has figured prominently. This complements my own urging to include "Wyatt" somewhere among our children's names.

"Sarah Wyatt?" I float hopefully in the direction of the couch.

This time Donna concurs.

"Hannah" is Hebrew for "graceful." It was by the grace of gratitude that the biblical Hannah, barren like Sarah, honored her pledge to give over her own miracle son to the service of the temple at Shiloh. Once weaned, he was delivered to the Lord there and raised a Nazarite — one who takes a vow to an ascetic life, forswearing haircuts, strong drink, and the like. His name was Samuel, "God has heard," and he grew to become the first priest of the nation Israel.

We have no Hannahs in our family, but my grandfather Samuel Bowles once dedicated his own life to the work of God, and I more or less have done the same. True, my grandfather and I both inherited the baldness gene and I appreciate the taste of a good Merlot, but in spirit at least the connection to Samuel stands.

PRIMOGENITURE

Adam knew his wife again, and she bore a son and
named him Seth, for she said, "God has appointed
for me another child instead of Abel, because
Cain killed him." To Seth also a son was born,
and he named him Enosh. At that time, people
began to invoke the name of the Lord.

— GENESIS 4:25–26

Now we have girls' names, but Donna is falling asleep on the couch. At this pace and with our luck she'll deliver twin boys before we ever reach the second half of the book, and so I hurry ahead to the male end of things.

There, midvolume, dividing girl names from boy, is a third brief category — "Gender-Neutral Names." I begin to read: "Austin, Bailey, Blaine, Blair, Bryce..." Donna perks up long enough to add to the list her own B contribution: "Bland!" These names do seem to smack of faddish mass appeal. They are terse, one- or two-syllable words that seem somehow almost interchangeable.

And yet, many on the list are ancient names, traceable to Gaelic or Celtic roots. In many of these names is embedded the so-called way not taken: ancient Celtic Christianity — gentle, mystical, and exceedingly deep. One of these is even listed in two variant spellings: "Cameron" and "Kameron." This is also the name of one of our dearest friends, an unusually kind and peaceable soul. Its meaning is equally unpretentious: "from the crooked stream." It gets me thinking.

But now we abandon the gender-free list to move on to the boys' names section. Whether out of desperation or fatigue, I begin to flip through these pages arbitrarily, letting my finger fall on a name, as some Christians turn blindly to a random verse of Scripture in search of God's will for the day. This time, as happens frequently enough to keep the doubtful habit alive, it works!

"Seth," I read, "Appointed one. Third son of Adam." Biblically speaking, we have found our way nearly back to the beginning of names. Donna and I warm to it instantly. It goes well with "Sarah," the S name in the girl-girl scenario, along with "Hannah." Further, it alliterates with "Staton," the family name Donna would like to include somewhere in our naming decisions. Finally, it holds meaning. Seth is the compensation Adam and Eve receive after the murder of one son and the exile of another (Gen. 4:25). "Seth" is a name of new and gracious beginnings. Perhaps it will serve such a purpose for us as well.

But the name Seth also bears within it the dark past. It holds the truth of the world's fallenness and shame. We choose it with our eyes open to the risks involved in all attempts at naming the world. After six days of creation, God named that world "good." Human events ever since have served both to vindicate and revile this divine act of boldness.

Yet each new day arrives bright with promise. Every Seth is a child named in hope. To quarrel with this truth is to declare God wrong about the world from the beginning, to claim that God has named in vain.

> Joshua son of Nun was full of the spirit of wisdom,
>   because Moses had laid his hands on him;
>   and the Israelites obeyed him, doing as the
>   Lord had commanded Moses.

— DEUTERONOMY 34:9

After the time of Moses, Hebrew parents began to name their children with amended forms of the name Yahweh: "Josiah" means "Yahweh supports"; "Johanan" means "Yahweh is gracious"; "Jesus" means "Yahweh is salvation." This has helped to settle the debate among scholars over just when the name Yahweh actually came into use. Thus it is more likely to have been after the time of Moses — not from virtually the beginning of biblical history as Genesis 4:26 suggests. So names for God have dawned over time, slow baked in the womb of religious consciousness.

More than that, this practice of naming has aided interpre-
tation of the Third Commandment itself. One could reasonably
suppose that "You shall not take the name of the Lord your God
in vain" would prohibit its use in proper naming, but this
apparently has not been the case. The Bible does not condemn
the use of God's name outright, only its abuse, its invocation to
justify evil. But how to define that evil — there is the rub!

The finger falls again and we consider the result. It is not a
name we cozy up to readily. There are no instances of it in
our own family lineages, and perhaps too many among our
friends and acquaintances. It smacks of the trendy. Still, it is
a pleasant-sounding name of biblical weight and theological
depth. For "Joshua" means "Yahweh is salvation."

Joshua was the heir to Moses, appointed by God at the
end of the Exodus. His task, meted out in the very first verse
of the biblical book bearing his name, was to lead the people
across the Jordan and into the Promised Land. Such an
assignment appeared daunting and dangerous, but like
Moses before him, Joshua had the pledge of Yahweh's presence. The name of God would deliver victory, for "Yahweh
is salvation."

The story of Joshua's crossing to the land and subduing
it is well known. It is a sanguinary affair. Holy war is waged
against the land's inhabitants in a battle of annihilation.
Men, women, children, slaves, homes, livestock, idols — all
are destroyed. No spoils will spoil the new beginning of
God's people. They will embark on their new life pure and
undefiled. But such an aim of holiness is also the justification for carnage: it is not the people's will but God's that

wipes the land clean. And it is not Joshua but Yahweh who wages unsparing victory.

This is among those biblical accounts that preachers avoid like the plagues of Egypt. We do not embrace such an image of God, whether known by "Yahweh" or some other name. Nor do we equate the rejection of such carnage with taking Yahweh's name in vain. "Joshua" may mean "Yahweh is salvation," but Israel's true salvation story was her deliverance from bondage, not the Canaanite genocide that followed.

Some today still revel in hegemony. They turn to their gods for aid in the destruction of others. No doubt some of my own forebears, Wyatts among them, viewed the settling of America and its resulting displacement of Native peoples with a sense of manifest destiny, akin to that of the conquering Israelites. They paraded the name of God like a banner along their way. Missionary enterprises, past and present, likewise have assumed God's will in their quest for converts by often disagreeable means. Present-day theologies of every stripe posit a God who takes sides in wars, both actual and ideological. There are many ways to take God's name in vain.

I try to keep the equivalence of the names "Joshua" and "Jesus" in view. Both mean "Yahweh saves." Both point to a God of grace and hope. But when the moment arrives to choose between brute force and sacrifice, Jesus takes up the cross, turning on its head the whole meaning of salvation.

In the end Donna and I decide to abandon our clean sweep of biblical names. We settle on "Cameron" as a second boy's name. Compared to "Joshua" or "Jesus" it is far less grand, but perhaps far more grounded in our own daily reality. "Crooked streams" — our lives are full of these, full of meandering paths and confounding choices. And so perhaps we'll raise a crooked stream. Why not? Meanwhile, we'll honor the name of God by not choosing it.

SO HELP US GOD!

They came to the other side of the sea . . . and when
[Jesus] stepped out of the boat, immediately a
man . . . with an unclean spirit met him . . . and he
shouted at the top of his voice, "What have you to
do with me, Jesus, Son of the Most High God?
I adjure you by God, do not torment me."
. . . Then Jesus asked him, "What is your name?"
He replied, "My name is Legion; for we are many."

— MARK 5:1–2, 7, 9

Western history is, by God's will, indissolubly
linked with the people of Israel, not only genetically
but also in a genuine uninterrupted encounter. The
Jews keep open the question of Christ.

— DIETRICH BONHOEFFER, ETHICS

The New Testament evangelist Mark tells a tale of two namings. A demon-possessed man identifies Jesus as "Son of God." Jesus wrests from him the name of his evil spirit — Legion. Each seeks to bind the other by the mastery of a name.

Still today, names can be tools of dominance. Learn my name and gain an advantage over me. Speak my name and I am compelled to turn and listen. The normal sting or charm of words is all the more potent when they are spoken in connection with my name. The mere mention of some names can strike

hearts down in fear: "Idi Amin," "Pol Pot," "Jack the Ripper";
or cause them to race in gladness: "Mother Teresa," "Mohandas
Gandhi," "Saint Francis."

Sometimes a name holds the power of life and death.
Sometimes that name is "Jesus."

It is Spain in the late fifteenth century. Ferdinand and
Isabella rule; Columbus is soon to sail to the New World. The
Spanish Inquisition is in full flame; its special target: Jews, both
practicing Jews and New Christian "converts" struggling
against the odds to prove their conversions genuine. From
Segovia to Ciudad to Córdoba, they are imprisoned and tor-
tured until they confess or die. A forced confession is itself a
death sentence. There is no mercy. But their torturers exact still
more, stealing from their current victims the names of their
next: Jonah, Mordecai, Gabrielle, Miriam. . . . To speak these
names is to murder their owners. Children incriminate parents,
the weak implicate the strong, and all die together.

Meanwhile, the inquisitors carry out their cruelty with
another name on their lips — "Jesu Christe." Pious devotion to
this name fuels their righteous indignation. Wielded as a
weapon, the name itself is the justification. The inquisitors have
attached it to their victims. They have christened them "Christ
killers."

In the gospel according to Mark, Jesus' purpose in naming a
man's spirit Legion is to restore the man's life, to free him from
his demons; the purposes of those who have wielded the name of
Jesus since are as mixed as the human heart.

Rachael and Rebecca sit on the carpet at our feet. Rachael is
playing a cassette tape of a nonsensical naming song called

"Willoby-Walloby." "Willoby-Walloby-Woo," it begins, "an elephant sat on you. Willoby-Walloby-Wee, an elephant sat on me." From there, verses move through a comical course of proper naming until half the world has been sat upon: "Willoby-Walloby-Wam, an elephant sat on Sam. Willoby-Walloby-Wark, an elephant sat on Mark," and so forth. Rachael giggles as it goes. She sings along and we join her. The patent absurdity of it is fetching — decreeing "death by elephant" through a simple act of naming.

The tension builds in this game. Who will be next? But Rachael has sung it through many times. She has her own goal in view. Toward the end of the tune comes the verse she has awaited. She holds her sister's hands and claps them together to the words: "Willoby-Walloby-Wecca, an elephant sat on Rebecca!" Rachael croons with delight and Rebecca joins her irresistibly, unaware that in her big sister's eyes she has just been flattened like a pancake.

Yet the song always ends the same: "Willoby-Walloby-Wus, an elephant sat on *all of us!*" No one escapes elephant demise. This little ditty is utterly democratic. All names get squished together.

In the real world, of course, names are not treated equally. Every generation has its roll call of unpopular names. Our baby book includes the main losers of the last century. "Abishag," "Babberly," "Clapham," and "Dozer" all make the list. It takes little imagination to appreciate why! Yet in some times and places the status of a name has pointed to things far more sinister: Protestant and Catholic names in Northern Ireland; Bosnian, Croatian, and Serbian names in the former Yugoslavia; Tutsi and Hutu names in Rwanda — all link to hatred and bloodshed and their aftermath of despair. In India, names in the service of the caste system still check the prospects of many. Family feuds can span generations, the names involved living on in the popular imagination. Descendants of the Hatfields and McCoys in and around Matewan, West Virginia, have turned their family feud of the 1880s into a major tourist attraction. Their names now generate cash. Modern DNA analysis has linked Arabs and Jews genetically as close family. Yet in the long-standing Middle East conflict, their disparate naming of its causes and effects, solutions, concessions, and even views of the sacred and divine make them avowed enemies.

Indeed, the place of God in the naming wars is large and prominent. In Nazi Germany, Jewish names and families were systematically catalogued with the calculating aim of extermination, "the final solution." Captive to centuries of anti-Semitism and notions of Jews as responsible for the death of Christ, Christians in Germany and around Europe often collaborated with or passively sanctioned the cause. Those who took a stand against it, from Dietrich Bonhoeffer to Corrie Ten Boom, suffered persecution. While the German fascists were hardly theists, they harnessed the spirit of religiosity like every other raw material at their disposal. The Jewish-Christian God became but another rung on Adolf Hitler's ladder of ascendancy.

"You shall not take the name of the Lord your God in vain" is pressed into the service of many causes: clean and tidy speech, courtroom oath taking ("So help me God"), narrow views of religious piety. But the Third Commandment means more; the name Yahweh is given to Moses with grave intent — to lift up the fallen, to set at liberty the oppressed, to bless the future with renewed hope. Should not the same aims govern our use of the name? Above all, not to take the name of Yahweh, of God, in vain means to resist its use in the service of death and despair. It means living lives of grace and mercy in keeping with the name's Giver, whose love will not be compromised.

To do otherwise, the commandment concludes, will carry consequences: "For the Lord will not acquit anyone who misuses his name." These consequences are not always quick to follow. They may delay a lifetime, a generation, even an era. Names endure all three.

The once-popular name "Adolph" does not appear in our baby-naming book. Over five hundred Hebrew names do.

NAMING LIFE

A man lives one generation; a name,
to the end of all generations.

— ANCIENT JAPANESE PROVERB

Months have passed, nearly the number that bring a womb to fruit. The baby-naming book is now long buried on our library floor beneath other volumes, each of which in one way or another purports to name our world. Just now they all matter little. In this moment all names are left behind — all but two!

I don a hospital gown, cap, and gloves and am escorted into a room. It is warm here and flooded with light. All lamps are trained on an operating table in the center of the room, where a cluster of disposable gowns now hovers, occluding my view. Neonatologists, OB-GYNs, anesthesiologists, surgical nurses, newborn nurse practitioners — all are present, huddled under the light. I, meanwhile, am relegated to the sidelines, but I wish desperately to draw near, to see.

For on the table lies my wife, and inside of her, our future. There is a double miracle in the offing.

Only two minutes separate their passages from womb to world. Each tiny body is lifted from the cut folds of flesh that for nine months have defined its existence. Their cords are cut and they are whisked to heated tables, where their mouths are suctioned until gurgles give way to the first cries of protest. Then their cheesy, pink skin is wiped clean of blood and fluid from head to toe, making plain at last that definitive word on gender. The ultrasound more than hinted at the truth, but this new evidence is irrefutable. Our twins are male and female, boy and girl. The boy shall be Seth, the girl, Sarah. All deliberation and anticipation are ended.

Gingerly, we lay the names Hannah and Cameron to rest, wrapped in the receiving blanket of memory. They have not been offered the most precious gift of actuality. A mere name never can. What is real is the flesh and blood before us, the painful gush into the world of the living, the thrill-packed, agony-racked adventure of years listing ever toward death.

Now I remember that "Seth" means "appointed one" — appointed to pleasure and pain, chosen to embrace the ambiguity inherent in the gift. I recall that "Sarah" means "one who laughs" — she who will both chuckle at life's irony and shriek at life's sting. Such laughter will be one measure of her humanity. My fondest hope is that my twins will better their names with their lives. Every name is a borrowed one, taken for the mere span of a life. Each has belonged to others before and will belong to others after. To honor these names is in some way to honor all who have borne them. Perhaps even more so, it is to honor the God who has made us all.

This is only as it should be for those who bear the names of the Hebrews, who know God by the unknowable name of Yahweh. To honor that name is to live in consonance with the gracious story of its revealing, the story of deliverance, redemption, and love. To do so is to honor life itself. It is, above all, not to take *life* in vain.

> The name is endless, and by it one gains
> the endless world.

> — UPANISHAD

KEEPING THE BEAT

REMEMBER THE SABBATH DAY BY KEEPING IT HOLY

For in six days the Lord made heaven and earth,
the sea, and all that is in them,
but rested the seventh day...

— EXODUS 20:11

More than the Jews have kept Shabbat,
Shabbat has kept the Jews.

— OLD HEBREW SAYING

BLESSED RAGE FOR ORDER

In Egypt, before the Exodus, time did not exist. Israel's life of slavery there is now a seamless memory of servitude, of ceaseless toil, still stinging like an open wound. The desert, too, is void of time. Sand blows night and day across a vast landscape of indetermination. Here, as in Egypt, the world is a flatland, dry, still, and colorless.

But the Hebrews carry with them a tale of time, the story of creation in six days, passed down by the elders over generations. It is a parable of grace: Yahweh named the new world "good," then rested on the seventh day to prove it. No need for last-minute changes. All that creation was required to be, it already was.

The grace is this: for all its adversity and grief, the world of the Hebrews remains a place of great beauty and promise. It is a work of art to be cherished, a window to the majesty of God.

Slowly, desert life takes on a rhythm. The making and breaking of camp, the daily collection of water and food, the rituals of sacrifice — with these, events begin to unfold in meaningful sequence. Time is reinvented in the bare act of survival. But it is not toil alone that resurrects time. It is Shabbat, the Sabbath rest, that brings order to this wilderness. Every seventh day, the Hebrews hear again that they are precious in God's sight. Keeping Shabbat, these former slaves resist thinking of themselves or others as objects, instruments, or means to other ends. On the Sabbath, the Hebrews cease to be nomadic wanderers, blown about like bits of sand. Now they are a people, a priestly nation, the Israel of God.

June 21, the summer solstice, marks the outset of a momentous experiment in the management of time. I am staying home to complete a book manuscript, due to the publisher before the first leaf falls. My four children are joining me over their summer break. I will write every day. They will play nearby, but at such distance as the tedium of word harvesting requires. Still, I will keep them in my sights. We'll share breaks, eat lunch together on the patio. Here at home, the cradle of creativity, I will nurse both my offspring of flesh and my offspring of words. It will be a magnificent summer, one I imagine my children will celebrate in memory long after I am gone.

This I think on the first day of summer, as I carry morning coffee to the computer keyboard and compose all of one sentence before flinching at the first bloodcurdling cries of my children at war. They have wasted no time. Soon I'm like Moses, who sat in the desert on the judgment seat from dawn to dusk, settling the disputes of his people. My people, ages five to ten, number only four, yet court seems always to be in session. My intention was to write myself ragged, but already I'm refereeing myself ragged instead. Within a week I discover that a house of harmless children with time on their hands is more trouble than a jail full of juvenile delinquents kept busy.

To the school aged, of course, summer break is like the Exodus all over again. The prisoners gain release from their classroom captivity, leaving behind the shackles of straight-backed chairs and straightlaced behavior, of tests and term papers. For the next nine weeks, they will bathe themselves in the wild perfume of anarchy. Yet, for all its allure, naked liberty doesn't live up to its billing. Within days if not hours, summer vacation imposes a new and suffocating bondage: boredom!

My children are not exempt from this phenomenon. They crave structure, a harness for their unbridled vim and vigor. So I seize upon the only tenable solution, summer school! I piece together a simple curriculum of math, linguistics, art, and recreation. Soon, I have recruited my eldest daughter Rachael into the organizational scheme. Rachael makes the ideal lieutenant, loyal yet born to command. Quickly she whips up the troops into a frenzy of enthusiasm for the cause. She draws a poster-size schedule for the week and displays it. We get specific. Math will cover addition and subtraction, telling time, and counting currency with — what else? — Monopoly money. In linguistics, we'll get hooked on phonics, revel in Dr. Seuss classics, and read the great stories of the Bible. In art, we will experiment with several of the less messy media — no finger paints, please! Bike riding and ball games will round out the schedule. We'll inject some routine into the mix, and discover the deeper freedom of daily order. Together, my children and I have made up lists of stories to explore over the summer. I view this attention to biblical texts as a normal part of a healthy diet. I am far from a fundamentalist of scriptural interpretation, and find often as much in Scripture to question as to embrace. I have waited hopefully before some texts for clarity to strike. In some cases, the wait still isn't over. Yet through it all, I have sustained a conviction that, despite their perplexity, the Scriptures are shot through with holiness. As we ponder them, we are snatching little glimpses of God. I don't wish my own children to nurse illusions of ease in biblical understanding. I hope rather that they will honor the text by wrestling with it deeply, as Jacob wrestled with God at Peniel (Gen. 32). God touched Jacob's hip, throwing it from its socket, but Jacob refused to let go without first receiving a blessing. He got the blessing, and walked with a limp thereafter. According to some, battling with a biblical text will put a limp in your faith. But I tend to think that to wrestle with the text is to be blessed in the end.

We have chosen passages from the Bible that are accessible to children and contain some palpable message: the Beatitudes of Jesus as ways of grace to live by; Jonah in the whale as a lesson on forgiveness; the story of the rich young ruler as a look at priorities in everyday life under the reign of God.

Even the creation story is included. Personally, I am closer to an evolutionist than to a biblical creationist. At times, I've found myself quite taken with the thought of my ancestors swinging from trees in some pristine jungle. Yet I continue to read with wonder and awe the account of creation from Genesis 1, which builds a world through a rhythmic structure of novelty and repetition reminiscent of a musical composition: "...and then there was evening and there was morning..." — each day the same, and yet each utterly different. Here is a story not only tightly packed with truth, but a transcendent truth that sings.

But the Genesis story of creation is so much more besides. There are the broad, sweeping strokes of creative endeavor, the miraculous power of words to bring things into being ex nihilo, from nothing, and the sheer fact of efficiency. Eden is the embodiment of perfection! Only in Eden does everything work precisely as it should. In our world of false starts, unrealized expectations, and broken dreams, a textbook start and photo finish are a wonder to behold.

Best of all is that, day by day, stroke by stroke, God surveys all that has been accomplished and calls it by its name. God says, "It is good," finally declaring at the end of the sixth day that everything together is "very good."

Then, almost as a reflexive response, God initiates the Sabbath. God rests, hallows the moment of perfection, then and there and always. In this model of creation, Sabbath comes as a standard feature, not as an option. It seals the world's destiny in God's gracious regard for all that is indeed "good."

In fact, I have chosen to include the story of creation in our Bible reading schedule for this very purpose: that my own dear children can hear it declared — of them! I want them to acknowledge that God's sure hand has wrought them, too, without blemish. I want them to bask in the glow of their own loveliness.

And yet, the linchpin of the Watkins academy curriculum will be something else entirely. Any day that holds an ounce of promise must include music. Music is food for the brain, oxygen for the soul. This summer, I will pursue a long-held ambition. I will teach my children to play the violin!

Not a few benefits follow from the study of music in general and the violin in particular. Music can stimulate the mind, titillate the imagination, and possibly even raise the IQ by several numbers. And my children's exposure to the greatest musical instrument of all time (in one father's view) will enrich their appreciation for all art and their soul's yearning to "speak in the tongues of angels." Whether they dabble or delve deeply, Rachael, Rebecca, Seth, and Sarah will profit from violin study in ways they cannot now begin to imagine. And someday, when they're grown up and I'm grown old, they'll thank me for it.

I discovered the violin at the age of six. On a Sunday after church, my parents took me to a nursing home, where a group of young Suzuki-method violinists were serenading the elderly residents. Following the recital, I cried all the way home. One might suppose I had been spooked by the piteous sights and sounds of nursing home life, was in mourning over the loss of a promising afternoon of neighborhood play or, more likely, reeling from the shrill screeching of a dozen E strings. Instead, I had been smitten, swept away by a passion I had never before known.

"I want to do that!" I blubbered between shrieks. "I want to play the violin!" With that, as I imagine it now, my parents patted one another on the back, exchanging satisfied winks, though at the time my eyes were too blurred by tears to notice. Within a week, I had a violin under my chin and my lessons were under way. I have been a violinist ever since.

On a long-ago Sabbath, in a setting reserved for the end of life, I had experienced my all-important musical birth. Doubtless there was serendipity at play that day. Mystery was at work, the kind that infects so many matters of life, both common and consequential. I hope for more of the same here and now, as I line up violin cases along the wall like conscripts. I wish for the beauty of music to bring my own children to tears, to inflame their young passions. But I don't dwell on this. Such things cannot be programmed. When they do occur, it is through a slow, almost imperceptible process. This is the usual way of things wondrous.

For now, my plans are laid. Blessed order will soon pay our wayward summer a visit. It will come kindly, auspiciously, riding on the wings of song.

THE MEANING OF REST

Remember that you were a slave in the land
of Egypt, and the Lord your God brought you
out from there with a mighty hand and an
outstretched arm; therefore the Lord your God
commanded you to keep the sabbath day.

— DEUTERONOMY 5:15

Over their forty years of wandering, the Hebrews have much to manage. Maintaining a city on wheels is a logistical feat of dizzying precision. If in doubt on this point, ask Barnum or

Bailey. Given this difficulty, how do we explain the seeming lunacy of such an added burden as construction of the tabernacle — God's "mobile home" in the desert — occupying nearly a third of the entire Exodus account (Exod. 25–30, 35–40)? It is difficult enough just to get through the instructions. Imagine trying to build it! And so, in the middle of the wilderness, surrounded by warring tribes and endless requirements of daily sustenance, why bother?

Fear, perhaps?

In the Sinai wilderness there is much cause for worry — deprivation, starvation, annihilation at the hands of enemies. Anxieties like these are spirit crushers, authors of inertia. Imagine then that someone says, "Yes, it is an anxious lot we've got on our hands. Better keep them busy or they'll worry themselves insane."

Nothing quells anxiety like the adrenaline of purposeful activity. Suppose that, toward this end, orders are drawn up for acacia wood chests and tables, curtains of goat hair and twisted linen, and an ark of gold. Families collect their treasures and donate them to the cause. Every artisan and craftsperson among the desert host is recruited for the work. Soon, the whole wandering multitude is caught up in the consuming business. After its construction, of course, the tabernacle will need to be moved, dissembled, and reassembled ad infinitum — another colossal distraction absorbing all the energy that might otherwise feed panic and fear. This would be a wise strategy. Work them like slaves so they'll leave all worry behind. They may end up back in the Egypt of their minds, but at least they will survive.

And yet, such a clever ruse could never stand. For just as all the intricate preparations are assigned and the arduous work of construction is set to commence, a decree of another sort sounds: "Keep the sabbath," says the Lord, "because it is holy for you.... Six days shall work be done, but the seventh day is a sabbath of solemn rest, holy to the Lord; whoever does any work on the sabbath day shall be put to death" (Exod. 31:12–18).

Yes, their life in the desert brings anxiety, but the Israelites will not conquer their fears through work without ceasing. They won't find peace of mind through a return to slavery. They must learn to live with their fears, for these are nothing in the face of Fear itself: Yahweh, who made the heavens and the earth, who delivered the people from bondage. The God of Israel is like a "consuming fire." Keep your distance! "Otherwise," says God, I will "break out against" you (Exod. 19:21, 22). Here is the Hebrews' dilemma: this is a God one can neither live with nor live without. How will they dwell under Yahweh's protective shadow without dying in the process?

Suddenly, the real purpose of the tabernacle becomes clear. It is not a burden, but a grace — "that [Yahweh] may dwell [tabernacle] among them" (Exod. 25:8). Likewise work, for all its necessity, is not an end in itself. Its purpose is to honor God. In Egypt, the Hebrews found no rest from their labors. Weekends and holidays do not exist for slaves. But the Israelites are no longer slaves. They shall not live in Egypt; Egypt shall not live in them. For six days, they will labor for all they are worth. Then, in the shade of the tabernacle, they will loaf to God's good pleasure.

My children have finished breakfast and cleared the dishes from the kitchen table. I am saving my work to disk before shutting down the computer for the morning. I have been writing since dawn but am now resigned to an empty harvest of words until after sunset.

Besides, I have music on my mind.

Violin playing is a dance with time, a subtle game of impulse and release. It begins with the equipment — two curious chunks of wood, one fat, the other skinny, one with the voluptuous curves of a woman, the other a bony stick with hair attached. Yet it is said of some violin virtuosi that when they picked up instrument and bow for the first time, it was as if they were long-lost appendages. Everything fit, everything clicked. Their rapid progress appeared effortless, destined.

Most find such a thought incredible. The violin, whether or not the most remarkable musical instrument ever devised, is undeniably the most awkward. There is no natural way to hold it; our hands were not designed to play it, and it leaves the arms dangling in midair like puppets on a string. In short, violin playing is a chiropractic appointment in the making.

Consider as evidence that the vast majority of those who have ever held a fiddle under their chin now describe themselves as *former violinists*. Practically all pianists still play, even if their skill and repertoire are limited. Not so violinists. Usually by high school, occasionally as late as early adulthood, these one-time violinists simply loosened their bows and closed their cases for the last time. Many still own their instruments, which lie forgotten in drafty basements or steamy attics, cracking and swelling with the seasons. To open one of these cases now would be like exhuming the dead.

Why? What is it about the violin that provokes such animus, even prompting its owners to, in effect, bury it alive? Demanding as a tyrant, unforgiving as a greedy creditor, fickle as a faithless lover...are there any questions?

I hold out little hope that any of my own children will prove prodigious. I doubt that my son is a young Jascha Heifetz, or that among my daughters is a budding Midori. Like their father, my children are endowed with a fine sense of pitch, an affinity for rhythmic precision, and emotion to burn. Why, then, would I not expect them to inherit as well my inclination toward intensity, the proclivity to clutch and grasp at mastery rather than waiting for mastery to come home wagging its tail behind it? Of course, diligence pays a dividend in the end, but not before a battle waged in blood. It is a battle my kids and I will wage all summer. Hopefully, we'll swap less blood than beauty.

> God saw everything that he had made, and indeed,
> it was very good.... [A]nd he rested on the seventh
> day from all the work that he had done. So God
> blessed the seventh day and hallowed it...
>
> — GENESIS 1:31, 2:2B–3A

Morning work commences with art time. As my children create watercolor masterpieces at the kitchen table, I summon them one at a time to our library-turned-music room. I greet them as they enter the room, holding a tiny violin under my chin and adjusting the tuners to proper pitch. They stare up at me doubtfully, like I'm a drill-happy dentist. But my enthusiastic smile catches them off guard. "This'll be fun!" I tell them — part lie, part wishful thinking. I plan with extreme care their first encounter with fiddle and stick.

"This is your violin!" I begin. I proceed to explain the instrument's anatomy — its top, back, sides, scroll, neck, fingerboard, bridge, tailpiece, chin rest, tuners, strings. Next

I place its neck gingerly into their left hand and have them hold it down at their side like a strangled goose. "Now, gently swing the violin back and forth," I instruct. "Feel the weight of the violin. Imagine that it's part of you." They obey. We do the same with the bow, on which I correctly position their thumb and fingers. They swing the bow cautiously through the air.

We go slowly at first. I spent years of my earlier life undoing the bad habits of my own misguided efforts. Too late, I learned to create vibrato like a hummingbird hums, to trill like a woodpecker pecks, and to shift like a leaping cat. Go too fast and my children will suffer the same fate, I fear.

The kids and I endure days of this. On a rotation, they join me in the library for what soon ceases to be "fun." We tune, talk about the instrument, practice holding it. They pull the bow across the strings, up and down, in rhythms. They pivot the left hand on its thumb and rock the fingers over the fingerboard, tapping on the other side. Yet progress seems grudging. They grow impatient with their teacher. They want action, real music to bite into. They long for the concert stage. At last I bow to the pressure. We begin a one octave A-major scale, then launch at last into "Twinkle, Twinkle, Little Star" to the rhythms of "bicycle, bicycle, peanut butter sandwich" and "Mississippi, Mississippi." My children have now officially "gone Suzuki."

A new energy is released in the library, and I take full advantage of it. Soon we are adding "Twinkle" variations and doubling up on string-crossing and left hand–tapping exercises, on simple scales and finger strength and independence work. The greater their compliance, the more I push. Our lessons grow longer, spilling over into math and linguistics time. The Monopoly banker is left staring at his pocket watch, the Cat in the Hat stands out in the rain all "that cold, cold, wet day." T-ball and kick ball get booted to the back side of the afternoon. Bible lessons have lost out entirely.

There is no longer any time for them. In order that my children can progress on the violin this summer, I have begun to devote entire mornings to music. Rachael is incensed by this breach of contract. Free-spirited Rebecca is bending under the added weight of obligation. Even the twins, who have learned to tell time, are studying its slow passage with agitation. But I persist. It will take more than a few idle protests for me to question the wisdom of my chosen path. The Watkins Academy of Music will carry forward, whatever the cost.

FOR LOVE OF LOVELINESS

The law of the Sabbath forms a bridge between those commandments in the Decalogue concerned with honoring God and those concerned with honoring others. Like the first three laws, the Sabbath command addresses the question of idolatry, that is, imaging God in ways that distort God's nature. Here for the first time, however, the edict is stated positively: "Do keep the Sabbath because God does!"

The implication is powerful. It is in God's deepest nature to rest, to bask in the loveliness of what is. This, of course, is contrary to how God is often depicted: God, the ultimate tyrant, the impossible-to-please parent, the cosmic beat cop, eager to catch us in the slightest act of capriciousness. Many of our own cherished views of work, progress, and accomplishment have been shaped by such images of God, conscious or unconscious. Here, at last, they are exposed and rejected so that a new and gracious view of things might emerge.

Sabbath law also addresses our relationship with others in the world, specifically our penchant for treating God's creatures as objects instead of subjects, to exploit their instrumental value for selfish ends. In answer to this tendency, Sabbath law asserts the intrinsic worth of all creation. "And God saw that it was good."

The Fourth Commandment thus invites a reappraisal of work and leisure that is both theological and practical. To heed it is to be set free from the twin slavery of worshipping our own deeds and abusing the work of others, and set free for the joy of collective effort and shared success. It is to link arms with the creative impulse of the cosmos.

It is a Monday, five weeks into summer vacation. An alarm is going off in my head. Recently, I have begun to observe a new physical tightness in my children's violin playing. Thumbs press so firmly against the violin neck that they turn white. Bow hands begin to resemble ugly spiders. More telling still are the grimaces on my four angels' faces, as their young bodies and minds strain to perform a dozen demanding motions at once. In truth, I am tired myself.

This all comes home to me as my middle daughter Rebecca struggles to pull her bow "between the muddy bank and the sandy bank" — the fingerboard and bridge. Of all my children, Rebecca is most desirous to please. Just now she is fighting back tears. At last, the force of nature overtakes her spirit of deference, and she cries, "I need to rest, Daddy! Now!" With that, she falls back into a chair, violin in her lap, head bowed as if in prayer. I stand speechless, staring down at this vision of sweet innocence.

All at once, a single word pops into my head. It is like a missing puzzle piece, falling into place from a source unknown. It is "Sabbath."

Today, of course, is neither a Saturday nor a Sunday. But Sabbath is beckoning to me nonetheless in the slouched figure of my Rebecca. Now, finally, I understand. If I deny my children the gift of Sabbath for much longer, there will be consequences. I probably won't be put to death — the ancient penalty for a Sabbath violation. It is doubtful whether such a capital sentence was ever carried out, anyway. But I might well have killed all hope of my children's love affair with the violin, possibly even with music itself, for a time.

For though we've attended worship each Sunday of the summer, during the week I have violated the spirit of Sabbath as if I'd joined some new anti-Sabbatarian cult. I have worked my children like slaves. I have exploited their young bodies, asking them to master feats of contortion while ignoring the rhythms those same bodies require to remain healthy and fit. I have asked them to think about the violin but not to wonder at the sheer miracle of music itself. I have dissected individual notes down to their pitch, duration, and timbre, yet neglected to instill in my children a sense of delight in the musical line or phrase. All this I have done while knowing full well that decisions to pursue any musical instrument seriously are made ultimately on aesthetic, not analytic, grounds. They are decisions of the heart. The sacrifice made for music's sake is a sacrifice of love.

I recall wise words I heard in college, when I practiced violin for five or six hours a day. Toward the end of my senior year, my professor suddenly thought to ask me about my practice regimen. When I told him, he reacted with alarm. "That's too much," he said. "After four hours, you have wasted your time."

But more than the voices of the past ring in my ears. The Lord of the Sabbath is speaking, and the message comes less by words than by intuition. In a summer of self-imposed frenzy, I am poised to rediscover the natural rhythms around and within us and to honor them. This, too, I am learning, is the meaning of Shabbat.

I think of the world-class percussionist Evelyn Glennie, admired not only for her talent but for pursuing her musical career despite deafness. Once, when the chamber orchestra in which I play shared the stage with her, I marveled at her rhythmic precision in the absence of sound. For twenty solid minutes of music she stayed with us beat for beat. It was more than her astonishing visual concentration that allowed her to pull it off. She, by her own testimony, "hears" by feel. The beat lives deep in her gut. Perhaps it is through something akin to Plato's music, sounding from the beginning of time, that Glennie, in her deafness, has tapped into the very throb of the cosmos. Whatever the source, she hears so well that it causes the world to listen. This also answers to Sabbath, to a hidden rhythm revealed.

My Christian faith names God as the author of that rhythm, the same God who for love of company created a world, and for love of mercy once set at liberty a nation of slaves. The same God who, according to Jesus, made the Sabbath for us and not the other way around, so that once and for all we might discover true peace.

It was the New England Puritans, often cited for the distortion of the Sabbath through the strict enforcement of blue laws and the like, who defined salvation as falling in love with God. Love of God, love of neighbor, love of music and beauty, love of life itself — these things touch the core of the meaning of Sabbath. They are, after all, what make us human.

It is not as if Sabbath means that all is complete and novelty is at an end. The very word "rest" implies that work is normative in our lives. I think of God as creating constantly, and us as creating along with God. So Sabbath is a grand pause from the strain of creativity, a long fermata amid the din of daily endeavor. This is how it will be with us, I decide. From now on in my music room, Orpheus, the poet-musician, and Morpheus, Greek god of dreams, will work side by side. A portion of each violin lesson will be devoted to Sabbath. On weekday mornings, my children and I will master the art of musical loafing!

A PRACTICE OF SABBATH

Three months into their desert odyssey, the Israelites arrive at the foot of Mount Sinai. On the mountain, the earth and the heavens touch. God and humankind meet in the clouds. But some restrictions apply. Some may travel high up the mountain, while others must remain low. Only Moses makes it to the top.

All alike, though, shall be consecrated. They have to wash up, look their best, abstain from sex for three days. They must take care not to tread too near holiness. Last, the Israelites must make a pledge to obey all that God will command. Only then will there be a theophany. Only then will God appear.

On the third day, fire and smoke envelop the mountain. Lightning flashes, thunder clashes. A trumpet blast sounds so loudly it causes the people to tremble. They grow fearful and contemplate a hasty retreat. "Moses, take it from here!" they cry. "Later on you can tell us how it all came out."

But God has other plans. "Come up to the Lord," God says. God has in mind not only Moses, but seventy-three elders of Israel. As representatives of the people, they, too, will climb into the presence of God.

More rituals follow: burnt offerings, sacrificed bulls, blood spattered about. Then the elders ascend. They go up and sit down on the side of the mountain. There, while eating and drinking their fill, upon a pavement of sapphire, clear as the sky itself, the Israelites gaze upon God (Exod. 24:9–11). It is an experience of Sabbath never to be repeated in Israel.

The practice of Sabbath assumes many forms. Some of us attend public worship, eager to share with others a message of grace that never grows tiresome; others kneel in prayer right where they are; still others simply assume a posture of rest that invites thanksgiving for the gifts of a day, or a week, or a lifetime. Tying all these activities together is a spirit of gratitude that opens like a window to the awesome presence of God. Sabbath is finally a formative expression of love for God and for neighbor. It is a practiced belief in God's goodness, a willingness to stop our busy acquisition of personal well-being in order to receive it from the Source.

Each morning in my library, my children and I are discovering our own forms of Sabbath keeping. On the first day of our new Sabbath observance, we play the dead weight game. In the middle of lessons, I stop what we have been doing and invite each child to put the instrument away for the day. Each one complies gladly.

"Now, let your arms rest at your sides," I instruct. "I'm going to raise your arm by the hand. Remain limp. I'll do

the lifting. When I release your arm, let it drop in a free fall."
For my girls, this is a cinch. They let out a giggle as their
arms swing like ropes before coming to rest. But Seth cannot
do it. When I lift his arm, he lifts with me. When I let go,
his arm remains in midair, flexed and tight. "Relax this
time," I command. But he cannot. I push his arm down,
massage his muscle, invite him to perform the procedure on
me. He crows with delight as he drops my arm like a dead
body. But still he cannot manage it himself. "My son, the
control freak," I think.

Yet there is something more behind his rigidness. It is
fear, I decide. It is as if he believes that if he lets go, his arm
will rip from its socket and spill to the floor. Seth dreads the
surrender of control the way adults fear death.

Here it dawns on me. Rest, relaxation, release — these
are not the natural acts we sometimes take them to be. From
the moment of birth, we are scrappers, programmed to com-
pete and prevail. We are not by nature Sabbatarians, keepers
of Sabbath. The instinct of ceaseless hunting and gathering
is embedded in our genes. Laziness and sloth exist in the
world, to be sure, but these are not habits of Sabbath. They
are merely alternative forms of striving, energy wasted on
the avoidance of risk, pain, and failure. Even our sincere
efforts not to strive are revealed as more striving. "I will
strive hard to relax!" we can say, but not with a straight face.
This is part of our dilemma.

There is more than genetics at work. Increasingly, young
people are being subjected to what one sociologist describes
as a "hurried childhood."[1] In the so-called curriculum of

---

[1] David Elkind, *The Hurried Child: Growing Up Too Fast Too Soon*
(Reading, Mass.: Addison-Wesley, 1981).

modern life, we are forcing on our children cognitive demands that they are unable to comply with. I reflect on my own childhood in the sixties. Whole summers were spent out-of-doors, barely supervised. My only teachers were kids, barely my senior, whose simple expectations were that I hit the ball and throw the other team out. My own children, by contrast, have been in some form of structured day care or summer program since before they learned to walk. Typically, today's young people parade from place to place, event to event, as if the journey from youth to adulthood were a constant stream of obligations and destinations. Since my childhood the lives of American middle-class children, from toddlers to teenagers, have become enormously complicated. Meanwhile, those same lives seem increasingly void of the vital sense of grace and assurance so closely associated with spiritual well-being.

Back in our library, my Seth and I are scratching our heads. How will we convince his brain to set the muscles of his arm free? Then I remember the quintessential exercise in trust from my church youth group days — the faith fall. With feet together and eyes tightly shut, we fell back into the arms of a friend. If we hedged by thrusting one foot back to catch ourselves, then we had to begin again. At first, we would catch each other early in a fall. Eventually, though, we would wait until the last minute to cushion the falling body in our outstretched arms. By then, we had each grown confident of a timely rescue.

I explain the faith fall to Seth, and we begin to practice it. He is petrified. In stages, though, he learns to let go. He comes to trust in his father's trustworthiness. Finally, it becomes great fun and attracts the other children, who soon join in. Once, I even fall back myself as eight skinny arms collude to catch me. We all end up on the floor, laughing to the point of tears.

"Now, Seth," I begin again. "Let your arms drop to your sides like dead weight!" This time, Seth succeeds with the limber ease of true belief.

To keep Sabbath is, in a sense, to surrender, to fall back into loving arms, assured of their will to embrace you. And ultimately, keeping Sabbath is acknowledging that those loving arms belong to God.

Soon, we find ways to keep Sabbath in our violin pieces as well. Far and away the most difficult variation of "Twinkle, Twinkle, Little Star" is the infamous "Variation B." The problem is negotiating the rests that fall on the second and fourth beats of every bar and achieving the changed pitches on beats one and three, two eighth notes *after* each rest. To my children, the rest beat is anything but restful; it is nerve-racking torture. My selection of it is routinely greeted with frowns, followed by the telltale stiffness of preordained failure.

Every "Twinkle" variation has a lyric to accompany it, a phrase with just the right number of syllables that have stuck to it like a "pea-nut-but-ter-sand-wich." But an "official" lyric for "Variation B" has been difficult to establish. With the eighth rest in the middle, few apt phrases have been thought of. The one I favor is "prac-tice-shh!-please-prac-tice!" The "shh!" of course is for the eighth rest. It means "Stop! Don't play!"

I teach this lyric to my children. Like most kids, they make the most of the "sh!" — chanting it loud and long and obliterating the meter entirely. But this is when it occurs to me that the key to success with this rhythm could be deep breathing. A long inhalation on the first beat of rest, followed by a long exhalation on the next, and so forth, might serve both to punctuate the rhythm and to calm the body. A second of Sabbath in a busy string of notes. We try it, and in no time they have each mastered their first rhythmic challenge. I watch the tension leave their bodies like so much expelled air.

Breathing itself is akin to Sabbath. Respiration is the most elemental form of labor giving way to rest. No wonder that the way we signal the end of any strenuous task is with a great expiratory sigh. No wonder that, on the sixth day, God created human beings by exhaling into their nostrils the breath of life — and then God rested.

Yet among the many forms the Sabbath takes in our music room, nothing rivals our discovery of pure listening pleasure. On a scorching hot day in July, I cut lessons in half and gather everyone together for a by-now familiar exercise in meditative listening.

"Sit down and get comfortable," I tell them, "and listen to this." A violinist is performing pieces from volume 1 of the Suzuki Violin School on compact disk. We come to a piece the children know, called "May Song," and I say, "Let's sing along!" A fine violin sound is the envy of every singer on the planet, but long before their strings sound velvet, violinists must themselves learn to sing. And so we sing: "All the birds have come again. Hear the happy chorus! Robin, bluebird, on the wing; thrush and wren this message bring. Spring will soon come marching in. Come with joyous singing."

But this is only a teaser.

"Now here's something you've got to hear." I turn on our old record player and lower the stylus on a favorite vinyl recording of my youth — violinist Henryk Szeryng performing unaccompanied Bach. "Let's lie down," I suggest, "and relax every muscle in our bodies." I know this is a recipe for a late-morning nap, but they stretch out on their backs and I join them. "Now close your eyes." Our vision, the dominant sense, tends to command a lion's share of the brain's attention. With the eyes closed, the ears begin to greet sound like a long-lost lover. We actually begin to hear!

What our ears encounter this day is arguably the greatest work ever composed for the instrument I love, the chaconne from Bach's D Minor Partita. At his post in Leipzig, Germany, J. S. Bach composed, copied parts for, rehearsed, and performed an entire cantata each week. Yet he also found time to master the organ and harpsichord, pen hundreds of compositions, many for the violin, and father twenty children to boot! At the end of each musical work, Bach was in the habit of adding three words in Latin: "Soli Deo Gloria," to the glory of God alone.

We lie in a circle on the living room floor, heads together, legs outstretched. We are holding hands. We probably resemble the folded paper cutouts of a string of dolls the kids have been making in art time, although with my eyes closed I cannot tell for sure. The D Minor Partita is a long work, so I announce the movements as each one arrives: allemande, courante, sarabande, gigue, chaconne.

After a while, my children begin to fidget. This is not a form of Sabbath keeping universally relished by the young. Sometimes they would just as soon get on with the lesson and get out-of-doors sooner. I don't blame them.

But when we reach the chaconne, the work's final movement, all wriggles and jiggles cease. From its opening chords, my children register recognition. They have heard these chords before. They know this music, for I have practiced it often. Like every serious violinist, I visit and revisit this chaconne with all the solemnity of a religious supplicant on pilgrimage to Jerusalem or Mecca. Never, though, have they heard it like this, void of all interruptions, all mishaps. Never until now have they heard these notes played to such heavenly perfection.

Over the next fourteen minutes, the length of the chaconne, something astonishing happens. It is as if we are no longer lying prostrate on the floor but have begun to climb slowly into the air, coaxed higher and higher by the alluring lilt of the musical line, up and up until we have touched the clouds. And while moments before we were five separate entities, joined only by the hand, my children and I seem now to have become as one body, locked in a union of soul-stirring sound.

I can see none of this. It is a felt thing — in the pulses of the hands holding mine and at a depth of spirit rarely reached. I wonder if my children feel it, too, for it is a thing defying description, impervious to the manipulation of language.

The music ends. We lie still for a long while. I begin to think my children may be asleep. But then, they are up. "Let's eat," they say. The moment has passed, never to be repeated again. There will be other such experiences, but this one is unique. Indeed, meaningful encounters with the Holy are scattered at best — a rare experience of formal worship when pilgrims transcend ritual and climb the mountain to God; a priceless moment of contemplative clarity when the spiritual senses awaken to the divine in our midst; the time a father and his children lie on a carpet with their eyes shut tight and see the Lord, high and lifted up, riding on the music of the spheres. *Soli Deo Gloria.*

AND THE BEAT GOES ON

The day after our encounter with Bach, Sarah, first on the roster, reports to the music room following breakfast. Dutifully, she reaches for her violin case. "No, Sarah," I stop her. "Not today. Today is a free day. Today you may do what you want."

Sarah looks confused. She says nothing, nor does she move. "Well, what do you want to do, Sarah?" Silence. Then, like all five-year-olds, Sarah looks to the ceiling for the answer.

"I wanna color," she says at last. For visual Sarah, coloring is next to nirvana. She promptly removes five clean sheets of paper from our computer printer, a practice long accepted in our household in the interest of artistic expression. Then she is gone.

Sarah's siblings are soon off on their own as well. Not even Commandante Rachael questions this latest glitch in the routine. My children are far from slaves, but today they bask in the grace of deliverance.

Sadly, Sabbath is often mistaken for just one more requirement in a universe of requirements, one additional weight of obligation to bear. But biblical Shabbat is instead the radical suspension of all requirements, the temporary removal of obligation. As the Hebrews learned early and well, another word for "Sabbath" is "grace."

Meanwhile, we will continue to work, and, like God, I will continue to name my children and their efforts "good." I know I'll always be a striver. As their violinist father, I will remain sorely tempted to chase my children up the mountain of musical success. Rachael has recently threatened to switch to the clarinet. To a violinist, this is nothing short of blasphemy. But, more importantly, I will continue to offer to each of them the gift of the Sabbath. I will affirm to them that they are all that they need to be, that they have attained the level of perfection appropriate to that moment among all moments in time. The next day or the next hour, our work shall resume. We'll labor on toward perfection. But, then and there, we will rejoice at where and who we are. We will exult in the manifold gifts of grace. And the Lord of the Sabbath will join us.

Be still, and know that I am God!

— PSALM 46:10A

5

LOVE, HATE, AND DIGNITY

HONOR YOUR FATHER AND YOUR MOTHER

Honor your father and your mother so that your
days may be long in the land that the Lord
your God is giving you.

— EXODUS 20:12

Remember the days of old, consider the years long
past; ask your father, and he will inform you;
your elders, and they will tell you.

— DEUTERONOMY 32:7

PARLEY WITH THE PAST

*For the Hebrews, memory all but starts over in the wilderness.
Israel is like an infant who looks out onto the world for the first
time, etching wrinkles in the virgin tissue of the brain. But
now the initial memory is not a wrinkle but a great cleavage
with the past: "You were Pharaoh's slaves in Egypt, but the Lord
brought you out with a mighty hand." Exodus is Israel's salvation story. The rest is a bonus.*

The years in the desert proceed in sameness. Manna falls,

offerings are made, feast days come and go. Yet with each passing day, the Israelites are further from that seminal event of liberation. The defining act of their existence is slipping slowly, unremittingly, into the recesses of the mind.

Meanwhile, the Israelites are dropping like flies. Life expectancy in the ancient Near East averages perhaps forty years, and survival in the wilderness is especially tenuous. Every day, Israelites die and are buried. Parents and grandparents, priests and Levites, artisans, designers, and weavers — all who had worn the shackles of Egypt and beheld the wonders of deliverance and had heard the trumpeting thunder and had seen the smoke billow off the face of Mount Sinai — all breathe their last and return to the ground. And the slow caravan to Canaan, the Promised Land, moves on, leaving their graves behind.

With each death of an elder of Israel, the collective memory of the Exodus event grows fainter. Over the length of the journey to the Jordan and into the new land, virtually the whole liberation generation expires. Even Moses himself will never set foot there. He stands atop Mount Nebo opposite Jericho and peers into the Promised Land, but he is destined to die in the plains of Moab, on the wrong side of paradise (Exod. 32:48–52).

So the chief problem for Israel is memory. How will succeeding generations recall the hardship of a past now fading and learn gratitude for a plenteous present? How will they take into account what has been, even as they help shape what is yet to be? How will they honor their elders in a land that those elders will not see? This is not only Israel's challenge, of course. It belongs to us all.

"Can I divorce my mom?" my wife Donna asks. Her long postponement of this question is laudable but has likely been detrimental to her health. I am no attorney, I tell her, but it seems to me that the one person in your life you may never divorce is your own mother.

The mother in question is sixty-five and suffers from crippling rheumatoid arthritis. For a decade, her small-town doctor prescribed megadoses of cortisone. Now she has Cushing's disease and severe osteoporosis. As her cartilage has deteriorated, the bones of her spine have been compressing and fracturing, robbing inches from her stature. When I first met her, she stood a proud 5 feet, 2 inches tall. Now, she has shrunk to 4 feet, 9 inches. When I don't call her by her birth name, Estella, I refer to her affectionately as "my little munchkin mom."

Of course, it is far from a laughing matter. Her tiny compression fractures bring on monstrous spasms. She can be confined to bed for days at a time, barely able to move for fear of unleashing another barrage of keen and relentless pain. These days, the bed of her confinement is ours. She is a guest in the home of her daughter, my wife, who as a result is on a fast track to insanity. Estella's residency has become our experiment in the life application of the Fifth Commandment: "Honor your father and your mother" — including in-laws!

This commandment is the first of the so-called neighbor laws that follow those more specifically concerned with our relation to God and the realm of the spirit. Here at the outset, the neighbors in question are none other than one's own parents. Neighbor relations begin close to home. If we can manage to love and honor those bound to us most intimately, perhaps we can learn to practice these same virtues among strangers. At times, this seems like a very big *if.* Speaking as a son-in-law, this appears to be one of those times.

Not long ago, Estella's husband Charles, Donna's father, suffered a stroke, leading to paralysis and acute cognitive aphasia. Up until that time, he alone had cared for his wife, managing the affairs of their lives from their home two hours south of us. On the day of the stroke, he was under the kitchen sink battling with a backed up drain line. He cleared the drain, and then everything went black; one of Chuck's arteries had cleared itself out as well. His life changed for good in one mad dash of clotted tissue to the brain. His thoughts, his memories, his emotional makeup were reduced to Swiss cheese. Weeks of rehabilitation brought limited progress, but not enough to alter the new, stark reality: the caregiver now required care. Chuck clung to his life in a nursing home for awhile before a second stroke claimed it outright.

Estella, meanwhile, bemoaned her pitiful predicament. While grieving her husband's loss, driven by temperament and naked necessity, she soon moved on to the next logical ground for gloom — her utter vulnerability. Estella was alone and wholly dependent on a daughter and son with lives, loves, and loyalties of their own. Her life had changed for good. "One day, you're bouncing the future on your knee," a disgruntled elder once confided to me, "next day, the future is hammering you over the head."

Donna and I were far from ecstatic over this turn of events. Nearly everyone faces responsibility for the well-being of elders at some point in life. We had deemed this or some similar situation inevitable. But it had not occurred to us that it would happen in our early thirties, just as we were embarking on the renovation of a hundred-year-old home and welcoming our first child into the world. And all who have borne responsibility for the elderly or infirm know that just as difficult as making decisions about care is adjusting to the changes that inevitably follow; rarely does any single decision stand for long.

The people at the center had called it "catered living," which had such a comforting ring to it that we quickly had made up our minds. The one-bedroom efficiency apartment had implied independence, while the dining, housecleaning, and bathing services had promised care at Estella's level of need. Soon after her arrival in Indianapolis, we had moved Estella into the center, with her consent.

But she was not happy. The help was cranky, she cranked. The elevator down to the dining level was shaky, she shuddered. And the residents, she complained, were a bunch of nitpicky complainers. Worse, her back spasms were growing more severe. Soon she was unable to dress herself. The staff agreed to assist her with this while her back improved, but instead things moved the other way. The morning arrived when she could no longer get out of bed without assistance. We were alerted that her residency was in jeopardy. Her options were to move into the nursing home wing or vacate the center entirely.

On a frigid February day, as our new daughter Rachael was poised to begin toddling about the torn-up rooms of our endless home renovation, we wheeled Estella up the front steps and into her temporary quarters in the first-floor library. The most difficult decision of our married life was made. Its consequences were yet to be discovered.

GRABBING THE BATON

He established a decree in Jacob,
and appointed a law in Israel,
which he commanded our ancestors
to teach to their children;
that the next generation might know them,
and the children yet unborn,
and rise up and tell them to their children,
so that they should set their hope in God,
and not forget the works of God,
but keep his commandments.

— PSALMS 78:5–7

Now the sons of Eli were scoundrels...

— 1 SAMUEL 2:12A

For much of human history, the passing of power from one generation to the next has been problematic at best. Embedded in the human psyche is a sense of entitlement that accompanies one's coming-of-age. The Greeks examined this process in the Oedipus myth. The Babylonians had their own myth of seven generations of gods, each murdered in succession by their sons, who then marry their own mothers. A scholar of the ancient Near East points out that the seventh god isn't murdered, only chained. I suppose it's comforting to know that even the Babylonians gave a nod to progress.

In Genesis, the entire record of the Patriarchs centers on primogeniture, the pattern of inheritance from one generation to the next. The ancient paradigm, of course, is that the eldest son takes all, leaving the younger siblings to fend for themselves. From the very outset of Jewish history, however, the pattern is broken. Jacob, younger son of Isaac, tries to steal the blessing from his elder brother, Esau. He ends up fleeing for his life, leaving the family fortune behind, but the promise of Abraham passes through his seed nonetheless.

Joseph, eleventh son of Jacob by his second wife, becomes the most favored son of the next generation, but it is the fourth in line, Judah, who ultimately carries forward the seed of Abraham. Meanwhile, in an oedipal move of his own, Jacob's eldest son, Reuben, sleeps with his father's concubine, Bilhah, thus forfeiting the blessing of the firstborn forever.

Through it all runs the thread of a novel idea: the God of the Hebrews confers blessing freely and at will. Inheritance is not a matter of chance, prerogative, or manipulation. It is God's gift, pure and simple. To seize upon this is to conquer fear and greed. In a world of constant grasping, it is to relinquish that control over lives and outcomes that denies the natural limits of human power. It is to find a deep-centered peace.

Donna signs the papers with a trembling hand. She would avoid it altogether were there really any choice, but there is not. Someone needs to assume power of attorney over her parent's estate. Her brother, while willing and able, lives a thousand miles away. With his consent, we see an attorney and Donna signs. Her mother signs with her. Estella's hand trembles, too, but hers answers to the further indignity of rheumatoid arthritis. Each of her fingers bends impossibly backwards and sideways in a grotesque reshaping, called the swan effect. Her autograph resembles a child's connect-the-dots puzzle.

Still shaken by events and affected emotionally by her

illness, Estella is glad to leave behind the burden of managing her financial and legal affairs. And yet, she remains thoroughly engaged in the day-to-day concerns of her own life. Her likes and dislikes, her pet peeves, her long list of phobias are all still in play. It is a familiar scenario: while reticent to make decisions on her own, she is frightfully alert to each one made in her stead. Donna is justifiably anxious. It is hard enough to assume responsibility for another adult without also shouldering the blame when things go awry. Nothing could have prepared Donna for this experience, at any age. But she signs, because after all, there really is no choice.

Donna's first task is to get her mother's affairs in order. We drive down to the family home and rummage through her parents' records. Estella has been a saver all her life. Her desktop is buried in clutter — invoices, receipts, recipes, letters, notes to herself, countless scraps of paper with barely decipherable scribbles. Donna's task is a combination of excavation and detective work.

The desk drawers, too, hold old secrets, a book's worth of quotes and musings. Born with one blind eye, Estella is nevertheless a voracious reader. For years she had given talks on all subjects at church women's circle meetings, collecting and culling data, writing out draft after draft by hand. Estella has a talent for this, an aptitude for bringing big thoughts down to a common level, not to mention a great gift of gab. But sadly, she has ventured almost nowhere for years. She has been a hermit in her own home, bound by a crippling illness and a cautious husband.

The manuscripts of her devotional talks lie in unmarked folders, deep in the recesses of her desk. Glancing through them, I come across a favorite topic of church women's devotional meetings: the power of prayer. "Don't pray for miracles," a quote jumps out at me. "Prayer is the miracle." In her talk, Estella had been making a compelling case for peaceful repose in the face of trial. Sometimes, those most eloquent on a subject have the greatest difficulty taking their own advice.

Estella's struggle for inner peace is only understandable. We keep reminding ourselves of this as we search for some peace of our own. As Estella loses control, we are being asked to assume it. This power shift is fueling anxiety on every side, and peace is becoming an elusive commodity. Just how a mother, a daughter, and a son-in-law will find some I cannot tell. I'm beginning to suspect, though, that some order of miracle or another may be required.

THE PRICE OF INHERITANCE

Israel's kinship with the land runs deep. Adam, the first man, and all others with him are formed from the very dust, quickened by the breath of God. Paradise is a garden where everything grows. But with their fall from grace, Adam and Eve are driven from the garden to till the stubborn earth from whence they came. And when they die and their breath returns to God, the dust that they are returns to the ground. It is a wondrous, grievous saga of gain and loss. It is everyone's saga.

Later, as Abraham sojourns in the land of Canaan, God promises to make of his descendants a nation and deeds to them a land, running "from the river of Egypt to the great river, the river Euphrates" (Gen. 15:18). And Abraham believes God's promise.

Later still, in her Exodus wanderings, a homeless Israel grows even closer to the land through the sheer intensity of yearning after it. To have a bit of earth is the fondest hope of every Hebrew blown about in a barren wind-swept desert. Just some fertile ground — not too much — to build a home and plant a vineyard, graze cattle and dig a well. As it turns out, the Israelites get more ground than their dreams can grasp — thousands of square miles of it, enough for twelve separate tribes to inhabit at once. They come into more than a homestead; they acquire a nation. God's promise to Abraham is fulfilled.

The land doesn't come cheap. It is acquired at the price of many lives. The ground is bathed in blood. But Israel comes to see this ground as sacred, because a people with no land have found a land, and because God, they believe, has delivered it to them. But the land that is given can also be taken. Isreal's hold on it also comes with a price and a promise. The price: "honor your father and your mother," and the promise: "that you may live long in the land."

It is 7:00 A.M. on Saturday, a lousy day for an auction. Though already mid-April, winter is making a cameo appearance, chasing the southern Indiana hills back into a deep freeze. Tulips and crocuses will suffer, and so will we.

Arriving on a gust of wind, the auctioneer climbs from his truck, feels the chill, and grimaces. It is a bad omen. But we have been at work for two solid days. The entire contents of Chuck and Estella's split-level ranch-style house sits sprawling on the front lawn. During his final visit to their home, shortly before his death, Chuck had given his blessing to the deed we carry out today. Looking around with a long face, gesturing with his one good arm like a priest at the Eucharist, he had managed in halting speech, "This can all go. . . . It don't matter now. . . . All of it . . . can go."

Estella has not offered a similar assent. Unable to travel, she remains in our home in Indianapolis. But she is a palpable presence still. Over every scrap of furniture, every trinket, every remnant of the past, right down to the davenport doilies, she has cast a pall of uneasiness. These are her things; they tell her story. Yet here we are, preparing to dispense them among strangers for pocket change. We have already removed all the items that the space of our own lives will hold, and yet so many artifacts of her life remain. And the gall of it — to divide them up like orphaned siblings, turn over the keys of the empty house to a realtor, and drive away. Estella is not here to voice these things, but they sound deep in my conscience nonetheless.

The auctioneer surveys the merchandise, grouping items by type for the auction block. Small, inexpensive pieces will go first, sometimes combined with others of a similar variety: assorted flatware, miscellaneous china, ceramic bric-a-brac, and the like. Pricier items will follow, leading gradually to large furniture and appliances.

A propane heater sits near the auctioneer's table, holding the chill at bay. Inside the house, hot coffee percolates. We are bracing for a bitter day in more ways than one. By 8 A.M. people begin to arrive, first in a trickle but soon in a steady stream. They peruse the makeshift aisles with a cold objectivity we find off-putting, even offensive. Their dismissive airs begin to awaken in Donna a renewed feeling for these articles of her past. Even I, a relative stranger here, begin to contemplate their priceless value: a pair of fancy golf shoes Chuck brought from Chicago when they moved to southern Indiana in the early seventies; the rusty patio glider where Estella swung on her better days, watching the martins flit and flutter the summers away; even the many garish ceramic pieces

Chuck painted and fired in the kiln at the local pottery barn. All these and more suddenly assume a subtle beauty. Why don't others see it? But already I know the answer. The real value of things is not visible to the eye. It accrues through every life encounter and is tallied over time in the human heart.

When bidding commences, snowflakes have begun to fall. Bodies huddle close to the auction block, both to place bids and share the warmth of the propane heater. But Donna and I retreat to the background, reluctant to witness up close this crude parceling of possessions. We take a walk in the woods out back, drink coffee sitting cross-legged on the empty living room floor, swap recollections of our courtship within those walls. Here, we cuddled on the basement couch after Chuck and Estella were asleep, exchanged intimate secrets, and hatched improbable dreams of a shared future, many of which have come true. As much as we have complained about coming back here to visit, more of this place than we realized has been living inside us all along.

At last we return to the front yard to assess the auctioneer's progress. We had told him that everything must go. We requested neither minimum bids nor reserve to deny sale of items that have gone too cheaply. Anything left at the end of the day is to be given to charity. But these instructions are easier to abide by in theory than in practice. Donna cringes as the gavel falls on a small curio cabinet. It is a cheap piece — pressed wood with a thin mahogany veneer — but the highest bid of fifteen dollars seems an affront to the memorabilia long on display inside of it.

Suddenly, Donna spies a piece of her childhood in an old wooden crate and grabs it up. It is Estella's Spritz cookie maker. Cookie dough was pressed through it to form the festive shapes of stars, bells, angels, and the like. Each holiday season, Donna and her mother mixed, shaped, and baked themselves silly, filling Christmas tins with rows of cookies neatly stacked between layers of waxed paper. These would be given as gifts or nibbled down to the last crumb in the privacy of their own kitchen.

Estella has not baked for years. Sitting idly in her wheelchair or rocker, she used to vaunt the average Christmas cookie yield in those days at better than five hundred, but even her boasts have since slackened. Donna has rarely spoken of it at all. Yet just now, the Spritz has sparked in her a wistful nostalgia. She places the cookie maker along with all its attachments in a paper bag and lays it aside. The death of one more precious morsel of the past has been narrowly averted.

Meanwhile, the day is wearing on. The auctioneer glances at his watch. Though the cold has thinned the crowd, there is still much to dispose of. We look on in shock as dozens of like items are now grouped together for a single bidding war and as the few hangers-on carry off whole truckloads of merchandise. In the end, articles are haphazardly tossed together — old shoes with magazines, clothespins with pie tins and egg timers.

A new chill comes over me, the feeling that I'm selling Chuck and Estella down the river for a hot cup of coffee. My thoughts turn to farm families, watching with shame as the legacy of generations falls with one stroke of the gavel. And back even further, to the original tenants of this land, Native peoples who were forcibly displaced by pioneer settlers, with their armies and diseases. Suddenly, I wish to stop these proceedings, haul everything back and set them just as they had been.

But even as I wish for this the last vehicle drives away, laden with the final scraps of a family's past. We watch it until it passes the first curve in the street, then turn our gaze back into the yard, now bare except for a few empty boxes and bits of litter strewn across the grass. The auctioneer's wife is busily counting up cash and coin, preparing to hand over our thirty pieces of silver. Too late for regrets. This deed is done.

Over the next several years, the sun will rarely set without at least one inquiry about this infamous day. "Whatever happened to my avocado egg timer?" Estella will ask. "Did it go in the auction, too, I suppose?" We will rarely respond. The answer is already known, and such questions, though heavy on rhetoric, arise from the pain of long-borne grief. They act like a sweat valve on some piece of machinery, allowing a little excess pain to escape. They allow Estella to grieve one kitchen gadget at a time.

Now and then, however, when Estella will pop such a question, we'll come up with an answer of happy chance. On a snowy December day, watching a Betty Crocker commercial between segments of *As the World Turns,* she'll say, "What about my Spritz cookie maker? What ever happened to that?"

"It's here," we'll say, "right here in the kitchen cabinet!"

"Oh!" she'll respond in surprise. "We used to make five hundred cookies at Christmas, you know!"

"Right," we will answer. "Maybe we'll make some more with it real soon."

And maybe we will.

THE GREAT ARC OF LIFE

For the son treats the father with contempt, the
daughter rises up against her mother, the daughter-
in-law against her mother-in-law; your enemies are
members of your own household.

— MICAH 7:6

Down the generations, the Hebrews endure wars and rumors of war, scarcity, pestilence, and corruption. But nothing tears at the fabric of Israel like the cruelty and indifference of the rich and powerful toward the vulnerable to whom they are obligated. From the first days in the Promised Land to the fall of the kingdoms of Israel and Judah, a period of over seven hundred years, God's prophets continually accuse the Chosen People of neglecting their own weak. The poor, the widow, the alien, the orphan — Moses' law provides for each of these and more, but the law is often ignored.

Arguably the Israelites' greatest concern for one another lies in the treatment of their elders, whose strength has faded like the setting sun. To disavow one's father or mother in need not only robs them of their dignity but also steals a part of oneself. Conversely, when Israel responds with compassion to the needs of her elders, she may be embracing her true identity. Thus it is that prophets like Micah interpret the neglect of elders as the forfeiture of inheritance itself, the very death knell of a nation.

My heart is thumping with anticipation. After three months of exile from my library, I am about to get it back. This is the day Estella moves into her new second-floor bedroom. We knew from the beginning that the twenty spiraling steps of our entryway staircase would never serve as Estella's route upstairs. And so we have redirected the old servant's staircase from the second floor, originally exiting to a carriage porch, into the first-floor den. But even with this, Estella requires an assist.

The Golden Glide 5000 is the latest in chair lift design, the Cadillac of stairway locomotion. It boasts rack-and-pinion drive, obstruction sensors, a swiveling seat with folding arms and footrests, and a custom-formed helical track

able to negotiate the tightest curves. Just now it is anchored
to the wall and floor of our new back staircase, swallowing
up half the width of each stair tread. The installer is running the padded chair up and down the track at its top
speed of 1 mile an hour. Estella is watching from her wheelchair below, her one good eye squinting cynically through
thick spectacles. Estella is a tough sell. Even after three
months in the library, she is not anxious to take a trip to
greater comfort on something that resembles an amusement park ride.

And there is more to dislike, for we have purchased the
Golden Glide with some of Estella's life savings, the nest egg
she and Donna's father scrimped and sacrificed for over
decades. These and other financial decisions we have made
with her knowledge but not her unqualified consent. We
have made them with our interests as well as hers in mind.
And even if her interests have comprised the better part of
this equation, our views of her best interests have prevailed.
She knows all of this, and we know she knows it as we watch
her squint up the stairs at the lift chair, disappearing on the
staircase to her future. "The stairway to heaven," I imagine
she is thinking. In an eerie way it is true, for each day is
bringing her closer to eternity through the constant compression of her spine.

To demonstrate our own confidence in the device, we
strap our daughter Rachael into the seat and flip on the
switch. Rachael crows all the way up to the top and down
again while Estella begins visibly to break out in hives. "Your
turn!" we tell her. She only squints. Then I have a brainstorm. "Ride up with Rachael on your lap. We'll strap you
in together!" Rachael, who is still light enough to pose no
real threat to her grandmother's brittle bones, follows my

words and is eager for another ride. So she beams a glance at the squinting eye — a glance it cannot resist.

"Wheeee!" screams Rachael, as she and Estella round the bend and ascend to the second floor. Both Estella's eyes are tightly shut. Donna waits at the top to help daughter and mother off. She will also be the first to introduce her mother to her new room, with its freshly painted walls and ceiling, just-purchased carpet and curtains, and furnishings both familiar and new, carefully arranged for Estella's convenience. Donna lifts Rachael off her mother's lap and lowers Estella's legs gingerly to the floor. I, meanwhile, have followed behind them and help Donna guide her mother into the hallway. Estella's groans of pain reverberate around the cavernous space. Four steps ahead is her bedroom. We shuffle Estella across the threshold, over the pristine carpet to her favorite rocker, and down. At long last, she is home. Only time will tell whether she'll christen it a haven or a prison.

Donna has displayed familiar photographs here and there around the room. Two in particular catch Estella's attention. The squint opens to a wide-eyed gaze. One photo is a 1940s black-and-white shot of her and Chuck. Young, thin, attractive newlyweds, elegantly dressed, they lean toward one another affectionately so their heads touch. They are glamour defined — celebrities from the cover of *People* magazine.

In the other picture we see Estella at the age of four. This photo is somewhat faded, yellowed by the years. She is sitting in a painted wooden wagon, holding a floppy-eared puppy in her arms. The child-sized wagon is hitched to a white goat. On the front of the wagon is stenciled "Indianapolis, 1929." Estella is a bit chubby and her hair is short cropped, closer to its current length — not long, as in the photograph with Chuck. All in all, in this earlier shot she more closely resembles her current self, except that in the photograph she looks happy, not to mention healthy. Now she is trauma worn, beaten down by the daily ordeal of living.

Yet this photo is significant not only for the little girl pictured there, but for the figures who are absent: a doting mother and father who must have placed Estella gingerly into the wagon that day, over her squinty-eyed protest, and who returned to lift her gently out when the photographer was finished.

Every normal life follows a progressive arc up and then down again, from birth to old age, frailty to frailty, need to need. In between, we may offer the world our labor and claim our dignity, but on either end we must receive these from others. We require surrogates, willing to confer upon us with the gift of wholeness.

Donna and I are learning to accept our new parental roles in Estella's life — to stand at the side, ready to rush in whenever her eye begins to squint or her nerve to fail, to offer grace and solace as the picture fades slowly away into night.

THE BETTER PART OF BLESSING

But Israel stretched out his right hand and laid it
on the head of Ephraim, who was the younger,
and his left on the head of Manasseh,
crossing his hands, for Manasseh was the firstborn.
He blessed Joseph, and said:
"The God before whom my ancestors
Abraham and Isaac walked,

the God who has been my shepherd
all my life to this day,
the angel who has redeemed me from all harm,
bless the boys;
and in them let my name be perpetuated, and the
name of my ancestors Abraham and Isaac,
and let them grow into a multitude on the earth."
When Joseph saw that his father laid his right hand
on the head of Ephraim, it displeased him;
so he took his father's hand, to remove it...
But his father refused...

— GENESIS 48:14–17, 19A

Long before the Israelites are even a glint in God's eye, Jacob, called Israel, blesses his children and grandchildren. This is the way of fathers with their progeny, to lay their right hands on their firstborn and heirs.

But Jacob has the habit of conferring blessing as it pleases him. After all, it was Jacob who once finagled his elder brother Esau out of their father Isaac's blessing. Jacob's son Joseph is enraged when his father crosses his arms so that his right hand falls on Ephraim, the younger of Joseph's sons, instead of on Manasseh, the elder. Father and son tangle, but in the end Jacob has his way. And who should be surprised? The blessing will be given as it is given. The coming generation cannot control it. Like life itself, blessing is not a transaction but a gift — free, clear, and nonnegotiable.

There appears to be a pattern of late childbearing in my family. My mother was thirty-eight when I was born. I, in turn, was thirty-one when our first child, Rachael, came along. There is surely good in this, but not good only. At my birth, my parents had long settled in as individuals and as a couple, as had their parents before them and as Donna and I had upon Rachael's birth. The children of my family have therefore faced less of the turmoil of instability that often marks younger households. In her role as a newborn nurse practitioner, Donna is constantly meeting grandmothers still in their thirties. They appear old beyond their years and are almost always poor. It comes as no great surprise that grand-babies like theirs have a disproportionately large presence in the ICU, or that their prospects for normal health and home life are, statistically speaking, dim.

There is also a downside to my family pattern. By the time I met Donna, all four of my grandparents had already died. In endeavoring to convey to her what they were like, I have had to face the fact that I carry with me few reliable memories of them. One grandfather died before I was born; my remaining grandparents lived some distance from us, and all were gone before I reached adulthood.

Curiously, my most intimate acquaintance with their lives has been through events I cannot recall, but which have been faithfully told and retold to me through the years until the event and the recollection are indistinguishable. Or per-haps this is how memory always works — each reflection on an original experience alters the next until the experience itself is but a single drop in a vast sea of memory.

My most vivid memory of my mother's mother concerns an event at which I was not even present. Shortly before her death in 1979, Grandmother Bapa, as we called her, stepped into the kitchen to make her famed boiled custard for the last time. Only a cousin of mine was there to witness the deed, but in an act of great foresight, she created what has become the crown jewel of the family archives. Cousin Mary set a cassette tape player on the kitchen counter, pressed *play,* and got Grandmother talking. Recently, I have dug out my copy of the tape to listen to it again. In these awkward days, something has told me that I should.

The interview starts slowly. Initially, one hears only a cacophony of clanking pots and pans. Then, Mary's questions begin: "Where did you and Grandfather meet? How did you fall in love? What was your life together like?"

Soon, Bapa is waxing eloquent on themes of life and love, grace and goodness. She tells us how our grandfather Samuel proposed to her. She initially accepted but later broke the engagement. "Oh, how he cried and cried!" she says. Yet, not long after, she recalls, when he had become engaged to another girl, Bapa realized she'd made a grievous mistake. By the time he ended that engagement and found the courage once more to profess his love for her, Grandmother Bapa's heart had opened wide in gratitude, never to close again. "That's how it was," she says. And there can be know doubt about it. I can hear it in her voice. That time around, she answered yes — a word of sheer grace in my own life, I confess, for apart from it I would not be.

The whole time she talks, Bapa cooks her boiled custard. "It takes eight eggs," she announces, "eight or nine." It doesn't matter; either will do. I can hear the eggs cracking against the side of a bowl, as 2 quarts of milk and 2 cups of sugar are brought to a boil on the stove:

1, 2, 3 cracks, and Bapa tells of their long engagement and careful saving for the future, for a house and livelihood and family.

4, 5, 6 cracks, and she has learned of Samuel's urgent desire to enter seminary and, someday, become a preacher.

7, 8, 9 cracks, and suddenly I am with them through a still more pressing circumstance: Samuel's father has cancer, and Samuel is now responsible for his care. He must continue to live at home, and so his marriage to Bapa is delayed still longer. What I am facing with self-pity in my thirties, he confronted in his early twenties with all his dreams and aspirations still ahead of him, meeting it gracefully by all accounts, without undue doubt or deliberation. He met it as a man you would want to fall in love with, answer "Yes!" to, resolve to wait for.

10, 11, 12 cracks, and apparently Grandmother Bapa has completely lost track of the eggs. These extra eggs have long been a source of good-natured amusement in my family. But we smile more than laugh as we listen and keep count. After all, Bapa was old and easily distracted. Or might each cracked egg have stood for some sage advice? Such as, you can always expect one more breach in life's best-laid plans, so don't get cocky! Or the golden truth that from the shards of broken dreams even finer things are fashioned.

Then, as the tape runs out, it dawns on me: I've just listened to the sound of the thickest boiled custard ever made. It is surpassingly rich in more than broken eggs.

13, 14, 15 cracks, and I hear how the Rev. Samuel P. Bowles preached for thirty years before dying in his sleep at age fifty-eight. He is the grandfather I never knew. Today, thanks to a cousin and a cassette tape player, his story lives on inside of me.

My Grandmother Bapa was right; gratitude does open wide the heart. For the first time, I have begun to take measure of another soul now backlisted to memory, my own father-in-law, Charles.

In Chuck's case, I know more than may be good for me.

A quiet, complex man, Donna's father endured his share of demons. While he lived, I often found little in him to respect. In those days, of course, I was still learning to respect myself. Mark Twain's quip about turning twenty-one only to be astonished at how much his father had learned in a few short years was true of me. Now, aided by hindsight, I can write a long list of posthumous commendations: handy, helpful, honest, knowledgeable, reliable, dedicated, true. Chuck could make almost anything worth making, fix almost anything worth fixing, and he had the knack for finding the most practical route between two steps in any process. "I wish I had him here now," I've often said aloud, and that may be the highest form of praise there is.

Yet, strangely, the recollection that has sealed my affection for him, now and always, is of something that took place after his stroke. On his final Thanksgiving, as Donna worked the day shift, Chuck and I shared turkey dinner on the hospital rehab floor. He cried a lot that day, I recall. It was an average day. Along with everything else it had altered, the stroke had released his usually bottled up emotions. For the first time, they flowed freely, naturally. I recall having thought it odd that, though he now could barely talk, Chuck and I were communicating on a deeper level than ever before. Even considering the clear tragedy of it all, something about this made me glad. Somehow, despite all he had lost, he seemed to me more fully alive and human, and I seemed more fully like a son of his own.

I realize now that, whether by will or design, he finally let his family in during those last days. That was what he had to give. That was how he blessed us.

Yet, for all their force, at the moment these instances of blessing seem mere anecdotal abstractions, not day-by-day realities. The daily elder in our lives just now is Estella. It is her groans that greet us early each morning and wear on throughout the day. It is her deep-sighed snoring that intrudes upon our love-making in a bed just one wall away. And it is she, my little munchkin mom, who holds within her porous bones the power over all my pique and pity. I know that the better part of my life with my mother-in-law Estella is a graced affair, that in her own way she is raising a rickety right hand to bless us. Yet I strain to see it. I'm still standing before her like Jacob's son Joseph, intent to know whether it will be the right or left hand that finally comes to rest upon our heads for good.

HONORING THE HONORABLE

Remember the law of my servant Moses,
the statutes and ordinances that I
commanded him at Horeb for all Israel.
Lo, I will send you the prophet Elijah . . .
He will turn the hearts of parents to their children
and the hearts of children to their parents so that
I will not come and strike the land with a curse.

— MALACHI 4:4–6

The book of Malachi is the last prophetic word spoken in either the Hebrew Bible or the Christian Old Testament. Nearly one thousand years of Jewish history lie between Malachi and God's covenant with the Hebrews on Mount Sinai, called Horeb. Spanning all that time, through victory and defeat, glory and humiliation, sovereignty and vassalage, the basic charter of Israel remains: "Remember the law of Moses . . ." Neither have the stakes changed: "... or else I will come and strike the land with a curse." The blessings of the earth are still tied to Hebrew obedience to the law. That obedience still depends upon the hearts of children turned to their parents, to the spirit of the Fifth Commandment itself. It is as we honor the past that the future discloses itself, bright with promise.

Yet here in Malachi, called the "seal of the prophets," we see something more. We see that "the hearts of the fathers ... and the hearts of children" must turn to each other. Relationship is a reciprocal business, a two-way street. Parents as well as children are responsible. The hearts of parents must incline to their children. If the heart of an elder is turned from a child, then that child's heart may shrivel, and the future dim in a curse of depravity and forgetfulness.

I have been reading in the newspaper of a man my own age on death row for a brutal murder. He has spent the last fourteen years of his life behind bars. Now his day of reckoning is at hand. But as always with capital punishment, there are grave misgivings. His guilt is not at issue, for he admits to the crime. Rather, his intellectual capacity is in question. He possesses the mental acumen of a seven-year-old. When informed recently that he could yet avoid the death penalty, he wondered aloud whether he would still get his final meal request of a double cheeseburger and fries.

There are further mitigating circumstances. As a child, he was severely abused by his own mother. After hearing his tormented screams for a long period, concerned neighbors finally intervened, demanding to see the child. What they found was a five-year-old body bejeweled with bruises, scars,

and burns. Some marks were fresh; others were emblems of
old torture. All were visible to the naked eye, but the scars
on his soul were too deep to fathom. The civil authority left
the boy with his abusive birth mother anyway, perhaps seal-
ing his sad, destructive fate.

To honor, *kabed* in the Hebrew, means "to give weight
to." It has less to do with *obeying* than with *taking seriously.*
Children honor parents by entrusting to them their fundamental sense of security and well-being. There is no greater
honor that one person can offer to another. When parents
fail to be honorable, they violate that trust. If the failure is
complete, a lucky child will find other elders to honor
instead. Those less fortunate may become unable to follow
any good example, or, worse, they may surrender their allegiance to the very accursed things that have brought them
suffering and despair in the first place.

Now this has happened to a simple soul of my own age,
sitting on death row in the dark. In a single brutal act,
he "gave weight to" the example of his mother. He "out-
mothered" her, in effect. This is how he brought her honor.
For this eerie deed of devotion, we will probably put him to
death. If the hearts of parents and children are not turned
back to one another, Malachi warned, then the land will be
stricken again with a curse — not a far-fetched view at all, I
think.

In his commentary on the Epistle to the Ephesians, John
Calvin points out that the admonishment for children to
obey their parents (Eph. 6:1) is qualified with the phrase "in
the Lord," that is, according to God's will. The door is thus
left open to the possibility that children may disobey when
their parents are behaving other than "in the Lord" — that
is, *dis*honorably.

The bitter truth is that, in one way or another, we all fail to honor the highest standards of parenthood. Some just fail more successfully than others do. Thankfully, my own parents failed quite admirably. Their chief infraction was the sometimes excessive richness and complexity of the lives they led. To compensate, my brother rebelled, while I excelled. Each was in part a bid for a bit more attention. In the aftermath, we both lead lives of richness and complexity. For us, the experience has yielded a net gain.

All of this has me thinking about my own parenthood. Will it be honorable? I imagine that my chief failing as a parent, like that of my own parents, will be distraction. I suspect that my children, like me, will suffer from the frenetic pace of the lives we lead, and I hope that they, too, will reap a net gain in richness. But just in case, I'm bracing for rebellion.

Meanwhile, in these matters I welcome all the help I can get. As we contemplate an expanding family, additional helping hands and giving hearts have come to appear indispensable. My own aging parents have retired hundreds of miles from our home. Who will fill the gap of modern life, with its two-career families living time zones away from the nearest next of kin? What ever happened to the venerable village elder? Could we not honor our parents by enlisting them in the service of their juniors, whoever and wherever they are?

Of course, such a solution should involve more than child care. Eric Erickson has coined the term "generativity" to describe that process whereby our elders bequeath to us the sum of their life knowledge and expertise. Naturally, generativity requires several things. Seniors must be willing to extend themselves in this way. Young people must wish for them to. Society must be structured in a manner that both allows and facilitates it.

There is hope. Already being challenged is the old assumption that everyone after a certain age should be retired and put out to pasture. Alongside America's rapidly aging population is the dawning realization that our long-term socioeconomic security may hinge on the discovery of the new tribal elder. Here and now, three millennia after Moses first pitched it to the people of Israel, the linkage between the honoring of elders and the well-being of the land still holds firm.

Such matters have been crowding my thoughts on a lovely gardening day in May. Daughter Rachael had helped Donna and me dig and plant, weed and water. But after a time she lost interest in dirt and was ready to move on. And so we chose to deliver her to Estella's room, where Grandma has been holed up more or less since the day of her arrival. Twice she has come down the stairway lift to rejoin civilization — once on Rachael's birthday, and again for a tornado warning. Yet something quite different has just recently begun to develop, something in fact that touches close to home on this very matter of tribal eldership. Rachael and her grandma have begun to bond.

We take turns checking on the pair at intervals. Now it is my turn. Not wishing to distract my daughter, I sneak up the front staircase and peek around the corner at the rocking chair where daily my mother-in-law's life totters in place. There, on grandma's lap, sits Rachael. A book is propped up between them. Rachael is pointing eagerly at a picture on the page. She coos and caws at every object, every shape, and Estella joins her. With full voice and wide eye, Grandma reads with thespian flair, with the animated innocence of a child yet the poise of a grand madame, and Rachael is mesmerized by the sound. This is Estella's true gift, this escape into a world apart. For a magical moment, all the layers of anguish and regret peel away. There, at the core of things, sit a grandmother and granddaughter. And when our young heiress cocks her head and lifts her own precocious eyes up into Estella's pain-worn face, the universe of possibility again opens wide. Estella regains the truest part of her namesake, becoming a twinkling star, shining light into dark surrounds. Or perhaps she is shot back in time to her own pristine childhood, back onto that donkey cart of innocence in 1929 Indianapolis. Either way, for the first time in a long time, Estella is home again. A withering soul reclaims her dignity. Sitting there, she almost begins to look like a tribal elder herself.

Then I know it: this is the very blessing I have sought. It is a right-handed blessing. And I vow, here and now, to tell this tale, to take care that it will not be lost. Over the course of time, this, as all tales, will pass away from the world of memory. But here is a pledge I intend to keep: this tale will not die with me.

6

IN A CHILD'S WORLD OF LIFE AND DEATH

YOU SHALL NOT KILL

Whoever sheds the blood of a human,
by a human shall that person's blood be shed;
for in his own image God made humankind.

— GENESIS 9:6

THE LEGACY OF VIOLENCE

Violence saturates both sides of the Exodus journey. The Hebrew slaves in Egypt live under a murderous cloud. Pharaoh's chief dilemma is whether to exploit them further or be rid of them for good. Fearful of their rapid increase, he chooses murder. When God raises up Moses to gain their liberation, Moses is already a murderer himself. Through the series of ten plagues, the circle of violence and murder widens. Only when Pharaoh's own hardened heart is broken by the death of his son does the sad cycle end. It is undeniable: suffering and death set God's people free.

After forty years in the desert, the Hebrews embark upon the conquest of Canaan. Following God's directive, they practice holy war. No prisoners. No spoils. All must die. Former

141

slaves may not become the masters of others, nor may they grow
fat on their bounty. The change of residency must be clean. As
a consequence, it is all the more murderous. This is an eerie
logic that we will never puzzle out.

Between these scenes of carnage are years of relative peace.
Desert life is severe and dangerous for the Hebrews; conflicts
surface and resolve only painfully. But the people are on a jour-
ney of new being. All steps lead up a mountain, Sinai, to a
covenant with the Living God, and then down again and on to
the Promised Land. At the zenith of the journey comes a word
that at once clarifies and mystifies all the death dealing that
surrounds it: you shall not kill!

It is just past dawn on a summer Saturday. I am sitting at the
kitchen table watching five-year-old Seth slurp down a bowl
of instant Cream of Wheat. Though full of earth's golden
grain, his mouth still finds room for rich chatter over urgent
matters — Power Rangers and space aliens, dilithium crys-
tals and quantum blasters. I strain to take it all in between
bites but find it as confusing as advanced physics. It is barely
past dawn, and I am already weary.

I had planned to rise early and enjoy some time to
myself before making a leisurely midmorning breakfast of
pancakes and sausage when everyone else was up. I almost
made it; was shaved and dressed and heading down the front
staircase to safety. For I covet such moments to myself, when
my dreams have all but washed away the previous day's disappointment and strife. These press me down gradually over
a day, down several notches into my reptilian brain. There,
anxiety mounts to the point of a hair trigger's release. By the

end of the day, I'm Clint Eastwood, thirsty to fire one off at a deserving target.

But each morning, I awaken from sleep a new creation. I am St. Francis of Assisi, a lamb of a nice guy. I am master of my passions, seated firmly again in the rational hub of my cerebral cortex. I am a centered soul, a righted being. Then unfolds the day. The sun crests on the morning's endeavor and begins its slow dissent. Events distill into fresh history, but the history is mixed. Grace and promise give way to need and regret. Heartache and fear again rattle the gate, and I am swept east of Eden for the ten-thousandth time. This is my daily destiny.

Still, this Saturday is another new day begun in the Garden, and I wish to forestall its withering for as long as can be. I want at the very least to lay out some of the terms of the daily fall. And so I tiptoe in stocking feet down the edge of the stair treads, where they are least likely to creak. I don't want another creature to stir, not for at least half an hour.

But Seth sleeps like a dragon, with one eye open. His senses are on twenty-four-hour alert. From his room next to mine, he searches the dark for any sign of my stirring. He hears my feet hit the floor and the clank of my belt buckle. He smells the shaving cream on my face and intercepts the sound of the comb running though my hair. When I am halfway down our winding staircase, Seth appears on the landing above, his arms outstretched. I'm had. For Seth is my second Adam and I am constrained to embrace him, to welcome him into my own private Eden before breakfast. I swoop him up, and together we brave the brand new world.

Now we are sitting on the back porch swing. I am watching him outfit himself for an excursion into our backyard. He

uncouples socks and untangles shoelaces before tying them.
All the while he is sizing up the state of his world. He notes
the position of toys in the yard and what lies in the sandbox.
He wonders whether yesterday's loot still resides up in the
swing-set fortress where he had stashed it before supper. Most
of all, he listens across the fence for his best buddy, Mattie,
who will be similarly preparing to challenge the day. Soon,
from twin watchtowers, they will call out to each other and
hatch plans for shared exploits.

Now Seth is ready to break free, but there remains one
crucial matter to address. He opens a toy chest and pulls out
a long plastic saber. This he spears through a loop in his
jeans. At last, he bounds into the yard, armed and dangerous. He has learned early and well. It may be a squirt gun or
an imitation sword, a bow and rubber-tipped arrow, or a
plastic knife, or just a stick off the ground. It may be still
only morning, but Seth never leaves home without arming
himself.

I scratch my head as he serpentines to his command
post, dodging attack and slicing up villains. Has his daddy
taught him this? It is true that I enjoy a good James Bond
flick. I watch at least the second half of a close Super Bowl,
and I like to recite *Jabberwocky* with children present. Each
night I set the house alarm on maximum and disarm it again
first thing every morning.

This habit is not without cause. According to FBI statis-
tics, crime is down nationwide, including homicides. But
Americans seem to feel no safer. My own street is a thoroughfare between two neighborhoods notorious for drug
dealing. We suffer porch theft, gang graffiti, and minor van-
dalism. We recount to any who will listen the story of our
return from the movies one summer evening to a driveway

of squad cars and the pitiless screech of the alarm, broad-
casting victory up and down the street. The housebreakers
had kicked in the backdoor but were so startled by the
sound they never even crossed the threshold before fleeing
the scene. I do not lie awake at night contemplating *whether*
I should hope to kill the intruder who would cause my
family harm, only *how* best to accomplish the deed without
getting myself killed instead. I don't think of this as an
enlightened preoccupation, just an unavoidably compelling
one. While the odds of having to act on such a plan are
slim to none, the fact of the plan itself points up a staunch
reality: we do not feel safe in our own skins. We are each
haunted by the specter of a violent and murderous world.

On this day, my first concern is for my only son. Will he
be well today? Will he live out the spirit of Cain or that of
Abel? Or shall I perhaps recognize in him a bit of the promise of his namesake, the third way, the hope of new life —
Seth, third son of Adam?

Is it "You shall not kill" or "You shall not murder"?
Everyone has an opinion. The question seems to hinge on
motivation. Some take the command to mean, "Don't take
life without moral justification," only to prevent harm, to
uphold freedom, to right a wrong. Those who take a broader
view of life taking read the command to mean, "All killing
is wrong." To participate in killing of any kind is to join
forces with evil and death.

Most of us squirm between the extremes. The Old
Testament itself refuses to decide for us. Biblical meanings of
"murder" and "kill," "murderer" and "killer," are anything
but clear. Indeed, they are layered with contradiction. Is
someone who kills accidentally a murderer? Or does murder
mean only intentional killing? Is a killer a heartless monster,

or a victim of circumstance? The Bible has no single answer.
I think it favors the confusion.

To live is to be tempted to take life and to sometimes
follow through on that temptation. The philosopher Alfred
North Whitehead wrote of life itself as robbery: to live at all
is to commit murder. The matter of intention grows irrelevant because more than human life is at stake. You may not
feel like a murderer while crunching on a stick of celery. As
proudly as you string together a crowded catch of bluegill,
the fact that you have killed them may be the furthest thing
from your mind. And you are thinking only generous
thoughts as you purchase for a son or daughter a garment
assembled in the developing world by some malnourished
child in a sweatshop. Indeed, you carry in your very genes
the triumph of your ancestors in the brutal contest for
human survival. This is the only reason you exist at all.
Whether the command prohibits murder or killing, we each
live closer than we know to the daily taking of life.

IN THE WORLD OF A DAY

By 9:00 A.M., households up and down the street are astir.
Children are prodding parents to pass a verdict on the day's
doings. Trips to the pool, the zoo, or the children's museum
are on every child's A-list. Hikes and picnics lag not far
behind. Yet the mere mention of such excursions is like pressure on a weary parent's chest. The prospect of planning,
gathering, and packing for a family outing has a fearsome
edge to it. Moms and dads are hoping simply to cross off a
few items on daunting to-do lists. Meanwhile, the city is
experiencing a heat wave. Temperatures this Saturday will
top out near 90 degrees. I decide that today has a decidedly

stay-at-home feel about it. Still, a child's weekend appetite for thrill and carnival must be satisfied.

My original plan for solitude has clearly been usurped by Plan B. Phones begin to ring. Children and parents alike commence between-household negotiations over most desirable play sites. Her house, his house, their house; his swing set, her pool, their basketball hoop; her Barbies, his cars, their Sega Genesis. Parents push their own agendas. The bank closes at noon; the toilet won't flush without a new tank kit; the lawn must be mowed before it rains. Scores are added up like a game of bridge. They factor both type and level of need. The highest scores win.

At 9:45, negotiations have ended. A decision has been made: today the neighbor kids will play at our house. I will oversee their play as I do lawn work, and Donna will catch up on a week's worth of laundry. We will fill the inflatable pool with fresh tap water that will heat through the morning to an acceptable warmth. Lunch will be served on the patio — grilled cheese sandwiches with apple wedges and chips and plenty of juice packets, available throughout the day. The parents of our young guests will enjoy a day of rare liberation. They will run errands, shop, or carry out projects long delayed. Perhaps they will reserve some moments to exercise or make love, to nap or read. Whatever they do, they will do it with peace of mind, knowing where their children are.

By 10 A.M. the children begin to arrive. Hastily, we make final preparations. Gather towels by the pool: check; ice and juice in the cooler: check; sunscreen: check; list of home and cell-phone numbers: check; review house rules: check; medication and allergy check: check! All is in order. Let the games begin.

MURDER WITH WORDS AND
OTHER WEAPONS

You have heard that it was said to those of ancient
times, "You shall not murder"; and "whoever
murders shall be liable to judgment." But I say to
you that if you are angry with a brother or sister,
you will be liable to judgment.

— MATTHEW 5:21–22A

My only childhood pledge to my parents as I went out to
play was to stay on our side of the street. Adults laid out few
other rules to govern our play. Playmates worked out their
differences among themselves. When this proved impossible
and things came to blows, usually verbal, the losers went
home, tail between their legs, and that was it. But they were
almost always back in the fray by the very next day.

My children's pledge is to stay on our side of the fence.
Because they honor the pledge, I find myself the reluctant
negotiator of every conceivable dispute. Unlike my parents,
I am present for all conflicts. My chief interest is that children have fun without getting hurt in the process. Most of
the time, these are compatible expectations.

Perfunctory greetings dispensed with, the four boys are
already busy inventorying weaponry. My eyes fix on two
scary-looking plastic firearms that have entered my yard in
the hands of a kid named Charlie. One is a giant aquama-
rine water cannon. I think to myself that we would have
killed for it back on the block of my youth, where water
fights were frequent and primitive. No one ever got very
wet with a water pistol. But getting drenched seemed like
half the fun, so someone invented the water balloon. On a

sizzling summer day, nothing felt better than one of these bursting across your middle, splashing refreshment up into your face. Yet now I fear the cannon spray from this new-fangled piece could put an eye out. I pass an edict that its reservoir shall remain empty this day.

The other weapon is a camouflaged semiautomatic rifle Seth's eyes have stuck to like superglue. He has never seen one of these up close before. Donna has banned all toy guns from our home on principle, a policy I both concur with and question constantly. Just now, all my doubts kick in. The seduction of this gun and my son's wide-eyed excitement over it are almost unbearable. If I take away the camouflage and the extra gadgetry, it brings to mind the seminal weapon of war in my own childhood: the M16 Marauder. In the late sixties, at the height of the Vietnam War, the Marauder was deemed essential gear. Popguns only went "pop." Toy six-shooters made a pitiful little clicking noise. Cap guns were louder, but their ammo was always in short supply. The M16 let out an intimidating "rat-tat-tat" that caused others to fall down dead with delight. If you were going to die in battle, this was the gun you wished to accomplish the deed. War was never so good as when Mattel dreamed up the Marauder.

I wonder again whether it is fair to deny my own son this passion of my boyhood — gunplay. Through formative years, I aimed and fired on countless human targets. I personally died in cold blood hundreds of times. Yet I have never owned a real firearm and have only fired one once. I deplore the proliferation of handguns. I favor safety locks and a mandatory waiting period on gun purchases. I grew up to disdain the war in Vietnam and am leery of any U.S. military engagement that overlooks even the remotest opportunity for negotiated peace.

I amass the evidence in favor of a toy gun policy review. But I remain torn. Much as I would like to, I cannot escape the stark reality of these days. This is not only about my son. It concerns the obscenity of three hundred thousand child conscripts worldwide. It is about our own culture of violence and the mounting possibilities for its expression. Violence in the media, in the workplace, in the school, and in the home all play a part. It is young male rage, a volcano of hurt and confusion poised to erupt at any moment. It is anger looking down a barrel, the unprecedented willingness of mere children to seek solace in a trigger squeezed with disquieting ease. It is a hole in our collective soul.

Nonetheless, on this day I choose to leave the guns in play. Call it an experiment, a bid to discover what life lessons still lurk in molded plastic destruction. Soon, the four boys have divided into two teams. They load their gear and march to opposite ends of the yard. Within moments they will meet in the middle and explore new meanings of life and death.

Five young girls, meanwhile, are holding Barbie Hour on the patio. They dress, primp, and accessorize. Theirs is a genteel play, far removed from the weightiness of war. But it is not devoid of conflict. Sarah and her friends have ambitions. Each wishes to produce the most beautiful Barbie of the day. Amassed between them are no fewer than twenty-five dolls: fifteen Barbies, four Kens, a couple of Skippers, plus a Mulan and a Pocahontas or two. I listen in amazement as a Peyton Place web of relations grows up among them — daughters and mothers, children and grandchildren, husbands and wives, girl- and boyfriends, ex-girl- and boyfriends. If they listen to their children playing, parents will discover richer plots than all the daytime soaps combined.

Soon, personalities begin to clash like mismatched skirts and blouses. The girls fight over shoes, boyfriends, and who will ride in today's equestrian meet. Tempers flare and words grow terse and unkind. My Sarah always wins this match. She is only five but was born with the brawn of a Brunnhilde. Her stare can slay a crowd, and her voice shoots daggers to the heart. It is not the words themselves but the delivery that counts. My middle child, Rebecca, is caught on the receiving end of both. She flees the scene with melodramatic flair.

I catch the eye of my eldest daughter Rachael. She has been put in charge of girl play for the day. She only shrugs her shoulders and lets out a helpless sigh. It is a familiar scene. Sarah is chin to chest, her arms crossed tightly. The awkward strain of the moment will go away only when she releases it.

All violence seems to commence with words. Unlike guns, knives, or fists, hurtful words don't coerce, they invade. They do not work all at once, but slowly and insidiously they wither the soul. Once uttered, they replay in memory, again and again, until at last the hearer becomes the speaker. This is how they kill.

Growing up, I was like Rebecca. Children like Sarah were my bane. I took their cold judgments as gospel. Even today I carry them within me, like a splinter long ago buried deep in the skin. Old words still pack a murderous punch.

Like it was yesterday, I recall the occasion when I first went to war against hurtful words. There was a boy on my block named Jimmy who I determined was in league with Satan. Time spent in Jimmy's company was only a shade better than playing alone. He had three overprotective older

sisters, so that he was more spoiled than an only child. Now
and then, we played well together, but most of the time we
wrangled over all matters, great and small. Every argument
ended the same. When backed into a verbal corner, he
would raise his final defense. It was one word, spoken like a
mantra over and over, a wall thrown up against reason itself.
The word was "Huh!" and Jimmy was prepared to chant it
until an opponent was either rendered speechless or driven
to tears.

"But you just had it!" I had declared, referring to a GI
Joe flamethrower we had agreed to share.

"No, I want it!" Jimmy answered.

"But it's my turn to use it now!"

"Huh!" was his reply, and then, with my every insis-
tence, more of these were added until they formed a long
string: "Huh, huh, huh, huh, HUH!"

On this particular occasion, after months of aggravation,
something had snapped inside me. I chose to lay aside words
and fight. I punched him in the chest and sent him screaming home.

When remorse set in a half hour later, I decided to walk
to his house and apologize. I was greeted on the way by his
three irate sisters, come to extract blood vengeance, accompanied by what seemed to me to be the whole angry neighborhood. The sisters could wield "Huh!" as well as their
brother, but on this occasion they led a loud chorus of stock
modifiers: "stupid," "stinky," "smelly," "scrawny," "sickly" —
and those were only the S words.

Mild pushing and shoving rounded out the assault, but
it was their words that drew blood. I knew them all to be
untrue yet took to heart every last one of them. For days
after I could barely step outside. The sting of the experience

has never quite gone numb. At moments of doubt I still utter their words, resigning myself to the condemning truth of them. Only slowly in my life have the words by which I know myself become charitable and life giving instead.

I am thinking of all this as my heart aches for both Rebecca and Sarah. But I also recall the simple words my mother spoke to my pain on that day: "You know who you are," she said. "You know who loves you."

The Hebrews had once been known as low class, as mercenary, as slaves. This was their fate, their destiny. But when they came to worship the God of Israel, then they had become the Israel of God, the Chosen Ones, children of possibility and promise. More than that, they had delivered to the world a powerful gift, the message that we are not to be defined by those words of death around us, but by those words of life within us. Whenever my own children run to me in tears to report they have been dubbed dumb or dirty or deformed — and those only the D words — I respond simply, "Well? Are you?"

"No!" they invariably reply, "I'm not!"

"Well, then?!" I conclude.

And this is what I want — to listen to them hear themselves say it. I want them to believe it with all the strength of conviction they can muster — to know who they are, to know who loves them.

Now Rebecca is on my lap, facing outward. Her tears are all wiped dry, and her arms are outstretched. They are reaching to her little sister Sarah, whose finer nature has been coaxed into an apology. She waddles up to Rebecca and offers a hug. Compared to other sympathy-challenged children, Sarah is an angel. Her playmates are relieved. The Barbies are all smiles. Everything is back to normal.

The difference is that my girls have each gained stature through this experience.

All the while, the four boys have been crawling in different directions through the still unmowed grass. Now, without warning, they aim and open fire on each other, right over the heads of the girls and their dolls. Mortal combat is hell for young civilians and their middle-aged fathers, I think. But who is really safe in war anymore? Between ICBMs and chemical weapons, not to mention the new horizon of cyber warfare, we may all be living one dreadful decision away from annihilation.

At the moment, the soldier boys are too low on the ground and far away to dare claim a direct hit. They will need either to come into more intimate contact or start launching bigger bombs. These earnest little men in the grass suddenly bring to mind the miniature green soldiers of my childhood. There were dozens of men of each type, enough for a large-scale battle. Holding his proud pose, each soldier was indistinguishable from all others like him. Lined up together, they appeared like some great mound of army ants in suspended animation. Is this like real war? I had wondered. At least real soldiers had dog tags to tell them apart, I mused, but I didn't really understand a word I was saying.

On cold or rainy days, we gathered in someone's basement with all our plastic soldiers and emptied them into one big heap on the floor. We sorted them by type and dealt them out like a poker deck. Our troops amassed, we retreated to separate corners of the battlefield and prepared for all-out war. Soldiers were painstakingly situated on or under furniture, in shelves, on steps, or practically anywhere visible and freestanding. Finally, from our own great altitude, we would survey this remarkable assemblage of might we had made. These miniature men of war turned little boys into gods.

Once all was combat ready, war commenced. Our ammunition was rubber bands — whole boxes of them. The object was to leave standing not a single soldier of any opposing army. The machine gunners were our biggest challenge. They were stretched out flat on their stomachs and had to be turned belly up to count as casualties. Each turn was one rubber-band launch, and play proceeded clockwise around the room. Shots could be fired in any direction. It was a delightful way to kill off an afternoon.

But the thrill was short-lived. With every purchase of plastic soldiers, our armies grew in size until shooting every one dead became wearisome. We stopped taking turns and began to fire on one another indiscriminately. While this accelerated the killing somewhat, the cold, hard reality remained. We were kids with limited attention spans, and our wars were taking too long. The glory had petered out short of final victory.

As a matter of military necessity, we embarked on a search for more efficient and deadly forms of weaponry. First, we traded in our rubber bands for slingshots. We fired rocks of ever-greater girth, taking out whole platoons at once. Soon, however, not even the slingshots could satisfy our growing lust for collateral damage. We cast these aside and took up baseballs, then footballs, in an ever-widening campaign of destruction. Finally, we enlisted the most destructive force known in our basement up to that time, a bowling ball, and in the blink of an eye the war was over. Our thirst for carnage at last was quenched.

There was fallout over this, naturally. Bowling balls do more than flatten miniature battlefields in one atomic instant. They leave moon craters in the floor and cause the kind of clamor that sends mothers down to investigate. As things turned out, it was the war to end all war, and we were banished to the garage.

What we could not have comprehended at the time was the richness of the sources fueling our passion for this miniature holocaust. From our bird's-eye perch, we were playing out more than kid fantasies of war. We were the children of the Cold War, living under the great cloud of the atomic age. Once a quarter, the alarms rang and our grade school hallways became converted bomb shelters. We sat on the cold tile floors for long moments, our heads tucked between our knees. We knew of the canisters of stored water and soda crackers, and watched the films on emergency preparedness. We were more than curious about war. Ours was the generation that finally held within its grasp war's logical end: total annihilation. Although my playmates and I didn't know it, we had been groping for some means to glimpse Armageddon. We had found it playing God to a thousand green plastic men of war.

Back in the yard, a tennis ball is flying at me. On instinct I reach to catch it and spin around to see Seth's buddy, Mattie, grinning at me.

"Boom!" he says with clear amusement. "You're dead!"

My Seth arrives to wrest it from his father's hands. "No, he can't be dead, Mattie," Seth corrects. "He's not in it!"

"What, you mean you're not playing catch, now?" I ask naively.

"No, Dad," my son explains. "It's a hand grenade!"

Even here in my own yard the rules of engagement apply. Destructive weaponry must always graduate upward to current limits of imagination and possibility. Otherwise, war might go on indefinitely, and as I know, that can get terribly boring.

CAPITAL GRACE

Old Testament law made wide provision for the death penalty. In addition to murder and treason, capital punishment covered such offenses as kidnapping, blasphemy, idolatry, witchcraft, adultery, rape, incest, bearing false witness in death penalty cases, and cursing or striking a parent. What about "You shall not kill?" we are tempted to ask. And this question was consistently raised by the Israelites themselves.

Scribes and judges increasingly interpreted the death penalty statutes through a lens of mercy and grace. Capital trials allowed no circumstantial evidence. They required at least two witnesses who had observed that the crime was premeditated, was carried out in hate, and involved a deadly weapon. These witnesses must have heard the accused confirm an awareness of the penalty, and they must have tried to dissuade him or her from committing the crime.

If, after all this, the criminal was condemned to death by stoning, these same witnesses were required to cast the first stones. The bar of conviction was raised to such a point that one Sanhedrin, upon handing down its first death sentence in seven years, was accused of being "bloody." Long before the Jesus in John's Gospel says, "You who have not sinned, cast the first stone," Israel understood and acknowledged a principle more fundamental than retributive justice. If we are made in God's image, then every human life is sacred, even the lives of those who refuse to practice that sanctity. If God by nature is gracious, then we must be no less.

❧ ❧ ❧

The sun has been crossing the eastern sky to near its midday height. It has yet to clear the towering sugar maple over-hanging the corner of the yard where our inflatable pool sits. From noon to 3 P.M., pool water will bask in direct sunlight and temperatures will climb to ideal warmth. But the chil-dren will not last that long. They have felt sunshine on their shoulders all morning. By now they are hot. They have done their share of wistful gazing at our kid-size aquarium. Cold or not, our little tadpoles will not be denied their natural habitat for one more minute. The boys brave the water first, all but Seth.

"Get in, Seth!" his buddies urge. Seth is a great hero, but in things amphibious he is a coward. The back and forth of hot to cold is upsetting to his system. He sits on the perime-ter of the pool, too afraid to lower himself in.

I know how this feels. I am a cold-water coward myself. But Seth wants in the pool badly, and so we play out an unspoken pact: I will lower him in; he will kick and scream. When I finally let go of him, he turns and grabs the edge of the pool as if he will struggle back out again. But he doesn't. He cries for a minute or two, and then joins the play. I am as relieved as he is. A loving father cannot bear the sight of his own son suffering.

Soon the girls join the boys to mix and mingle, taunt and tussle. I have spelled out the rules: no splashing in the face; no spitting water; no pushing down; no mean talk. Yet almost at once I hear high-pitched screams. Charlie has sneaked in his water cannon and is taking aim at close range. Before I can stop him, a loud-mouthed girl suffers a direct hit. Reluctantly, Charlie and cannon exit the water. Charlie goes into time-out; the cannon goes into hiding. Charlie is sulking, and although I cannot blame him, I don't cut him loose. My one-strike-and-you're-out policy seems harsh, yet commensurate with the risk of serious pool accidents. Not on my watch, thank you.

Meanwhile, a pool game has taken shape. It is a toss-and-catch game called Ball-Call that the older girls have learned at school. Everyone stands around the perimeter of the pool. Someone throws a ball into the air and calls the name of another person. That person must catch the ball, and then take a turn. But if you drop the ball, you must sit out the remainder of the game. Instant elimination play. No second chances. I don't favor such games in a cold pool. Standing idle in chilly water turns your lips blue.

Ball-Call gets me thinking about a game of my childhood called Time Bomb. A bomb-shaped timer was tossed around a circle until it went "boom." It was the children's version of Russian roulette. I recall how I both loved the game and detested it. Time Bomb taught a wickedly valuable lesson: some things go around only once. No second chances.

As I keep my eye on the children, I am reading in the Saturday paper the account of a man who is on death row for the brutal killing of his own infant son. It is a common enough account these days. What catches my eye, though, are the words of the convicted man's own father, pleading in public for his son's life. His boy was a problem child, he tells the world, an alcoholic and a drug abuser. "He was his own worst victim, and while he should pay for his crime, he should not be put to death. He needs more time than the rest of us if he's ever gonna learn to love!"

I find that his words make great sense to me. When capital punishment was first reintroduced in the United States, I was in high school. Even then I struggled to understand why those most behind in the game of life should be the first ones taken out of it. Life was not a game of Time Bomb. Yes, persons have to atone for their misdeeds — but how can people pay for something if they are dead? And how could two dead persons be better than one? I was naive about these things. No one had yet explained to me that the death penalty for a heinous crime *was* the atonement. Today I understand this argument. But I do not accept it.

In the same paper is an article about my home state of Illinois, which had reinstituted the death penalty in 1977. Since that time, state authorities have exonerated, or found not guilty, more death row inmates than they have executed. Nationwide, the article continued, eighty-five persons on death row have been similarly acquitted in the last twenty-five years. Next to the greatly disproportionate number of poor minorities awaiting execution, this fact illustrates my greatest question about capital punishment: how many innocents aren't cleared in time? George Ryan, the governor of Illinois, has imposed a moratorium on all executions until authorities can determine why the courts are performing so poorly. Ryan is not from my generation. Still, I wonder whether he or his own children played Time Bomb, too.

Whether guilty or not, the man on death row for the murder of his son did not reside in Illinois. The date of his execution by lethal injection has been set, and the appeal process is at an end. His own father has asked to be at his side when the deed is carried out, but his request has been denied. I think to myself this is probably wise. No loving father can bear the sight of his own son suffering.

Suddenly I remember Charlie and realize the kids will not last much longer in this cold water. Charlie has paid his dues; he deserves some playtime, too. But even as I invite him to get into the pool, the other boys are getting out. They are chilled to the bone. The girls follow quickly. Now Charlie is in the pool alone and looking cheated. Time for lunch.

I help Charlie out of the pool and offer him a warm towel. "Sorry, Charlie," I offer. "Sandwich and chips?" Charlie nods his head affirmatively. He smiles. At least for Charlie there is the afternoon. The water will be a little warmer and Charlie may well be a better playmate for his lesson of the morning. In my backyard, we believe in second chances.

THE MEASURE OF A LIFE

A voice was heard in Ramah,
wailing and loud lamentation,
Rachel weeping for her children;
she refused to be consoled,
because they are no more.

— MATTHEW 2:18

"You shall not kill" surely applies above all to the killing of the very young, who require protection because of their innocence and their vulnerability. Children were especially vulnerable in the world of the Bible, which was fertile ground for the practice of infanticide. Pharaoh hatched two plans to rid the nation of all male Hebrew infants, and these plans met with the willing consent of his subjects. Double-crossed by the wise men, Herod the Great ordered all young Bethlehemite boys slain and found hands to carry out the deed. Greek and Roman cultures are

known to have tolerated the abandonment unto death of unwanted infants, probably mostly female. According to the Roman Tacitus, there were further grounds for anti-Semitism in the Jewish prohibition of the practice.

Infanticide has not yet been eradicated from the face of the earth. In certain corners of the globe, unwanted babies are still sacrificed on altars of desperation, gender preference, misguided notions of family honor, or mere convenience. In the United States, too, babies are still beaten and burned, shaken and strangled. But at least as a people we concur that when such things happen, evil has been done.

There is one exception to this consensus: the question of the unborn. This one appears beyond resolution, stretching as far as the eye can see into the new century.

It is just after lunch. Sandwiches and chips have given the children their second wind. I am anticipating that mine will come shortly. Finished with laundry, Donna has joined me on the patio, just in case.

The combatants have returned to the field. The afternoon is like a whole new day. There are fresh scenarios to invent, novel strategies to employ, new and sophisticated weaponry to dream up, ingenious hideouts to discover. But our boy warriors settle instead on a new and diabolical scheme.

Sarah and friends have climbed into the swing-set fort with their dolls and are setting up house. Seth and comrades have been watching and now arrive at a bold course of action. They rename our yard "the high seas" and enlist themselves in promising careers as pirates. The swing-set fort becomes a seafaring vessel, the girls, slaves in waiting, their babies, insufferable liabilities. Now the boys act. They climb the ladders and storm the deck, easily subduing the unsuspecting seafarers. High-pitched screams pervade the air, as sabers rattle and infants are toppled mercilessly to their deaths in the raging waters below. One plaintive voice soars above the rest. It is Sarah's voice, and I know its plea. My eldest daughter has been summoned to the rescue. Sarah is crying, "Rachael!"

I glance at the dolls lying on the ground. Rachael has come to their aid, pushing a plastic stroller. My eldest is a paragon of charity and grace. She scoops them up and lays them gently down on soft foam, shielded from the sun by a striped cotton canopy. These babies are a blessed batch. A pity they are not real. Too many little lives never know such tenderness on either side of the womb. But Sarah and the girls feel genuine relief. To them, these dolls are as vital as you and I. And herein lies the heart of the matter. Everything finally hinges on what it means to be human.

My mind races back several years to a family excursion. We took the Indiana-Illinois Skyway to Chicago and landed in the Loop, where we toured the famed Museum of Science and Industry. There our minds drank in the triumphant tale of human ingenuity in an inhospitable world.

But the museum had other stories to share, visual sagas of nature's own hidden wonders. One was a developmental chronology of life in the womb. The exhibit illustrated the stages of prenatal existence, from the tiniest embryo to a full-term fetus. Seth and Sarah, still in their twos, sat up in the double stroller and stared hard at these little bodies, entombed behind plate glass. Only then, as my eyes darted back and forth between these tiny offspring and my own, did it occur to me these were actual specimens of human life. They had been conceived and sheltered in, and ultimately severed from, a live womb. They were life. But were they human?

Where within this progressive soup of creation does human life first stir? Before conception? At conception? During the first, or the second, or the third trimester in utero? At the moment of birth? Or does the whole matter hinge, as some believe, on the question of fetal viability — when a baby can survive outside the womb?

It seems prudent for any father to assign special value to his wife's opinion on this subject. I have sought out Donna's views numerous times. After all, she bore in her body all four of our children. She is also a neonatal nurse practitioner, in the business of keeping the tiniest premature babies alive. She knows that any baby born at twenty-two weeks gestation or younger has a 100 percent chance of dying. Babies born at twenty-five weeks have an 80 percent mortality rate. But at twenty-six weeks gestation, a baby has a fifty-fifty chance of surviving to a normal life. Not very long ago, she tells me, such premature infants always died. Due to the rapid advance in medical science and technology, the viability of the fetus is itself in constant flux. Our question ends up where it started: when does human life begin?

At the very moment our stroller pulled away toward the next exhibit, Sarah had decided to stand up and stretch. She spilled out onto the floor and thwacked her noggin with considerable force. She began to wail as I pulled her to the safety of warm embrace. We fought back shame, as other moms and dads paused to scrutinize our hapless display of poor parenting. As I pulled her all the tighter to my heart, it occurred to me that just maybe the humanity of my Sarah and every other child, born or unborn, might finally have less to do with any physical status or developmental stage than with the sheer fact of its loveliness to someone else. Perhaps its intrinsic worth is tied both to the world of others who value it and to its enduring value to its Creator. A fetus is a person because there is a mother to love it like a baby, to delight in its growth, to grieve its loss. And should there be no single person to cherish such a life, its value, actual or potential, would continue to reside nonetheless in the heart of God.

"You shall not kill," spoken in the womb, is no easy, ironclad canon. Surely reproductive freedom, like all other freedoms, cannot be simply dismissed out of hand. Surely there are circumstances in which not being born could be viewed as a mercy: profound deformity, a brain stem with no brain, the prospect of certain death within the first excruciating months of life. And aren't children born daily into fates arguably worse than never having been born at all: extreme poverty, surpassing cruelty, unmitigated suffering? The question of a young life's sanctity seems endlessly complex. Perhaps the myriad ways to honor life — from its first stirrings to its finished shape, in its quality and its quantity, its proper freedoms and obligations — might converge at one point only: in a vision of a God who is at once creative and redemptive. Passions continue to divide, but God continues both to bring life into being and graciously to receive it home again. In this, indeed, lies the final value of any living thing.

Back in our yard, the girls come down from their house in the air to embrace their babies with fresh affection. This sweet reunion is decidedly short-lived. Our girls are young and flighty. They have yet to confront that truly solemn covenant called parenthood. In our society, they are not alone.

THE MERCY OF DEATH

Suddenly, all play stops. Children are running to the side of the house. In a tone of somber excitement, Rebecca has called everyone together. A young bird lies on the ground, fresh fallen from its nest, tucked precariously under the eaves of our house. Judging from its size and feathers, this was a bird on the verge of taking wing and soaring high above the earth. Instead, it is gasping its last shallow breaths from the ignominy of our sidewalk. The dog sniffs it. The girls sigh. The boys prod it with sticks. "Get up and fly!" one of them commands. The bird is limp, its only motion the beak opening and closing in pained rhythm. "Kill it!" says another young man, named Henry. He lifts a paving brick from a shallow stack against our foundation and raises it over the fallen fowl.

But just then I arrive on the sad scene with a shoe box. I offer instructions for the collection of leaves and grass to lay down a bed of mercy. Little feet race into action. One child returns with a plastic teacup filled with pool water. Another is all aflutter with her find of an earthworm. Down they go into the box along with the blades of grass. The cup is too tall, the worm too large, and the bird too weak to eat or drink. But these offerings ease our sadness.

Time is running short for our feathered friend. Perhaps the bird itself knows this but cannot say. Through years of pastoral ministry, I have hunkered down at death's door with many parishioners, and I know that the timing of death is hard to call. Some who have every prospect of recovery slip quietly away, almost unnoticed. Others who have borrowed heavily against the future through unwise living manage to cheat death time after time. Some die all at once. Others die one bad day at a time. A few, a growing number it seems, die long before their hearts stop beating, kept alive by means arguably more diabolical than miraculous.

All at once I am seeing, not a bird, but a woman named Jessie, the first victim in my experience of what I have come to dread most in life: the mindlessness of dementia, whether caused by Alzheimer's or some other illness. Jessie, I recall, had the look of a bird — all nose and no jaw, eyes set far apart, full body in the middle with skinny extremities. She lay all day in a nursing home bed, or sat up and drew blanks with her eyes. She no longer knew anyone, not even herself. She came to eat like a bird, as well, until a day of decision arrived.

As patients begin to lose the function of swallowing, they may aspirate, introducing food matter into the airway. Infection often follows. If this makes it to the lungs, pneumonia can develop. In chronic situations, the options are two: insert a feeding tube or allow them to continue on their own, risking infection and a slow withering. It is hard to find the dignity in either choice. But once inserted, the tube will very likely remain and the humility may be prolonged indefinitely.

One day Jessie's daughter called me in tears. The family had come to a decision but needed many shoulders to cry on. No feeding tube would be started. It was clear they deemed this the merciful choice, extended in love. Though it prompted a guilt they would struggle to endure, they seemed to view this a necessary price for their mother's

release. But was it? Was withholding food, bodily nourish-
ment, ever justified?

With a family's consent, hospitals routinely withdraw
patients from ventilators. Some cancer sufferers, near death,
are disconnected from all support, given large doses of mor-
phine, and allowed to die. Victims of severe head trauma are
sometimes pronounced brain-dead and unplugged from life
support, as their healthy organs are harvested for a donor
bank. Such decisions are widely regarded as prudent mer-
cies. But is food different from oxygen? Does it represent a
higher level of function, a more intact humanity, and is its
denial a greater cruelty?

Granted, there are those who view life of whatever quality, at whatever cost, for whatever duration, as the single
value. They believe that all means should be pursued to
preserve it. On the other side are those who pronounce
unnatural any and all uses of artificial means to sustain life.
Curiously, adherents on both extremes label any deviation
from their position as "playing God"! Still others argue the
rightness of mercy killing, or sanction the "Kevorkian solution," physician-assisted suicide. Here, not only is life not
prolonged, but proactive steps are taken to hasten its end. Is
this murder, or mercy? Who among us can ever be sure?

Six months after the family's decision, Jessie died. The
cause of death was never divulged to me. At her viewing, she
looked the same as always, except she was smiling. I chose to
take it as a good sign. In some situations, I have decided,
there is no clear path of compassion, no greater good to
achieve. There are only bad choices. Sometimes, the only
mercy is the love we feel as we choose among them, and it
falls to God to do the rest.

Now it is time to move our bird. We gently roll it onto a

magnolia leaf and bundle it up for safe transport. The bird chirps wildly with fear. Meanwhile, Henry has raised his paving brick in the air once more. He still pretends designs on this little bird's manner of demise. Others try to seize the brick from his grasp. In the struggle, it slips from his hands and lands on the leaf. The little bird falls silent. "Whoops!" he says.

There are accusations and denials, explanations and rebuttals, but these quickly run their course. Only tears are left. A bird had been dying. A bird is at peace. The bed is now a coffin. We lay the bird reverently to rest. Rebecca offers a prayer for one briefly a friend. She will pray for it often at night, as she does for the dead dogs and cats of our household, whether known to her in life or only through the stories and pictures of the past. In her prayers, they are all the same. Each of these creatures is hers, she believes, because all of them belong to God.

Now the shoe box lid; now off to the alley in solemn procession, out to the dumpster, and down.

THE WAY OF MERCY

It is half past 3:00. Out back, things have begun to unravel. Seth has killed Mattie, but he won't stay dead. Seth is certain he has finished off his best buddy fair and square, but Sarah has come onto the battlefield uninvited and assumed the role of triage nurse. She gives Mattie a kiss on the cheek and makes him all alive again. In retribution, Seth summarily cuts his sister's head off with his saber, but Sarah only sticks out her tongue at him. This enrages Seth, as everyone knows it's impolite for a girl to stick out her tongue at a boy, especially if that boy has just severed her head from her body fair and square. His rage is short-lived, for the newborn Mattie rises quickly to open fire on Seth and shoots him down in the dust. A now-mortified Seth begins to cry.

I feel for my fallen comrade. It doesn't seem fair that the dead should rise to slay again so easily. But then, just who does make the rules in killing? There is no justice in war.

History carries as many justifications for war as wars themselves. Francis Bacon thought war necessary for a nation to preserve its physical vitality. Hegel allowed for the right of "enlightened" nations to wage war over those deemed lesser. Christian thinkers have tended to raise the bar of justification: Augustine insisted that war be waged to avenge wrong and win peace. Aquinas validated it only in the resistance of evil. Calvin saw in war God's strategy to mete out punishment for injustice. A distinction has often been made between wars of principle (wars of the Lord), which are justified, and wars of mere conquest (wars of the king), which are not. The trouble is, every party to a war claims to be on the side of God. Which sort of war you are waging seems to be open to interpretation.

There have been other, contrary voices. Rousseau viewed any course but total pacifism as sheer stupidity. Groups like the Quakers have found war utterly irreconcilable with the core teachings of Jesus: "Love your enemies," "Pray for those who persecute you," "Turn the other cheek." I like this kind of thinking, until I wonder what the world would be like had Hitler been allowed to conquer. There would be no Jews, for one thing. No Michael Jordan, for another. And striking even closer to home, there would be no me. My parents met at college on the GI Bill. Without World War II, everything would be changed, and I would not be around to see it. I'm uncertain whether the world would be worse for my absence, but I sincerely doubt it would be any better.

Now daughter Sarah does a matronly thing. She picks herself up, mortal wounds and all, and plays nurse to her twin, kissing Seth right on the mouth, breathing newness into his breast. Seth springs to life and hugs his sister tightly. Seth and Sarah travel through life as soul mates. Their love is stronger than a thousand wars. The battle ends. Humanity is the victor. There is little justice in war, no winners or losers. But there is justice in mercy. For mercy knows only winners, and in mercy, all become more than they were.

THE END IS LIFE

Finally, it is late afternoon. The remaining playmates have been called home. The grownups and children of our household are all but finished off. Someone says we should measure out our lives over the length of one normal day, say, from birth at 7 A.M. to death at 11 P.M. It is 4:30 and I am forty years old. Already, I am not far from sunset, and just now I feel it.

Soon we begin dinner on the grill. I flip hamburgers and roast corn on the cob. Donna tosses a salad and cuts up fresh fruit. Rebecca sets the table. Rachael pours the drinks. At last, we sit down to dinner on our patio. We offer blessing for the food that even now sacrifices existence so that we might live another day. This is the Sabbath hour. As we eat, we glance around our yard and remember this day by the scenes that filled it — the pool, the swing set, the fort, the tall grass, the shrubbery and trees, the fence, weapons of war and weapons of mercy. These are the formative spaces in the lives of our children. All the meanings of their great journeys through time — successes and failures, beginnings and endings, cursing and blessing, living and dying — will all double back to here. For already, in the world of our backyard, they are learning to face death, and to choose life. And I am here to see it all, and this makes me glad.

Finished with supper, we bid farewell to the outside world. Soon our children are bathed and it is time for prayers. This was a good day, and we offer up thanksgiving for it. The grass never did get mowed, and a light rain has begun to fall. But our yard was a laboratory of life today, of living and dying and blessing. Neither Cain nor Abel were involved in murder while the sun was up. Instead, Seth and his siblings grew a day older, even wiser perhaps. Our prayers are for forgiveness as well this night, and I no less than my children have earned the need for them. But now comes the grace of sleep. And with sleep comes rest and peace, cleansing and release. Perhaps tomorrow I will rise to live a little longer in Eden.

The real grace of this day, I suppose, has been simply that in a murderous world, my precious children are still alive at the end of it. Here is a mercy I will take to my pillow, and I will spread it over me like a blanket, and sleep.

> They shall not hurt nor destroy
> in all my holy mountain...
>
> — ISAIAH 11:9

HIGH FIDELITY
YOU SHALL NOT COMMIT ADULTERY

BAGGAGE

Now Sarai, Abram's wife, bore him no children. She had an Egyptian slave-girl whose name was Hagar, and Sarai said to Abram, "You see that the Lord has prevented me from bearing children; go in to my slave-girl; it may be that I shall obtain children by her." And Abram listened to the voice of Sarai.

— GENESIS 16:1, 2

In the world of the Hebrew patriarchs, slaves are freely bought and sold. Serving a wandering tribe or clan, they are little more than beasts of burden, baggage handlers without pay.

Many slave women are concubines, sharing their masters' beds in a harem pecking order not of their choosing. Like the labor they perform, their bodies are not their own. The Bible condemns none of this, nor is God's wrath piqued. In the world of the Hebrew patriarchs, such things are expected, inevitable.

Hagar is an Egyptian slave girl in the possession of Abraham's wife, Sarah, who is barren. Desiring offspring for her husband, Sarah persuades Abraham to enter Hagar's tent.

Hagar's permission is never sought. But when Hagar conceives a child, Sarah turns jealous and resentful. Miserable, Hagar flees to the wilderness of Shur, en route back to her native Egypt. God visits her there with a word of consolation and hope.

This story is something like the Exodus itself, in reverse — an Egyptian slave escapes bondage from the Hebrews... The irony of it is not lost on the text: Sarah's mistreatment of Hagar presages Pharaoh's mistreatment of Israel; the Hebrews' cries of misery reverberate back to Hagar's own. And the God of Abraham, Isaac, and Jacob hears them both.

But here the similarity ends. Unlike Israel, Hagar is not set free. She is directed by God back into bondage, home to mistress and master, to Sarah and Abraham, whose child she bears. The story of Hagar turns at best on the fair treatment of slaves, not on the question of slavery itself. Hagar is the property of Sarah and the sexual property of Abraham. She possesses no freedom, reproductive or otherwise.

Rather, Hagar's consolation is God's promise that her son by Abraham, Ishmael, will have a share in God's future. There will be a people called Ishmaelites, and they will be too numerous to count. For Hagar, an Egyptian slave in Canaan, this is arguably better than freedom itself. Her salvation lies in a male offspring, a son. Meanwhile, the matter of the sexual autonomy of slaves — indeed of all women — awaits a further revelation.

The Seventh Commandment, "You shall not commit adultery," is conditioned by patriarchy. Abraham does not break it by taking a second wife, or even by taking two concubines. Ancient Hebrew law defines adultery as sexual relations between a man and woman when the woman, not the man, is married to another. Hebrew law also punishes husbands who have extramarital sexual relations, but this is not considered adultery, and lighter penalties apply. Men may *acquire multiple wives and lovers. Israel's kings enjoy them by the palace-full, but they are not adulterers. The chief biblical count against kings is the worship of other gods, the sin of idolatry. Extramarital sex doesn't rate, unless the woman is married to someone else.*

Such distinctions reveal the fault line of ancient gender roles and obligations. Women belong to their husbands like sheep to a shepherd. They are reproductive nurturers of the future, and the future is male.

The first task of interpreting the Seventh Commandment is to free ourselves from its patriarchal baggage. The second is to embrace the wisdom that remains to guide us in right human relationships, to let the law awaken us to the possibility of binding covenantal love. If we ignore this wisdom, we risk wandering through life as lonely relational vagabonds.

Late on a Friday afternoon, we are in the sanctuary of God. Two families are gathered in pews on opposite sides of a center aisle. I stand before them, convening a wedding party to rehearse for the next day's ceremony of marriage.

The bride-to-be is Gwen, the groom, Alan. In their early twenties, they represent an increasingly rare category among the couples I unite: never-marrieds. Over the course of our premarital counseling, I have found them to be a compatible, highly communicative pair — in contrast to other never-marrieds who have sat in my study with their eyes glazed over, stunned like deer in the headlights of infatuation. Those couples claim no interpersonal struggles, think no big thoughts, and glance frequently at the clock. It is hard to tell whether they are genuinely shallow or just faking it. They all but sit in one another's laps and cannot keep their hands to themselves. More than once it has made me nauseous.

But Alan and Gwen have taken seriously our time together. They speak candidly both of their personal peccadilloes and of their struggles as a couple. Gwen is strong-minded, sometimes to a fault. In a home of constant turmoil, she learned early to fend for herself and work out her own problems. She honed the art of self-assertion. Alan, by contrast, can be distant and avoids conflict. He stuffs his feelings. Alan, too, traces these inclinations to his childhood — to his insecure relationship with a distant mother and his thwarted desire to please her.

Gwen has been exploring the difference between assertiveness and combativeness. She is striving to become a better listener. Alan is learning to express emotion, to fight the urge to withdraw into silent stoicism. It is hard work, with no end in sight. Long-established patterns of behavior resist change, especially those habits formed as strategies of survival. The very existence of enduring relationships, fraught with difference, is a testament to the human social drive. It is also, I like to think, a compelling argument for the reality of grace.

Alan and Gwen have been monogamous sexual partners for much of their two-year courtship. Sexual intimacy has followed the same curve as other aspects of their deepening relationship, evolving into a thing of profound satisfaction and meaning. Yet, fearful of losing the critical distance of discernment before they make that final lifelong commitment, Gwen has resisted Alan's suggestion that they live together. Especially given her past, Gwen does not want to make a mistake.

Alan has struggled to follow her logic. For him, sexual

intimacy *is* commitment. I recall having been taken aback by this view, nowadays such a swim against the stream, rarely expressed. But who could dispute that sex possesses powers unfathomable and dangerous, capable of unleashing the restive energies of emotion and spirit, not to mention procreation and even death — as the AIDS pandemic has so starkly revealed. For all its good intentions isn't the phrase "safe sex" an oxymoron? How much critical distance can there really be in a relationship involving something as volatile as sex?

Still, I have no quarrel with Gwen's resolve to enter marriage with her head clear and her eyes open wide. Nor do I question the sincerity of Gwen's and Alan's love as expressed through sexuality. At least in our day, they are free to think through these matters openly and intentionally, without fear of reprisal. This in itself is a hopeful thing, just as they are a hopeful couple in the arduous quest of contemporary covenant keeping.

At the top of the hour we get the rehearsal under way. With Gwen's help, I take a head count of wedding participants: bride and groom, bridesmaids and groomsmen, ring bearer and flower girl, father of the bride, mothers of the bride and groom. All are present and accounted for.

Others are on hand as well, including the current wives of both the groom's father and the bride's father. There are six "parents" present in all, but this complication merely scratches the surface of the story. Alan and Gwen are the children of divorce many times over. Former spouses are seated at strategic distances apart, some on speaking terms, others not. The tension in the hall is palpable, swirling to the rafters like thick smoke. The irony is thick as well: two young lovers, products of their parents' long-failed covenants, are intent on forming a bond for life. They have come to stake their future on the possibility of permanence, the fond hope that promises made might be kept.

Formed of these families, the bond will need to have industrial strength. This thought leaps to mind just as I begin my opening remarks, but I withhold it. Instead, I explain our reason for gathering: "We are here to help Gwen and Alan celebrate before God their promise of everlasting love." In a room of broken covenants, every head nods approvingly. Nobody laughs!

TANGLED NATIVITY

> So God created humankind in his image,
> in the image of God he created them;
> male and female he created them.
> God blessed them, and God said to them,
> "Be fruitful and multiply..."
>
> — GENESIS 1:27–28A

Canaanite religion and the cult of Baal, god of storm and fertility, are highly sexual. Through erotic rituals, farmers mate with the rhythms of the land to entice the gods to release their productive powers. And for their trouble, the gods comply — rains will fall and crops will grow — granting survival for another season... perhaps. Maybe they do, maybe they don't. Like an anxious gambler whispering a prayer before a spin at roulette, the people can only hope for the best.

Yahweh is no prudish deity. In Hebrew faith, sex is good; it is God's creation and decree. But unlike Baal, the God of Israel won't be rolled. Yahweh's fancy cannot be tickled to fulfill some aim of the Hebrews' choosing. The problem with the religion of

Canaan is not its sexuality; it is the treatment of God and others as objects, as means of fertility to be prostituted for gain.

Faith in Yahweh begins with grateful obedience toward the God who is ever present and faithful. Worshipping the Lord of steadfast love is not an anxious affair. Rituals are more matters of the soul than the stomach. Rains may fall or not; seeds may sprout or remain buried in the ground; wombs will open or shut like a tomb. Either way, the God of salvation will be present to save. More than wishful thinking, this tenet is life itself.

The chief purpose of sexuality, like all else in Hebrew faith, is to glorify God. This implies the freedom to be faithful to others, to treat them not as objects but as subjects, just as Yahweh covenanted to treat the children of Israel. To take the purpose of sexuality lightly, on the other hand, is to forfeit its blessing. It is to play roulette with the future and watch it spin out of control.

I am struggling with names. There are too many to keep straight. Harder still to master is the intricate web of relations that bind them; uncovering the layer upon layer of intrigue is like tuning into a daily soap opera for the first time.

Alan's father and mother have both been married and divorced several times. Their union was the second marriage for each, and Alan was the sole product of this second go-round — a tryst lasting seven tumultuous years. After their breakup, Alan lived with his father and his third wife, Jennifer. Alan inherited a stepbrother and stepsister by that marriage, but since its dissolution he has scarcely seen them. Jennifer and the children were invited to the ceremony but are not expected. This is perhaps for the best. Even the joy of a wedding can heal only so much heartache.

Meanwhile, Alan's mother, Faith, has been in and out of relationships, some culminating in brief marriages. He has lived with her only sporadically over the years, and their relationship cannot be described as close. She is by all accounts a troubled soul. Still, she is his mother, and she is here. I can see Faith now out of the corner of my eye, sitting to the side like a high school girl at her first dance, terrified that she'll be sitting there alone all evening and also terrified that she won't.

In the arena of multiple marriage, Gwen's father, Rex, takes the prize. He is handsome in an age-defying way and has reportedly used this over the years to his lecherous advantage. A tall man, Rex towers above the crowd, looking down almost monarchically upon our proceedings as if deliberating his bestowal of blessing or disapproval.

To Rex's right is his fifth and current wife, Sherry, a plump, self-conscious blond with large, sad eyes and tanning-salon skin. The twenty-eight-year-old mother of Rex's seventh and eighth children, Sherry has been busy fussing with her number two, a bouncing young boy named Billy who has converted the church pew into a circus trampoline. Rex is oblivious to the scene, his attentions wandering the room — probably from female to female.

But now Billy has crawled onto the floor and is beginning to do what every child in church dreams of: to worm his way across the sanctuary from beneath the pews. Sherry calls him back in a muffled shout. I recognize the sound as the desperate shriek of a single parent in public, and Sherry qualifies for this distinction if anyone does. As usual, her command goes unheeded. At last she jumps up to chase

Billy down as if he were a hamster out of its cage. Rex either doesn't notice or doesn't care that they have gone.

Of all the divorcees present, only Gwen's mother June has remained steadfastly single. Gwen worships her mother. "My angel without wings," she calls her. Gwen is not alone in assigning the appellation.

After her marriage to Rex, June had embarked on a road of self-improvement, fighting her way through college while holding down a full-time job to support herself and her daughter. Several years later, she had earned a degree in nursing and was working in the trauma center of a Catholic hospital, volunteering for numerous Catholic charities on the side. At the same time she turned her attention to Gwen's college tuition, saving enough to fund four years at a state university.

All this she accomplished with virtually no help from Rex, to whom she had become a pesky enigma. Rex has his own names for her: "Saint June of Arc," "The bride of Christ," and "Florence Nightingale saving the whole damn world!"

At the moment June is living up to the billing. Having joined the search for Billy, she scoops him up deftly from under a pew and into his mother's arms. Sherry's sad eyes brighten with gratitude and perhaps with further insight into the real truth behind Rex's self-serving portrayals of his "cold-hearted and spiteful" ex-wives. Now June goes back to her seat, and Sherry, for better or worse, returns to Rex.

Such matters have served as mere sidelights to my opening remarks. I have offered introductions, spoken briefly about the church, and presented a short sketch of the ceremony. The gathered are now in possession of such critical information as the location of water fountains, changing rooms, and lavatories. But I have been the real learner here. I have come face-to-face with the collective intrigue of two family stories. Never-aired laundry, unresolved anger, cynicism about the future, even a hint of redemption have all been on display. And all will figure in the event we have come to witness: new love, rising from the family ashes like a phoenix.

HEART MATTERS

You have heard that it was said, "You shall not commit adultery." But I say to you that everyone who looks at a woman with lust has already committed adultery with her in his heart. . . . It was also said, "Whoever divorces his wife, let him give her a certificate of divorce." But I say to you that anyone who divorces his wife, except on the grounds of unchastity, causes her to commit adultery; and whoever marries a divorced woman commits adultery.

— MATTHEW 5:27–28, 31–32

In this scene in Matthew, Jesus has gone "up the mountain," like Moses before him (Deut. 9:9), and he, too, sits down. Crowds gather around him as he expounds upon matters both timely and provocative. Among his words is a new teaching on adultery. "You have heard that it was said," he begins, putting the crowd on notice for the corollary that follows: "But I say to you..."

One is tempted to portray the second teaching as the negation of the first, but this is not the case. Rather than repealing the law, Jesus expands it. He makes things, not easier, but more difficult: even look at a woman with lust and you commit adultery. Marry a divorcee, and you've broken the commandment. Even his closest disciples agree that this is one of Jesus' "hard sayings" — difficult to understand, and brutal to obey.

Its sting has endured the generations. Christians of every age have struggled to hear Jesus out and honor his wishes. Even today there remain those remarried divorcees willing to accept second-class church status as fair punishment for their sin, and pious eyes that still strain to look down or away whenever beauty draws near.

But times are changing. Divorce, while still a wrenching experience, no longer carries the social stigma it once did. Few begrudge divorcees a second chance. A better understanding of abuse and mental cruelty has bolstered the prevailing view of divorce as an indispensable option, often even a salvation. And while the dissolution of a marriage is still deemed a tragedy, especially where children are involved, subsequent remarriage is not labeled adultery. On the contrary, for the sake of children remarriage is strongly encouraged.

Jesus' equation of a lustful heart with adultery is equally in jeopardy. Following the sexual revolution, few pay this saying more than lip service. Instead, sexual explicitness is pervasive in our increasingly visual culture. Ads for swimsuits and lingerie are thinly veiled attempts to market attire through desire. Lust and beauty are woven into one seamless garment. Voyeurism is a trip to the mall or the grocery checkout line. It is enough to make Venus and Aphrodite blush, but we think little of it. We are a culture of lookers. Few consider, though, that their gazing is adulterous.

Where does this leave Jesus' teachings on adultery? Some view them as irrelevant to modern life; a few still wish to swallow them whole. Is there a middle ground, some means of appropriating their deeper wisdom without applying them prescriptively to the inscrutable world of human sexuality?

In his own day, Jesus' words had a liberating ring, challenging the widespread presumption in Judaism of a husband's right to divorce his wife for nearly any cause (Deut. 24:1–4). The often-cited teaching of the rabbinic school of Hillel, for instance, stated that if a wife burned her husband's dinner, it was grounds for divorce. Jesus' words also expanded the legal definition of adultery to include a husband's infidelity against his wife. No longer was adultery a glorified dispute over male property rights.

Yet more was at stake for Jesus than the well-being of women; his greater concern was the sacredness of the marital bond itself, as a God-given grace not to be squandered. This is not to deny that divorce and remarriage will occur; Jesus' own teaching provides for exceptions (Matt. 5:32). Rather, it is to suggest that the cost of severed covenant is always dear, exacting a price not only practical, but spiritual. Perhaps, in our culture of casual sex, serial marriage, and multiple partnering, such a truth still speaks.

I am assembling the bridesmaids and groomsmen. The bridesmaids will soon be lining up in the narthex to practice the procession. The groomsmen will wait in the stairwell by the chancel, their point of entry to the sanctuary.

Consulting my rehearsal notes under "wedding party," I call out ten names: "Dawn and Kyle, Linda and Paul, Melody and Jim, Tracy and Greg, Kerry and Matt. Men to my left, please," I tell them. "Women to my right." Five couples in all, I remind myself — actual couples, in fact. Gwen had made this clear. She and Alan had wanted their wedding party to model commitment; those standing with them are for them living examples of the life they intend to lead.

While on the one hand laudable, these intentions at first appeared quaint and overstated. Was this some strategy of rebellion? I had wondered. Did it point back to the absence of such commitment within Gwen's and Alan's families of origin? Was it like children of alcoholics responding to their past with teetotalism, or those raised in strictness adopting attitudes of leniency? But that was before the rehearsal.

I look up from my wedding notebook to an astonishing revelation. Bridesmaids and groomsmen have separated into groups just as I had requested, but instead of five to five, the ratio of men to women is six to four. I focus immediately on two of the men, standing off to the side, appearing by turns apprehensive and defiant. They are well groomed and nicely dressed. They wear simple gold wedding bands on their left ring fingers. They are holding hands.

Finally Gwen breaks the stunned silence. "Um, Kerry, Matt: I guess maybe one or the other of you is going to need to move to the other side."

"They're such a great couple!" Gwen had offered in one of our sessions. "So loving and committed, they're practically my role models for marriage. That's why we just have to have them in our wedding party." Alan had nodded in agreement, though with only a fraction of her enthusiasm, I remember.

I also recall having wondered why Gwen had singled out Matt and Kerry for comment. It had seemed to me there was even a kind of urgency in her voice, but this had not been explained in our conversation. Gwen hadn't told me that Matt and Kerry would each be dressing as groomsmen for the day. She had neglected to add that they were "unioned," not married. She had failed to mention that they were gay.

Our views of the world are formed over time from a rich panoply of influences: the cherished wisdom of an elder, a chance encounter with a stranger, the source books of faith, the cumulative force of daily ritual, the zeitgeist of the age, the power of a novel idea. Each of these and more mold our habits of belief and action.

My first direct encounter with homosexuality was in seminary. In some mainline Protestant settings at least, seminary life has afforded gay men and lesbians a safe haven of sorts, a spirit of tolerance in a hostile world. There they have encountered the gracious message of God's unconditional love for all, a message to claim, celebrate, and cling to for dear life.

Yet as was long the case for the pastoral gifts of women, openly gay and lesbian leadership remains a rarity in our churches, where fear and misunderstanding still prevail. Too often, the gospel is wielded like a club, while biblical texts are fashioned into tools of exclusion. As the church spins in the winds of controversy over the subject, I have sought to weigh the evidence for myself, scriptural and otherwise.

Biblical references to homosexuality are limited to a mere handful of passages. Among these is Genesis 19 — the account of the condemnation of Sodom. In this story, the residents of Sodom threaten with violent rape two male visitors to the city who are really God's angels in disguise. This is followed immediately by the city's destruction in a torrent of fire and brimstone. While it is often claimed that homosexual acts prompted Sodom's demise (hence the term "sodomy"), the context suggests otherwise. Gang rape, not homosexuality, appears to have been the sin of Sodom. The rape of males was an ancient tool of domination following military victory, intended to humiliate and subdue the vanquished. That the Sodomites were engaged in nasty business no one doubts; to conclude that this has any bearing on modern homosexuality appears mistaken.

The remaining texts on the subject in the Hebrew Bible concern ancient standards of ritual purity rooted in a singular view of the natural order (Lev. 18:22, 20:13). This view taboos all wastage of male seed, including the act of male penetration of male, as a slap in the face of God's gracious offer of procreativity. Lesbian acts are conspicuously absent from the list of prohibitions, probably because male sex organs do not figure there.

The same concern against religious defilement also forbids such things as eating pork (Lev. 11:7) and lying with a woman during menstruation (Lev. 15:19F). While still valid today for some, these are clearly matters of ritual purity, not ethics per se. Few Christians would think to label them sin.

References to homosexual acts in the Christian New Testament are found in lists of wrongdoing that condemn everything from lying to greed, envy to arrogance. The presence of sodomy on these lists appears to be prompted by such practices as pederasty, the physical exploitation of children, and idolatry, specifically temple cult prostitution — not by a direct concern about homosexuality.[1]

Meanwhile, Christians routinely violate far more prominent biblical prohibitions, and the churches barely bat an eye. Vices from guile to gossip to gluttony go virtually

[1] See Romans 1:24–31, 1 Corinthians 6:9–10, and 1 Timothy 1:9–10.

unquestioned. Indeed, the flouting of these and other sanctions is almost expected.

Add to this the growing weight of evidence for a strong genetic link to sexual orientation, the attestation of psychiatry and psychology to the ineffectual outcomes of treatments to "change" it, and the witness of gays and lesbians that by far the greatest trial of homosexuality is those who seek only to condemn and not to understand. When I cap all this off with the central message of the Christian gospel — the unconditional love of God and neighbor — I find my tutelage is nearly complete.

Yet there remains one final arbiter in my pursuit of answers, the simple, irrefutable test of all vice or virtue: the question of its fruit. Promiscuity aside (which exists of course without regard to sexual orientation), do *committed* homosexual couples constitute some inherent threat to themselves or society at large? Do their partnerships promulgate any more harm or good than those of their heterosexual counterparts? Is there any substantive basis at all for distinguishing between gay couples and straight in measuring the quality of relationships? To these questions, my own experience has shouted a resounding No! "You will know them by their fruits" — these words, too, are from Jesus (Matt. 7:16).

Yes, there is the matter of long-term commitment itself. "Is such a thing even possible among homosexuals?" many ask. Here, gays indeed appear to be at a statistical disadvantage, but not by much, I wager, given the high instance of infidelity and divorce among married couples. And this, of course, raises the great catch-22 for homosexuality and a burning dilemma for society today: marriage itself. How is it that gays and lesbians can be denounced as somehow incapable of long-term commitment yet denied the legal right to choose it even if they wish? The law against adultery is an invitation to practice sexual fidelity in covenant relationship — an invitation not yet extended in our society to gay men and lesbians. Meanwhile, the heterosexual divorce rate hovers near 50 percent.

Back in the sanctuary, the practical matter remains. I am still scratching my head when Gwen, a problem solver, poses an alternative plan for the wedding procession. I like it immediately and together we work out the logistics, calling over Matt and Kerry to secure their concurrence.

Now it is on to the narthex to practice the procession. Couples will march down the aisle, one immediately after the other, led off by Dawn and Kyle, the matron of honor and best man. Matt and Kerry will be the last in line before the ring bearer, the flower girl, and the bride, escorted by her father Rex. The wedding party will walk the aisle, minus the time-honored baggage of gender roles. No hands looped through arms, no silly stutter steps. Just couples on a quick stroll of solidarity.

Once down the aisle, the wedding party will fan out by couple, right and left, then up the steps onto either side of the chancel, where they will form one seamless curtain of togetherness, just behind the bride and groom — five faithful couples in all. Let the congregation draw its own conclusions.

Not surprisingly, Gwen's father Rex already has. He had got early wind of Matt and Kerry's likely participation and fixed his eye upon them the very moment they arrived. Now, as we make our way to the narthex, he pulls me aside for comment. "Can you believe them?" he starts, flicking a thumb over his shoulder in their general direction. "Makes you sick, doesn't it!" He's fishing for a reply, but I don't bite.

"One of 'em works with my Gwen," Rex continues. "Don't know how she stands it, but she claims to like him. Go figure!

"Can't believe, though, she asked 'em both to stand up at her wedding! 'Gwen, honey,' we said to her — Sherry and me — 'what in heaven's name were you thinking? You trying to embarrass the whole family here, or what?'

"Well," Rex concludes, "far as I'm concerned, these types can do whatever they want to — long as the rest of us don't have to *know* about it."

This, I note, from a four-time divorcee, a serial polygamist. Kerry and Matt, I will later learn, have been a couple already for eight years. Rex's record for one marriage is only five. "You will know them by their fruits..."

THE SINS OF THE FATHER

But the thing that David had done displeased the
Lord, and the Lord sent Nathan to David. He came
to him, and said to him, "There were two men in a
certain city, the one rich, the other poor.... [T]he
poor man had nothing but one little ewe
lamb...and it was like a daughter to him. Now there
came a traveler to the rich man, and he was loath to
take one of his flock or herd to prepare for the way-
farer...but he took the poor man's lamb, and prepared that for the guest...." Then David's anger was
greatly kindled against the man. He said to Nathan,
"As the Lord lives, the man who did this deserves to
die...." Nathan said to David, "You are the man!"

— 2 SAMUEL 12:1–7, PASSIM

This is the story of Bathsheba, the unwitting object of a king's lust. From the heights of his palace roof, David spies a beautiful woman bathing. She is, he learns, the wife of one of his own warriors, Uriah the Hittite, battling for Israel against the Ammonites. David nevertheless sends for Bathsheba and sleeps with her, and she becomes pregnant. Then he arranges for Uriah to become trapped in the heaviest fighting at the besieged city of Rabbah, where he is killed. After her period of mourning, Bathsheba is summoned to David and she becomes his wife. Then and there, the matter is settled. After all, David is king and more than king. David is Israel. What further need be said?

> Nathan said..., "Thus says the Lord: I will raise up trouble against you from within your own house...." David said to Nathan, "I have sinned against the Lord."
>
> — 2 SAMUEL 12:7, 11, 13 PASSIM
>
> *Every vice has its price.*

The line is forming up nicely. I call the flower girl and ring bearer to their places behind the bridesmaids and grooms-men. The young pair is Rex's five-year-old daughter Brenda and four-year-old son Billy, recently collected from beneath the sanctuary pews. Rex, of course, is old enough to be their grandpa and has more or less functioned as such since their births.

Brenda complies with my wishes, but not Billy, who wants to travel the aisle solo at roughly the speed of a Formula One racer. "Vroom, vroom!" he steers into place with his white satin wedding ring pillow. Gwen bends down to eye level for a half-brother–sister chat. She sweet-talks, bribes, threatens — all to no avail. Billy pushes the pillow into her face, then races away, squealing with pleasure. Gwen shoots an exasperated glance at her father, who is at the very back of the line. Rex is busy with Gale, a pretty young employee of Weddings Unlimited who is setting up a silk floral arrangement by the church entrance. Gale, in a halter top, is kneeling to arrange the flowers, and Rex swoops down on her like a lion on an antelope. He is describing to her the lobby of the Adventura Palace in Cancun — "the Mayan Riviera, they call it! You should see the way they decorate! Really ought to go there sometime, you know. I just might be going back sometime soon myself," he adds, almost suggestively, staring down at her with his deep blue ogling eyes.

Gwen rolls her own eyes in disgust. This is her father as she has always known him. Not until now, though, with his graying hair and growing paunch, has he appeared to her quite so pitifully ridiculous. It seems clear that nothing will come of this latest overture, but Rex has taken one more little step along his personal quest for Divorces Unlimited.

Time is slipping by. I decide to play hardball with Billy, forcing him in line next to Brenda, just in front of Gwen and Rex, who has temporarily reigned in his predatory instincts. Billy shoots me his best scowl, but the rest of him remains in place. It is Brenda who does the shifting, moving to the very outer edge of the aisle and away from Billy, for, sensibly, she prefers her brother at a safe distance. On my signal, the organist begins to play and the wedding party to process up the aisle to the strains of Bach's *Jesu, Joy of Man's Desiring*. Back in the sanctuary, Rex's wife Sherry has been gratefully oblivious to the carryings on of her husband and son. Just for once, it seems, she wants not to know. But the sudden bellow of the organ jars her loose from repose — and each of us with her — free from her daily disappointment and pain and the costly evasion of both, roused to something beyond faithless husbands and puerile sons. For a brief interval, as we witness this moving ritual of commitment, each of us is summoned back to goodness, back to joy, back to God.

> ... Then David went to [Bathsheba], and lay with her; and she bore a son, and he named him Solomon.
>
> — 2 SAMUEL 12:24

> Among [Solomon's] wives were seven hundred princesses and three hundred concubines; and his wives turned away his heart.
>
> — 1 KINGS 11:3

ABANDONMENT AND BLESSING

> If, however, this charge is true, that evidence of the young woman's virginity was not found, then they shall bring the young woman out to the entrance of her father's house and the men of her town shall stone her to death....
>
> — DEUTERONOMY 22:20

Lahore, Pakistan, is a principal site in the practice of "honor killing," the murder of innocent women whose sexuality is regarded as the property of family honor. Women who defy their family's wishes for marriage face isolation, torture, even death. Wives who attempt to escape domestic abuse are hunted down by their husbands and their own family and executed. With

*deep roots in a culture of arranged marriage and female sub-
missiveness, honor killings continue to be carried out in
Pakistan and other places with impunity. In some instances,
their perpetrators act with the sanction of local governing
bodies.*

*Even female victims of rape and incest are gunned down or
hacked to death by relatives who regard them as damaged goods,
holding no more value than a broken cup or saucer. Indeed,
their shame is their family's shame, their death and removal
from memory its only escape.*

*As governments and human rights groups struggle to force
Pakistan's compliance with CEDAW, the United Nations
Convention on the Elimination of All Forms of Discrimination
Against Women, the true basis of the problem persists: a view of
women as commodities whose value is derived from the men
who possess them. To satisfy this view, women suffer untold
anguish.*

*Although it appears to most as obviously wrong, to some this
idea remains completely valid. It has ruled, after all, throughout much of human civilization. And though the fog of misunderstanding seems to keep lifting over time, it is always too early
to celebrate. In matters of dim thought, no one is exempt from
the next round of folly.*

The procession has come off nearly without a hitch. The
couples — bridesmaids and groomsmen — now form a
human screen across the chancel of the church, with Gwen,
Alan, Rex, and me on the steps just in front. Brenda and
Billy have rejoined their mother in the second row of pews
according to the wise decision of the bride and groom.

There were no objections. The thought of Billy standing on the chancel steps with a captive audience for thirty minutes sent chills down the backs of family and friends alike.

This accomplished, we turn to the business of words. I talk through the elements of the ceremony, beginning with a greeting, remarks about marriage, Scripture readings, and prayer.

I merely mention the Declaration of Consent, that preliminary, formal inquiry into a couple's intention to be wed, answered simply, "I do." In a traditional rite of marriage, it stands as a gateway into the more intimate portion of the ceremony centering on the vows. It rarely requires rehearsal. This is not the case today, though, for what follows next.

"And who adds a blessing upon Gwen and Alan's intention to join in marriage?"

My question echoes, unanswered. Save for Alan, Gwen, and me, no one here has heard it before. The question Rex had anticipated was "Who gives this woman to be married to this man?" Indeed, he had long awaited it. It was to be his moment in the limelight, standing there, smack dab between the daughter he barely knows and the young man who has won her heart. Rex had thought it all out. He planned to hesitate slightly before making his pronouncement, "I do!" One brief moment of feigned deliberation would do it, he'd figured. A playful pause, just for the effect. But now, with these lame words of "blessing" — not "giving" — he could feel the moment slipping away. Blessing? Like a bad pitch, there was nothing solid here to swing at.

In truth, it had taken only a gentle prodding from me to convince Gwen to abandon that time-honored passing of the bride from father to groom routine. "I guess I should ask

Rex to give me away," she had remarked at one of our premarital counseling sessions. "Shouldn't I?"

Gwen appeared caught in a pitched battle between longing and loathing. While desirous of a loving father to offer
her hand in marriage, she was understandably reluctant to
entrust such an honor to *this* father. It had surprised me at
first to hear her refer to him by his first name, Rex, not as
"Dad" or "Daddy." She had abandoned those appellations
while still in high school, at a time when she was seeing
less and less of Rex, he being preoccupied with his fourth
wife and her own children. After that marriage ended, Rex
had made a concerted effort to involve himself again in his
daughter's life, but then his Sherry had come along and soon
thereafter the children she bore him. Sherry was scarcely
older than Gwen herself, and their relationship from the
start had resembled more that of stepsisters than anything
else. This had closed the coffin on "Daddy" for good.

But Rex remained her biological father, and here, on the
occasion of her wedding, the irony of this part of the liturgy
was thick: Rex had long since abandoned the role of the
father as the significant male presence in a daughter's life.
Now, as Gwen sought a permanent remedy to that breach of
custom through marriage to Alan, custom itself allotted to
Rex a key, if ceremonial, role in granting it!

Had Gwen thought it through, she might have passed
the privilege to her mother, June, perhaps even enlisting her
in the grand escort down the aisle. But I had begun to move
things in another direction. "Is it true?" I had asked at last.
"*Is* someone 'giving you away'?" I often ask this question at
this point in a couple's planning, but I asked it on this occasion with a special force of purpose. "Is that who you are,
Gwen — some commodity to be passed on to the next

owner? Or is this your mutual decision with Alan, a decision that seeks no permission but only the blessings of God and those who love you?"

She had not even needed to answer. We both knew who Gwen was, and after that the course had seemed clear enough.

"And who adds a blessing upon Gwen and Alan's intention to join in marriage?" I ask for the second time. Rex is still stuck in shock, but at last he manages, nearly in a whisper, "So, how am I supposed to answer?"

"You don't, Rex," Gwen replies. "Everyone says it together: 'We do!'"

WORDS

At last we have come to the core of the ceremony, the marriage vows. Gwen and Alan face one another. They join hands and stare earnestly into each other's eyes. A hush falls over the hall as every ear strains to hear these ancient oaths, the plightings of troth between lovers prepared to surrender their lives, half to a person, half to an ideal.

"I, Alan, take you, Gwen..." It is only a rehearsal, yet Alan's speech trembles. His voice is high, strained.

"A little louder, please, Alan" I coax. "You'll need to speak louder for anyone to hear you."

Alan nods in agreement. Then, all at once, his eyes break off their steady gaze into Gwen's. For a moment they search the floor, then look to me. Alan's lips are parted as if wrestling with some half-formed question. "Louder?" they seem to ask. "*Can* we be louder? *Should* we be?"

It is a curiosity of marriage vows that they represent at once the true inner sanctum of a wedding ceremony and its most public aspect — private promises exchanged in the glare of lights, flashbulbs, and the whites of a thousand eyes. Why should others overhear what a bride and groom pledge from their depths? And yet, this is precisely why friends and family have been invited: to witness Gwen and Alan exchange the most sacred espousal of commitment one can make to another.

My wife Donna and I were married in the same year as the most public wedding in history, the joining of Prince Charles and Lady Diana. It was happy timing for the spectator in me, as I was taking a real interest in weddings as never before in my life.

The royal wedding occurred in the summer of 1981, just after my graduation from college. I was living at home in Illinois, working to save money for married life. Five hours away in Indiana, Donna was doing the same. We were each on the night shift, she as a nurse's aid in a hospital and I as a technician on a psychiatric ward connected to a nursing home. The morning wedding aired live from London. Back in the States this was the dead of night, but millions of households around the nation tuned in anyway to witness the spectacle live. A reclusive prince and his mystery bride held the whole world in their sway.

It was a quiet night on the psychiatric ward. From a tele-vision set in the nursing home dining hall, I followed the proceedings with fascination: the long carriage procession from Buckingham Palace to St. Paul's Cathedral, the diamond-studded regalia and star-studded pageantry, the solemn, seamless liturgy, proclaimed by the archbishop of Canterbury himself. I took it all in, bemused by its contrast with our own modest wedding plans.

But when at last it came down to words, to vows, to a

prince vouchsafing his faithfulness unto death, it was not Charles speaking, but I, offering myself — mind, body, and soul — to Donna. And when his bride, blind to all the anguish fate is free to bring, in giddy innocence pledged to her prince the same, it was Donna speaking, linking her future unreservedly to mine — come what may.

We spoke of it on the phone the next day, of how a public marriage spectacle had evolved at our viewing into our own private wedding rehearsal. Though a world apart, we were present there in words, in oaths by which we took the true measure of our own devotion.

Now these memories have bubbled up unbidden, as if in answer to Alan's silent query. "Share the words, Alan!" they seem to say. "Belt them out for all the world to hear. Give the brokers of doubt cause to tremble and their clients cause to hope!"

I want to communicate these things to Alan directly but never get the chance. With a tight squeeze of his hand, Gwen has summoned him back — back to her, back to his senses. She smiles, and so now, it seems, do Alan's words.

"I, Alan, take you, Gwen, to be my wife." They are delivered in a clear, strong voice into a pin-drop silence.

THE ROAD TAKEN

Donna and I composed our own wedding vows. The minister typed them into the body of his text, right after the Declaration of Consent and Blessing. Following the ceremony, we received our own copy of it, including those vows. Now and then, usually over a glass of port wine, we pull it out of a desk drawer and read the vows through again, just to recall what it was we agreed to that day.

I still regard those words as the necessary and sufficient expressions of our heartfelt intentions at the time. Strangers might find them lacking in certain ways. My children will surely find them mushy one day, thumbing through our papers once we're either senseless or expired. But none of this matters. We recited them once in public among close family and friends and have no plans to do so again. They belong to Donna and me alone now, and to God.

They are no longer words to us anyway, but rather first flickers that long ago went to flame and have grown since to a great height — and heat. We need the words less now because for so long we've simply been living them. But then the words were urgent, and so we wrote them down and shared them with the world.

Now and then I have wondered what my life would be like had I chosen to spend it with someone else — an old flame, perhaps, or my first infatuation, or a relationship I broke off with someone, or the other way around. I play out scenarios in my mind: our lives as lovers, the children we might have birthed and raised, the tragedies endured, the plans for retirement, that senseless hedging against inevitable decline. I spin them out until they will spin no further. For every road seems to wind back to where I already am — to this place, this home, this life. And it is my life, all I know or would ever wish to know.

We should harbor no illusions: in this vast world of infinite possibility, each of us might have found happiness in countless places, along innumerable paths, with any one of a million different loves. There is no marked trail and no preordained companion along life's journey. Yet the path each of us has chosen is our own path. Though our futures remain open, they are closing fast with the passage of days.

And where we are in a given moment, whether good or bad, is increasingly revealed to us as the only place we might ever have been. The rest is hypothetical.

This is a strange paradox, good for considering now and again while sipping a glass of port.

LOOSE ENDS

Weak woman, poor woman who understands,
Sorrow of centuries I knew in the drinking of it:
Ah, this soul of mine cannot support
All of its weight!

— ALFONSINA STORNI

The rehearsal has nearly ended. Following the marriage vows were those of the rings. Gwen and Alan got through them nicely, I thought. At that point, the three of us, along with the matron of honor and the best man — the real ring bearers — had huddled in a circle. A ring of intimacy, you might call it. This clustering not only imitates the shape of the ring itself, but it greatly reduces the likelihood of dropping the thing and watching it roll under a pew in front of a few hundred spectators.

Rings themselves are emblems of permanence. They have no end. This is unlike everything and everyone else involved here. The finger a ring goes on has an end — the ring can come off! So do the beating of the heart that gives it and the breath of the soul that receives it. Even marriages themselves have ends — whether through death or divorce. But not rings. They keep right on ringing, as if in stubborn witness to the hunch of soul mates that their love will touch eternity.

The remainder of the ceremony is straightforward: a reading of a poem by a family member, a vocal solo from a friend, the pronouncement of marriage, the presentation of the couple, and the final blessing. Each of these requires little rehearsal time. Yet this time another matter comes to the fore unexpectedly, delivering in its wake perhaps the profoundest meaning marriage can boast.

The candle of unity seems innocuous enough on the surface of things — a large votive candle lighted by a bride and groom from two smaller, family tapers, representing two identities and traditions blending into one. The pair of candles is lighted prior to the ceremony by representatives from each family, usually the mothers of the bride and groom.

It is with this last detail that things have gotten dicey. Alan's mother, Faith, still sitting alone on the outside aisle, remains unaware of this portion of the ceremony or her part in it. Alan has never gotten around to asking her, and it takes no great insight to see why. On one level, Alan is simply happy his mother is here at all. But because she *is* here, something else is now possible, something for which Alan had hoped against hope, guardedly, tentatively, as a child who has learned the hard way to practice caution around a hot stove.

It had all started with Gwen's talk of honoring her own mother with a red rose. Gwen planned to present the rose to June just after lighting the unity candle. She would light the candle, turn from the chancel, retrace her steps down the stairs, and then would just keep right on going, right out to the second pew and to her mother's side. There, she would bend down to deliver a kiss to the strong but tender face of the woman she loves most in the world. Last, Gwen would press into June's hands a single red rose. And her mother would smile.

Alan had listened intently as Gwen shared this fancy, finding himself both inspired and dispirited by it. He realized anew just how estranged he remained from his own mother. What if Alan were to do the same for her? How would Faith respond? It frightened him just to ponder it. But he could not shake the thought that he should try it. And so Alan and Gwen had laid plans for the giving of roses, ordering them well in advance. Weddings Unlimited had placed them in a separate box to be refrigerated overnight in the church kitchen. Even now, as we rehearse the candle lighting, Gwen and Alan are beginning to choreograph the act, secretly of course, since it is to be a surprise.

I, on the other hand, am thinking about Alan's surprise if he should try to deliver a rose to a mother who isn't there. Faith, indeed, is the loose end in their planning. Already I had mentioned that the mothers would be seated just after lighting their candles and before the ceremony began. Alan had cast me a horrified look. Faith had not even seemed to hear it. "I haven't asked her about lighting the candle yet!" he told me moments later.

My fear now is that Faith may not even be planning to sit in the mother's place of honor, being gun shy of the limelight and the judgments it might bring. "It's time you talked to your mother," I whisper to Alan. "We'll wait," I say. He turns gloomy, but then he complies, Gwen on his tail. As he saunters to face his mother, it is clear there is more at stake than the fate of a single red rose.

I don't hear the words, nor am I likely ever to learn what is spoken. Instead, I simply watch. Alan approaches his mother. Her arms are crossed and her head is down as if caught in a trance, but she looks up suddenly at the sound of her son's voice. Alan kneels down to her eye level and speaks softly to her. He is trembling. Gwen places her hand on Alan's shoulder as if to steady him. They are working as a team. Now Alan is pointing to the chancel and Faith is following his hand, up to the table where three candles sit, ready to be lighted, then down and out to the second pew on the aisle, to the seat of honor reserved for mothers. And still Faith's eyes trail her son's hand.

But all at once she undergoes a transformation. The change is palpable and the cause apparent: it is fear. Faith's back stiffens, her shoulders tighten, her eyes bulge, and her head begins a pronounced shaking from side to side. The answer is no. But Alan is not finished. Now he has taken her hands in his and is shaking them firmly to the rhythm of words. "Please, Mom!" is what I imagine he says. "I need you. Please do this for me!" And before I can blink, Alan has embraced her, and has buried his head into her breast, and his back is heaving in the unmistakable pattern of sobs.

Caught off guard, Faith does not know how to respond. She pats his back lightly as if hoping to make him stop. But I can already glimpse her weakening resolve. Steadily, in the way of a quiet miracle, she begins to embrace him back, and the tears of years, it seems, stream down her cheeks. And Gwen, the daughter-in-law in waiting, waits no more, wrapping her arms around them both tightly and not letting go.

By now, others are aware of them, sobbing there at the edge of events. The side aisle has become the center, and the mother of the groom is seated in the place of honor. Perhaps, after all, it will be just as the bride and groom have envisaged it: Alan will turn from the chancel, walk down the steps and keep right on going, right to the second pew, where his mother will be seated. He'll bend down to deliver a kiss to that stern but somehow tender face of the woman whose love he has wanted most in the world. Then, Alan will press into his mother's hands a single red rose. And she will smile. It would be fair to say, it occurs to me, that at long last Alan has found Faith.

The covenant of marriage is more than a bond between two souls. It is a way of faithfulness that extends to all relationships, all realms of mutuality. While early, in love's infancy, couples may stand face-to-face, eye to eye, blind to the world about them, in time, if love matures, they will turn cheek to cheek and face the world as one. Marriage finds its raison d'être, a mission beyond itself. Why, I can't say, but Gwen and Alan are far down this road already, even before the wedding bells ring.

PAPER CHASE

The rehearsal is over and the wedding party is clearing out for the evening. Before they get away, I press Gwen and Alan for the marriage license application. I had asked for it before, but they never remembered to bring it for me to fill out. After today, however, there are no more chances.

"Got it!" Gwen says. She digs into an oversized purse and pulls out a white envelope, frayed at the edges, betraying the rough and tumble, not of days but months. I turn it over in my hands. The package is hard in the middle, and heavy. By its weight alone, I know that we have a problem. My face must betray my concern, for Gwen jumps on it immediately. "Is something wrong?" she asks.

What is wrong is that the bulge is that of the handsome keepsake license booklet included in every application — until recently, that is, when it was replaced with a simple broadside of thick parchment. It's a cost-saving measure no doubt, implemented at the same time the official license form was updated. But that had been nearly six months ago. A license signed by the clerk of the county court is valid for only ninety days. Without even looking, I know that this license has expired.

Gwen and Alan had picked it up shortly before their only serious falling out. The spat had sobered them up enough to postpone their nuptials by several months, and by that time, unknown to them, the license application had expired.

I pull out the book, responsible for the envelope's telltale bulge. "It's nice," I comment. "Much nicer than the new one they're using! Since it's only a keepsake, you're welcome to use it instead if you like. I can fill it out this evening. But this official license has expired" — I point to the date. "It's completely worthless, I'm afraid. You'll have to apply for another one."

Gwen looks distraught. "But the wedding's tomorrow!" she frets. "Our marriage won't be 'official,' will it? Without a license, I mean . . ."

It is a fascinating question. A license is a legal document, a formal representation of fact. Here, that fact is a couple's union, accomplished in the sight of God and other partisans, everyone whom Gwen and Alan love, who love Gwen and Alan. That union, these words, those rings to be worn and cherished, along with the prayers and well-wishes of live witnesses, their pledges of support, and their hugs and kisses and tears — these constitute the substance of the wedding.

The official license will be folded, filed, and forgotten, its significance tied at best to some future historical curiosity, to some day when both Alan and Gwen are already long gone. But their love will outlive both them and the paper. It will linger in the hearts of all they have touched, then go on to the love of the cosmos itself, home to the heart of God.

"Forget the license," I tell them. "When you get a new form, we'll have a signing party with Uncle Sam. But the next time you leave from here after tonight, it will be as husband and wife, as coupled as a couple can be!"

"I guess I knew that," Gwen says, "but thanks!"

THE ETERNAL COVENANT

As always, I am the last one out, left with the task of leaving God's house in darkness. I walk through the building, throwing switches. But I'm heartened to think that in the real work at hand, things have been moving the other way. New light is shining on old darkness. The rehearsal has gone well. Within hours, Gwen and Alan will finally bury their doubts and marry. Meanwhile, two families of estrangement are doing some burying of their own, laying to rest two quarrelsome pasts in the interest of one brighter future. Not every rift has closed, nor every old wound healed. Some never will, on this side of eternity at least.

There are no sure bets in marriage, not even for Gwen and Alan. But most who will gather on the coming day to hover near the mystery of holy covenant will depart in some small way changed. They will carry away a vision of faithfulness, a share of the love that endures, 'til-death-only parting. This is far from everything; but it is enough.

I flip off the last light and shut the door.

SWINDLING STINGINESS
YOU SHALL NOT STEAL

[W]hen you go, you will not go empty-handed;
each woman shall ask her neighbor and any
woman living in the neighbor's house for jewelry
of silver and of gold, and clothing, and you shall
put them on your sons and on your daughters;
and so you shall plunder the Egyptians.

— EXODUS 3:22

All life is robbery.

— ALFRED NORTH WHITEHEAD

GIVE AND TAKE

*Before the Exodus, the Hebrews had rights to nothing. Even their
scant belongings did not qualify as possessions. You cannot own
anything when you are owned yourself, when you are a slave.*

*When the Israelites escape into the desert, they bring with
them flocks and herds, jewelry of silver and gold, and Egyptian
clothes. These are the spoils of their hard-earned departure.
Overnight, they are transformed from property into property*

owners. This is a legacy of liberation. It is, likewise, a curse, a new burden to bear.

In no time, Moses finds himself judging the people, settling their disputes from sunup to sundown. It is tedious work, a new form of drudgery that prompts Moses' father-in-law, the priest of Midian, to suggest the appointment of judges to share the load. Their chief qualification, he says, should be an abhorrence of dishonest gain. This is not surprising, as one imagines that a high percentage of complaints involve personal possessions. In a court of law it is rarely otherwise.

Later, when Moses receives the law at Sinai, many of its statutes pertain to matters of property: stolen and damaged goods, lending practices, respect for the property of others, the care of bond servants, and the like. There are ordinances for nearly every circumstance imaginable. But the essential word is short and unadorned. It is clear, carved in stone even, yet possessing all the ambiguity of daily life: "You shall not steal."

The doorbell rings twice. We hear it the first time, but we are up in our attic beginning a long remodeling project. It is thirty-seven steps down to the first floor, and another eighteen paces from the back staircase to the front door. We are living in a veritable mansion.

Our doorbell plays the Westminster chimes. We have installed it as a festive alternative to "dingdong," but lately it has become more significant. Our vintage 1870s Victorian home harbors many secrets, and with the aid of our new doorbell, we have been giving them voice. The chime is pleasant to hear, so we have taken to ringing it ourselves for pleasure. Meanwhile, short lines of verse set to the six-note tune have suggested themselves, until we have come to imagine that it is our old house herself singing, "Glad to meet you. Let me greet you!" she says.

Over time, we get acquainted. Her tongue loosens up. Ours is a house of the world, it turns out. We have it on good authority that she once was a bordello. "As a lady, I've been jady," she confesses. And the more we ring, the more our old bell seems to like it. "I'm so happy... to be yappy!"

In truth, since installing the chimes, we have done most of the doorbell ringing ourselves. So when, from the attic, we hear them go off, it gives us quite a start: "Someone's ringing, so I'm singing!"

By the time I get to the first floor landing, our house has called again: "If it please you, someone needs you." At last, I make it to the front door. On our porch are a young man and woman. I recognize the woman right off as the daughter of a Hispanic couple who lives down the street. The young man is her boyfriend. I open the door to greet them as Donna arrives from the attic. She and I are both perspiring heavily. The attic is hot and we have been cutting and hanging sheets of drywall. Most of the drywall has yet to be hoisted up the three flights of stairs to its new home. I have done this sort of work before and share the widespread sentiment that it is among the least desirable of the trades.

The young man does all the talking. His name is Thurston, a respectable name if any is. The woman's name is Alicia. We know through the grapevine that she is pregnant, a fact that is already beginning to speak for itself. She herself keeps quiet, only smiling sweetly and shyly. We warm to her.

Thurston is attractive and articulate. It is not hard to see

why Alicia has fallen for him. But Alicia's parents, conserva-
tive Catholics, were crushed by her pregnancy. Thurston is
no longer welcome in their home. Yet Alicia is eighteen and
head over heels for him. She believes in her future with
Thurston the way she was raised to believe in heaven.

At the moment, she and Thurston are simply looking
for a place to live. They are interested in renting the old
apartment above our carriage house garage. The apartment
is dilapidated and generally unsuitable for tenants. The current occupants are mice and sparrows. We tell Thurston the
carriage house cannot be rented, but he persists. He will fix
it up for the price of rent, make it like new. He is a crafts-
man, a carpenter, a drywaller.

His last word steals into our ears like a siren song.
"Drywaller?" we repeat. "You do drywall?"

Within minutes we have settled upon terms. They will live
rent free while Thurston works for us, beginning with drywall
in the attic. We will spruce up the carriage house apartment as
best we can. Gradually, Thurston will do the rest. He is full of
bluster. "Yeah, really I can do about everything," he says. And
I believe him because I desire to desperately.

We shake on it. When they have gone, Donna and I
trade in our utility knives and drywall nails for mops and
brooms and head out back to the carriage house. We have
struck a good bargain. For us, cheap labor; for them, a roof
over their heads. Privately, we each have misgivings. Are we
taking advantage of this couple, of their vulnerability? After
all, the carriage house apartment was sitting abandoned.
Now we'll get it renovated for next to nothing. Isn't that
stealing? But we put such thoughts out of our minds.
Instead, blindsided by desire, we smile through the balance
of the day, happy as larks.

STEALTH

The problem of sin is that it is profitable.

— WALTER RAUSCHENBUSCH

At the bottom of our attic stairs sits an old desk. It belongs to Donna's mother Estella, but her second-floor bedroom is too full to accommodate it. The desk holds Estella's remaining papers — prospectuses, insurance information, old bank statements, and the like. Some of her deceased husband Chuck's personal effects are stored there as well — pocketknives, tie tacks, a little of everything.

A big desk in a narrow hallway leaves little room for drywall, which Thurston and his partner Jim have been hauling around the corner and up the attic stairs. By the time I check on them, the desk has already been moved down the hall, out of the path of traffic. I think no more about it as the pair begins to cut and hang drywall.

It is immediately apparent that Thurston and Jim are not compatible workers. They bicker like young siblings over every aspect of the task. They swear like sailors. Thankfully, our young daughter Rachael is with Donna, who is helping Alicia to settle into the carriage house. We have lent her a few furnishings to get started. The apartment has taken on a quaintness we had not thought possible. A sparrow's nest has been removed and a crack in the clapboard siding repaired. It is far from perfect, but it is home.

Meanwhile, Estella is growing exasperated. Thurston is loud and obnoxious. The volume on his portable radio, tuned to a local country station, is cranked high. Even with her door shut, Estella cannot hear herself think. The two young men continue to volley insults at each other over the din, almost without pause. Reluctantly, I climb to the attic to try and set them straight.

Jim seems genuinely regretful, chastened even. Thurston is uncharacteristically quiet. "It's too hot up here," he complains at last. It is late September but still quite humid. I have given them a fan, but he wants at least one more. I deliver a second one to the attic, then begin to look around. Drywall has been slapped up onto the angled walls with reckless abandon. Gaps exist everywhere. The floor is covered with chunks of broken plasterboard. I know in an instant that we have made a dreadful mistake.

I voice my displeasure, but Thurston has a ready answer. They'll mud it and tape it. "It'll look great," he boasts. I ask them again to keep it down and to be careful not to waste any more drywall. Then I go directly out to the carriage house to have a word with Donna.

Things are proceeding much better on this front. When I arrive, she and Alicia are hanging lace curtains in the small kitchen. The aging appliances have been scrubbed until they sparkle. New area rugs cover the wood floors, hiding years of wear and tear. Alicia looks tickled, almost exuberant. I want to pull Donna aside and spell out the attic situation. "He won't last a week," I am aching to tell her. But I restrain myself.

Then, from the carriage house window, I spot Thurston slip out the back door of our house. Jim is just behind him, calling him back, but Thurston is gone. Alicia doesn't notice. I go to investigate, but already both have disappeared.

For the next two days, there is no sign of Thurston. Our agreement had stipulated he would finish the attic without delay, then tackle the carriage house at his own pace. I am angry, yet I find myself relieved to be rid of him. We worry for Alicia, though. She has not seen or heard from him, either. By now, the apartment is all prettied up, but with Thurston away, Alicia slips into a funk. We loan her a small black-and-white television. She sits on an old sofa chair watching Ricki Lake and Sallie Jessie Raphael to pass the time. There is always someone who's got it worse, she consoles herself. Or is there? By Thurston's third day away, Alicia has begun to wonder.

But that is the day Thurston shows up at the carriage house door. He has returned with a new stereo system, we learn later. He hooks it up, cranks it up, then spends the rest of the day and night "making up" with Alicia. Next morning, he is back in our attic, minus Jim. "He wanted out," Thurston explains. "Too damn lazy, and he can't drywall for nothin'."

"So, where've you been lately?" I ask.

"Taking care of some things," he answers.

"And the stereo," I pry. "Where'd that come from?"

"Friend," he offers — no more.

"Well, please keep the volume down at night," I tell him. Thurston smiles contemptuously.

The work continues, poorly as before, but I let it go. I am beginning to feel like a hostage in my own home with no one but myself to blame.

BETRAYAL

Reporter: "Why do you rob all these banks, Willy?"
Willy Sutton: "Because that's where they keep
the money."

The phone is ringing. Our phone features an option that replaces the usual ring with a voice saying, "You have a telephone call." It is a male voice, clear and strong. Press a button

and he will announce, "You...have...three...messages."
Press another and hear, "I...have...saved...your...mes-
sages."

I pick up the receiver, soon to drop my jaw. It is a credit
card company. They have called to report an irregularity, a
sudden surge of activity in an old credit card account. The
account has been dormant for two years. Over the last week,
several thousand dollars have been spent against the
account. Then, the deeper mystery: the cardholder is a
Charles F. Usery — Donna's father, over two years deceased.

There is scarcely time to think when the doorbell rings,
our house chirping above the chimes of Westminster: "Come
and get it, or you'll regret it!" Over the phone, I tell the credit
card company employee that the card transactions were not
Estella's. She informs me that they would like to freeze the
account and investigate through a third-party firm.

The doorbell sounds a second time: "Stop your stalling,
someone's calling." I hang up the phone and go to the door.
Looking through the glass, I am surprised to see Jim,
Thurston's former sidekick. He has a nervous look. He keeps
craning his head back over his shoulder, left and right, as if
to see who might be watching.

Unlocking the door, I invite him in. Once we stand face-
to-face he can barely make eye contact. But as he begins to
speak, the words tumble out, solving our riddle instantly.
"It's about Thurst," Jim says. "He stole from you. He took
some knives — and a credit card."

I stand silent, stoic, as slowly the pieces fall into place:
the hallway desk, the papers yet to be organized, the rem-
nants of Chuck's life.

"I'm pretty sure he's used the card," Jim adds.

"*Thurst,* you call him, huh?" I ask.

"Well, yeah, sometimes people do."

"Why?" I could ask. But I don't need to. "Thurst" speaks for itself. The ideal epithet for such a man — a man with an unquenchable thirst for the things of others. Jim is right: it *is* about "thirst."

When the bank robber Willy Sutton offered his famous bank robber's raison d'être, America laughed aloud, mistaking it for a joke. But it seems to have been Sutton's sincere response to the question as he heard it: not "Why rob?" — a question that never entered his mind — but "Why banks?" His answer cut to the marrow of his moral incapacity. Willy and Thurston, I suspect, are pathological first cousins.

I thank Jim for his candor.

"Just don't tell him I told you," he asks before leaving.

Next morning, Thurston comes across the yard to work on what he thinks will be a normal day. I meet him at the backdoor and bar his entry. Thurston is caught short. "What's goin' on?" he asks.

"Thurston," I say, working hard to mask both anger and unease, "Did you take my father-in-law's credit card from the hallway desk?"

His look of surprise quickly gives way to one of cold contempt. "What in the hell makes you think that?"

I don't answer. *"Did* you?" I repeat. We eye each other uncomfortably. He is scrambling for an angle, for something to grab hold of. Then he finds it: "Jim told you that lie, didn't he?"

When he says Jim's name, I visibly react despite myself, and Thurston sees it. He knows now, and I know he knows, and Thurston knows I know he knows. I'm not as good at this game as he. "It doesn't matter," I tell him. "Did you do it?" I ask now for the third time.

"That bastard!" he mutters, still on Jim. "No, I didn't take nothin'! Did you ask him if *he* did?"

But now Thurston undergoes an eerie transformation. His face turns to stone. His eyes narrow to slits, admitting no light but letting off a steely pinpoint of rage, of fury approaching apoplexy. This fury is clearly trained on Jim.

The question of Thurston's guilt has ceased to be an issue. I no longer factor in his thoughts, either. Thurston has moved on. Betrayal! Thurston has assumed the indignation of a victim, of one who has suffered an unspeakable crime. While our loss at his hands has been material in nature, his loss concerns a secret, protected by an unwritten code. Jim has violated that code. He is a snitch, a thief of secrets. In Thurston's book, this makes him the lowest form of life. Thurston verbalizes none of this; his expression tells the tale. All at once, my adversary and I are married in a thought: the robber has been robbed!

I recall the story of a woman serving time in a women's correctional facility. She had been convicted of grand larceny, of cashing other people's welfare checks and making purchases on stolen credit cards. When asked why she engaged in these crimes she explained that, while generally stealing is wrong, she did it because *she* needed the money. What if someone did this to her, the questioner followed. That would be wrong, she explained, because she needed the money. There is an eerie consistency in such an argument that I can see mimicked in Thurston's own mind. What harm could there be in stealing from a dead man? What harm in taking from a cripple, confined to a room, with her simple needs already met? But steal his secret at your own risk! Betray him and pay!

Now, at the back door, things between Thurston and me

have reached a standoff. "Well, I'm sorry, but you're finished in the attic," I tell him at last.

"Yeah, I wouldn't come back here if you begged me!" he says.

"We'll talk about the carriage house later," I say.

"You can have your damn carriage house!" he cries, sauntering off. But with nowhere else to go, he heads back to the apartment anyway, and neither he nor Alicia comes out for the rest of the day.

STEALING AWAY

But Jehosheba, King Joram's daughter, Ahaziah's
sister, took Joash son of Ahaziah, and stole him
away from among the king's children who were
about to be killed; she put him and his nurse
in a bedroom. Thus she hid him from Athaliah,
so that he was not killed.

— 2 KINGS 11:1–2

Steal away, steal away, steal away to Jesus.

— TRADITIONAL SPIRITUAL

The biblical history of Israel the nation is the story of one, and later two, troubled monarchies. After the reigns of King David and his son Solomon, the kingdom divides, north and south. From there, the testimonies of historians and prophets spin a tale of titillating political intrigue, spanning the next 350 years, or to the end of Israelite nationhood.

But the Bible's interpretive lens is theological. Behind all human motive and effect is the will of God, far-reaching and decisive. Faithfulness toward God and the law is rewarded; unfaithfulness is punished. Among those laws is the Eighth Commandment, "You shall not steal."

Yet there is more than one way to steal. When Queen Athaliah, regarded by the Bible as an illegitimate ruler, attempts to murder all rivals to her throne, she misses one — an infant who is whisked away to safety like Moses in the bulrushes (Exod. 1, 2). In the Hebrew, he is ganab, *"stolen" away, later to return and claim his rightful throne. Through an act of stealth, of "stealing," a murder is averted. God's will for Israel is accomplished and the law preserved.*

Most of the time, stealing is a crime, an act of avarice. Occasionally, it is a deed of highest idealism. Pockets of courageous souls across the Third Reich steal Jews away from their Nazi pursuers. Escaped African American slaves, Southern property, are shepherded out of Dixie to safety in the North on the Underground Railroad. Those who remain enslaved, once stolen from homes across the continent of Africa, "steal away to Jesus" in song and spirit. The body may be in chains, but the spirit flies free.

Sometimes, stealing is intimately bound up with our own humanity and the deeper spirit of the law itself, and God seems to smile a blessing upon it.

There is shouting from across the driveway. Thurston and Alicia are quarreling. The windows slam shut, but the shouts carry on unabated. I remain silent but busy in my thoughts. My concern is for Alicia, for her well-being and that of the new life within her. But it is also for our own peace of mind. Donna and I had moved to this inner-city neighborhood fully cognizant of its social problems. To live here was to become unavoidably enmeshed in the life around us. Yet we had at least hoped to plant a small hedge around our own home, to keep the problems of the neighborhood at the fence line.

In fact, when Donna and I bought our Victorian fixer-upper back in the late 1980s, our first act of home ownership was to put up a French gothic picket fence around the property. This was prompted neither by fear nor by any particular desire for privacy. Rather, we owned dogs that we had no intention of walking. Once our fence was up and the new back gate to the alley was in place, we were surprised to discover that the steady flow of foot traffic through our yard continued unabated. The gate was constantly being left wide open, allowing our dogs to roam. Soon, we began to observe pedestrians trekking across our property as if we were camped along the Appalachian Trail.

Finally it sank in. For decades our home had been a boarding house, where an endless stream of souls had come and gone almost at will. Our driveway was more than a route for our cars to the garage. It was a major pedestrian thoroughfare. This long-established shortcut through our yard reduced significantly the average commute time on foot between neighborhood streets. Our driveway was providing a critical community service.

This posed a serious dilemma for us: how to reclaim a public access for our own private use and still manage to sleep at night? Who were we to steal away a perfectly good shortcut across the neighborhood? Though by law the drive was ours alone, as a matter of well-trodden tradition it belonged to everyone. Here was a fact we simply could not fence out. Finally, we opted to treat our trespassers kindly, offering a wave or greeting and a cheerful request that they remember to close the gate on the other side.

For whatever reason, foot traffic through our yard has gradually slowed to a trickle. Perhaps it was the sheer inconvenience of gates or a general fear of dogs, however friendly. Either way, traffic is now rerouted. Someone else's yard has become the new main pedestrian thoroughfare — someone who didn't keep dogs or never got around to putting up a picket fence. And yet we remain thankful for our decision and its companion realization that all boundaries are more permeable than we think.

This truth is serving us well now, as the social problem on our property is turning nasty. We have just gotten daughter Rachael down for a nap and are ready for some quiet time together when Westminster sounds and our house is singing again: "Stop your flirting. Someone's hurting!"

We hurry to the door. It is Alicia. There are welts on her face, conforming to the shape of Thurston's hand. Other bruises she exposes to Donna's eyes only. Thurston is an abuser of alcohol and, lately at least, women. While her injuries are not serious, Alicia is no longer safe in our carriage house. She is visibly exhausted, distraught. Living with Thurston's pathology, she has suffered an emotional beating as well. "I was so wrong about him," she moans.

Donna has Alicia lie down on the couch and applies ice packs to Thurston's most recent work. Then we pull up chairs beside her to talk. Should she consider filing assault charges? we ponder. Alicia resists the suggestion.

"Are you afraid?" I ask.

She assures us she is not. "I still love him," she says. "I just hate him more now. And I can't trust him anymore. I never will! I've just got to get away."

"Where can you go?" we ask.

Alicia retreats into her thoughts. Finally, she crooks her

head in order to gaze out the window in the direction of the street, up the street, in fact, where she imagines her parents sitting even now in cross-armed judgment. Before she supplies the answer, we already know. "I just wanna be back in my own home!" she exclaims, as fresh tears of stolen innocence stream from her eyes, down a face bearing the marks of consequence for recent choices. Some of these choices were hers. Others were made for her. Either way, her life will never be the same. She may indeed make it home, but she can never go "back." Alicia's world is changed forever.

Just now, home does appear to be Alicia's only real option. Recently we had run into her mother, Esperanza, on our street and had brought up her daughter's plan to move into our carriage house. While we had spared her mention of Thurston, she was not naive to the shape of things. We had feared the Garcias might be angry with us for offering any legitimacy to their daughter's recent life choices, but this was not the case. Instead, it had seemed to bring them considerable relief to learn Alicia was nearby. She is their youngest child and their only daughter. Although their decision to reject her relationship with Thurston seemed set in stone, they still loved her and were happy to at least know her whereabouts. They could cast a vigilant eye over her from only a few houses distant. We had offered to be of help in any way we might, and they had pledged the same. Now, the time has arrived to call in that pledge.

Dusk is falling fast as we walk Alicia up the street. A crescent moon hangs low on the horizon. Donna reaches her arm around Alicia's frail frame, holding her close, steadying her resolve. I carry Rachael, who coos in the still night air, unaware of our errand's intent and its sharp commentary on the darker perils of the heart.

Back in our carriage house, Thurston's new stereo blares. He has loud company, as well, but Thurston's own supercilious squawk rises above the din. It seems to reach toward us like a prison searchlight, combing the dark for would-be escapees. Alicia buries her head in her chest at the sound, though clearly she is far from Thurston's mind. With the help of his beer-guzzling buddies, Thurston's alcoholic bingeing has reached a new crescendo. Alcohol aside, his own arrogance renders him immune to the thought that Alicia could ever leave him. And yet, even now, under the cover of night, we are stealing her away, wresting her from his grip. For the time being she will be free from him — and, just maybe, for good . . .

The Garcias live in an Arts and Crafts–style home in poor repair. We climb the five steps to the porch, then hesitate. It is just after 9 P.M., and the house is already dark. "They always go to bed very early," she tells us. We might have phoned ahead, but they have no phone. Her father Julio is a proud, first-generation Mexican American who still speaks very little English. He works on a mostly Hispanic painting crew. Esperanza has never worked outside the home. Their close friends are other Latinos from a nearby Hispanic Catholic parish, and all have similar stories to tell. They live on the fringes of the wider culture in tightly knit communities, with little need for telephones. Alicia's parents had tried one once, but they soon discontinued the service.

For us, however, there is no turning back. This is the hour of reconciliation. The Garcias' front door is all wood. There is no doorbell, not even a "dingdong." Alicia knocks on the glass of an adjoining window, just as she and her older siblings have always done. Within moments the window curtain is pulled aside — once, then quickly again as in a gesture of disbelief. A yellow porch light switches on above our heads. Slowly, deliberately, the front door opens.

Alicia's mother is in a nightdress. She acknowledges us shyly, even forcing a smile, but then her eyes settle on her daughter. I watch them rush to Alicia's pain, caress her sense of shame. They regard her lovingly, critically — a mother's eyes. Then a change overtakes Esperanza, vivid as a sunrise. Her mother's heart opens wide, so that the part of her she had closed to her daughter is given back, and those feelings for her daughter she had dutifully suppressed, robbed her very soul of, are restored in full. Here, in our presence, mother and daughter are made whole again.

"Mamma!" Alicia sobs.

"Ah! Alicia! Alicia! Niña!" her mother answers in a voice that cracks with emotion.

Now Julio emerges from the darkness. He wears a crew neck T-shirt and work jeans. When he sees us and sees his wife and daughter wrapped in a tight embrace, he gasps, then commences with a long catechism directed at Esperanza. Soon mother, father, and daughter are caught up in a rapid-fire discourse in Spanish, all beyond our comprehension. Still, we get the gist of it. Alicia is the contrite defendant. Esperanza plays her advocate, Julio plays the devil's advocate. Each role is necessary in this drama of reconciliation. And when it is over, a sobbing daughter is back in her papa's arms. Anger and hurt have buckled under the superior weight of devotion.

Uncertain days lie ahead for this family. New boundaries

will be established, only to be continually altered. Soon, their little niña will be a mother herself. But for now, a family has rescued itself from rupture. It has disarmed the robbers of shame and disgrace with mercy and love.

From the porch steps of the Garcia home, Donna and I have been silent witnesses to this scene. Now, a teary-eyed but blissful Alicia motions us onto the porch and toward her parents, as though wishing to draw us into their intimate family circle. She offers Donna a deep embrace. Esperanza, too, remembers our presence and moves to supply us with her customary hospitality. She insists that we come in and sit with them. She offers us something to eat and drink.

"No, thank you," I reply. "It's late," I add, nodding at Rachael, now fast asleep on my shoulder.

"Ah!" she says, nodding. "Sí!"

At last, Julio himself approaches us, his own face welling up with emotion. He places his hands gently on Alicia's shoulders, nods his head, and manages an awkward grin. He doesn't speak. Shifting Rachael to my left, I extend a hand and Julio and I shake, father to father. Tonight, we have shared a rare prodigal moment. Such an experience creates a heart bond, bridging the gulfs of history, language, and life situation. Without exchanging a word, we have reached a deep understanding.

The flip side of "stealing away" is arriving home again. Alicia has made the journey, and her life will be freer for it. Now, we must make ours. With a final "adiós!" we step off the porch. The door closes, and the yellow porch light switches off.

Back at the carriage house, a party remains in full swing. The building still shakes with raucous sound. Tomorrow, we will deal with Thurston. But on this night, we will rest well.

Nothing can rob our dreams of the peaceful music of reconciliation.

PITY FOR THE PERPETRATOR

When someone steals an ox or a sheep, and
slaughters it or sells it, the thief shall pay five oxen
for an ox, and four sheep for a sheep. The thief
shall make restitution, but if unable to do so, shall
be sold for the theft. When the animal, whether an
ox or donkey or sheep, is found alive in the thief's
possession, the thief shall pay double.

— EXODUS 22:1

Thieves are not despised who steal only to satisfy
their appetite when they are hungry.

— PROVERBS 6:30

*Punishment of criminals in the ancient world was swift and
decisive. Mesopotamian law called for the death of thieves. The
custom of retributive justice took eyes, teeth, arms, or legs and
asked questions later. Vigilantism was a way of life. Penalties
appear merciless alongside our standard of presumed innocence.*

*Against this backdrop, even the law of Israel appears a
model of merciful restraint. The case in point is ink spilled in
concern for the well-being of thieves. While recompense for
thievery is costly (fivefold), when the stolen goods are recovered,
the penalty drops to a mere double indemnity. Debt slavery for
nonpayment, while harsh, is temporary; after working off a
debt, the indentured slave is released. And remarkably, if a thief
is killed in the act of discovery, the punishment for the thief's*

death depends upon the hour. If it occurs at night, in darkness, taking the life of a thief exacts no punishment. If in daylight, however, bloodguilt is incurred because the property owner should have exercised mercy. The stealing of property does not justify the robbing of life. Restitution, not retribution, is the goal. Behind the terse injunction "You shall not steal" is a principle of unrestricted scope — respect for the dignity and selfhood of every person.

The list of credit card transactions over the days of Thurston's disappearance comes in the morning mail: Best Buys, Sam Goodies, the Hyatt Regency Hotel, Escorts Unlimited, Indiana Limousine Company — a grand total of over four thousand dollars. The limo ride lasted eight hours and covered four counties. We do not know who accompanied Thurston on the jaunt, but it wasn't Alicia.

The cover letter brings us relief. Estella will not be out a dime of her own money. Liability insurance will cover the losses. The credit card company will pursue any legal options it deems viable. So far as we, the cardholders, need be concerned, the matter is settled.

But we are more than mere cardholders. Up in her bedroom, a widow still smarts from the sting of violation. Above her, an attic floor swims in a sea of broken plaster. And out back in our carriage house, a perpetrator slumbers the morning away.

It is not about the money. Yes, we are glad to learn Estella has suffered no financial loss. But Thurston has stolen something dearer. He has defrauded the name of Donna's deceased father, Charles. He has limousined through the state on the good name of a dead man. "Call me Chuck," I imagine him telling the chauffeur, the call girl, the sales clerk, as he whips out his Platinum Plus card, forges the signature, and throws the receipt in the trash.

Once, crimes of theft were intensely personal. Thieves faced their accusers. Today, in the case of fraud, at least, there is no resolution, no reconciliation. The awkwardness of face-to-face encounter is conveniently swept up into case files and paperwork.

In truth, Donna and I would prefer such an accommodation. We wish we could forget the whole thing. After all, had we not been seduced by the hope of quick, cheap dry-wall, we would not be here, preparing to go eyeball-to-eyeball with a con man. Yet there is something potentially redemptive in this nasty business of personal confrontation. We will voice our accusations, suffer his recriminations, then show him the carriage house door. Any legal action will remain in the unemotional hands of the justice system. But when we part company with Thurston, our good-byes will be spoken with no small investment of feeling — even a thief deserves that much.

At noon precisely, we knock on Thurston's door. There is a long pause. We hear creaks, moans, the flush of the toilet. Then, at last, feet clomp down the entry stairs and the door swings open. Thurston is barely awake. He stands with his legs crossed, leaning a forearm against the doorjamb, running his free hand through his tangled hair. He stinks of stale alcohol. The apartment reeks of stale smoke. "No smoking" had been one of our main stipulations, but this doesn't matter now.

Thurston squints out at us smugly. "What do you want?" he asks.

"To read you something," I answer. "This came in the mail today." I hold up the letter from the credit card people. "It's a list of things charged to Donna's father's Platinum Plus card."

Now Thurston awakens from his hungover stupor. "I told you I didn't have anything to do with that. You shouldn't accuse people when you don't know..." Thurston says more, and we listen. Once he is finished, though, Donna begins with the list: "Hyatt Regency," she reads. "Two nights... Room service... Other services..."

As she goes through the list, Thurston grows agitated. "I don't need this!" he cries.

"No, I need this!" Donna rejoins. And she keeps on. "Dinner at Hard Rock Café. A carriage ride around town..."

"I'm not listenin' to this pile a..."

"Best Buys!" Donna breaks in. "A stereo system — speakers and all — good, high-end ones. Well, my ears can sure vouch for that!" she adds.

At this, Thurston bristles. "That's it. I'm outta here," he cries.

"Yes," I agree. "It's time for you to go!"

"You're not really gonna kick me and Alicia out, are you?" he asks in his sardonic way.

"Not Alicia," Donna corrects. "Just you. Alicia's already gone, or didn't you miss her?"

"We had a fight. She'll come back."

"What makes you so sure?"

"She always does!" he says confidently. But now Thurston's guard is down, his interest roused. "Why, where is she?"

We drive it home: "You hit her! Beat her black-and-blue!"

"I was drinkin'...Hell, I don't even remember.... Where is she?"

"Where you can't hurt her."

He presses us further. "So, what, is she stayin' with you? Did she go home to 'Mama'? Nah! She wouldn't do that!...Would she?"

But we don't answer. "You have until 5:00 today to vacate," I tell him. "I don't want to call the police. Please don't force me to do that."

Thurston swears under his breath, but says no more. Donna walks away in disgust. Our conversation is finished.

Thurston falls to the floor and rests his head on his knees. "Oh, my head's poundin'!" he says.

Watching him there, wallowing in a mess of his own making, I find myself wooed by a new and unbidden emotion: pity. Thurston resembles a naughty child who turns to physical symptoms to avoid punishment. But he is not a child. He has done real damage to real human beings. He can do much more. Still, I can't help but wonder what dark secrets have brought him to this point. What of his own childhood, his family, his troubled past? Of what has he himself been irretrievably robbed? And what possible good might his future hold?

I will likely learn little of this. Neither can I keep his life from some long, precipitous fall into ruin. Ultimately, we have no power over those bent on self-destruction. But such questions as these, when we think to ask them, temper our judgments. They quell animosity and fuel mercy. We are enabled to offer back simple human dignity to those who have forfeited it. We become more human ourselves.

"Well, Thurston," I say, "Looks like you're really in pretty bad shape. So if you need 'til tomorrow to leave, that'll be okay. Tomorrow — no later! And Thurston," I manage, "I'm very sorry that things didn't work out here."

"Yeah," he says. "They never do..." And we leave it at that.

That same afternoon, Donna and I decide to contract out the attic refurbishment. We'll pay real money for real work, a fair price selected from reasonable bids. From Thurston we have learned much: avarice doesn't pay. Everything comes with a price. These are truisms that, though cast in doubt from time to time, always seem to get vindicated in the end. Add to them this truth: the real victim of theft is the thief. "It doesn't hurt money to get it that way," Steinbeck wrote, "but it hurts the person who gets it."

By 4 P.M. Thurston is gone, and we never see him again.

ROBBING REPUTATION

Who steals my purse, steals trash;
'tis something, nothing;
'Twas mine, 'tis his, and has been slave to thousands;
But he that filches from me my good name,
Robs me of that which not enriches him,
And makes me poor indeed.

— OTHELLO, 3.3.157–161

An early rabbinic interpretation of the Eighth Commandment suggests that the original meaning was "You shall not steal a person." Kidnapping, a once-lucrative enterprise and still so today in some places, was the primary prohibition. Material objects were secondary to the law's real purpose: to safeguard selfhood.

Most scholars dispute this notion, insisting that the theft of things, not people, is the focus of the command. However, the theory retains one great advantage: it ties the true value of possessions to persons and relationships. As in each of the so-called neighbor laws, it is people that ultimately matter. All else is incidental.

Out for an early evening stroll around the neighborhood, we see Julio and Esperanza, sitting on the top step of their porch stairs. Several weeks have passed since Alicia's return home. We have gotten busy in the interim, failing to check up on her progress back at home and in the family way.

We call to the couple, then make our way up their walk in the manner of old friends. But it is clear from the outset: something has come between us. The warm energy we had shared on the night of reconciliation has dissipated.

At first, we fear it concerns their daughter. "How is Alicia?" we ask.

"Good," Esperanza answers. "Working part-time. Up at the dollar store."

They don't mention the pregnancy. We want to bring it up but hesitate. Clearly, it holds a stigma, one we fear to tread on.

Neither, we guess, does this unease have anything to do with the situation at the carriage house. After Thurston's departure, we had contacted Alicia, inviting her to come and retrieve her things. She had arrived with her mother while Donna and I were cleaning up Thurston's mess. When the pair eyed the wreck and ruin there, they insisted on working with us until every last surface shined. On their departure, we had again embraced, and Esperanza's tender, kindhearted eyes had reached into my soul.

Yet just now, Esperanza can scarcely maintain eye contact. She looks down, then away. Finally, she speaks, and her strained words tell the tale. "We are so sorry about what Thurston did to you, how he took from you," she says, on the verge of tears. "We feel so badly — we feel responsible.... We feel ashamed."

Donna and I stare back incredulously. We have not mentioned the theft, even to Alicia. The matter has been long settled in our minds. How did they find out? With effort, we piece together a trail of discovery stretching from us to Thurston's friend Jim and then to Alicia. Her family has endured a long investigative interview by a detective on the credit card fraud case. This has caused them embarrassment in the extreme.

"We had no idea!" Donna assures them. "We are so very sorry!"

But it is too late. The damage is done. Julio and Esperanza have labored admirably to make a home in a foreign, sometimes inhospitable land. They have raised their children to become productive citizens of their adopted culture. They have built reputations of the highest integrity — only to have a louse like Thurston steal first their daughter's chastity, then their good name.

And yet, a mark of Cain is on *our* heads, a scarlet letter affixed to *our* chests. From now on, the very sight of us will only serve to conjure up their shame. Our friendship with the Garcias had once seemed a hopeful thing, a bridge across divides of culture and experience. Now it has been ripped away from us like an infant from its cradle.

Still I find myself wondering about the real life, beating even now inside Alicia's belly. That Alicia will choose to carry this pregnancy to term is beyond question. Just how such a child will be welcomed into the world of her parents is more difficult to predict. While Donna and I are busy grieving the seeming death of a friendship, Esperanza and Julio still face the prospect of new life to come — and a choice about how to greet it.

As Donna and I speak our awkward good-byes, I cannot help but imagine that their own saga holds a further chapter of pain. I pray it might also promise hope for redemption.

OF GRACE AND GREED

Joshua then said to the Israelites, "Draw near then
and hear the words of the Lord your God." Joshua
said, "By this you shall know that among you is the
living God who without fail will drive out from
before you the Canaanites, Hittites, Hivites,
Perizzites, Girgashites, Amorites, and Jebushites:
the ark of the covenant of the Lord of all the earth
is going to pass before you into the Jordan.

— JOSHUA 3:9–11

The Israelites stand on the east bank of the Jordan and peer over into the land of Canaan, their Promised Land. It is a country of rough terrain, of valleys punctuated by hills. Such a landscape does not lend itself to centralized governance. Hegemony is scattered among city-states across separate regions. Each of these boasts a major fortified city as well as a ring of lesser towns and villages. The peoples of these states celebrate diverse histories and customs. The Hebrews are poised to subdue them all, for Joshua holds a divine bill of sale. The land will be Israel's.

Historians ponder the nature of the Israelite conquest, asking whether it is more a rapid subjugation or a gradual occupation. Either way, a people without a land gain a land, while a people once at home become homeless.

The special means of Israel's success is provocative. The Ark of the Covenant is a gilded chest with a lid of gold. Above the lid, called the mercy seat, hovers Yahweh's divine presence. Beneath it, in the ark itself, are the tablets of the law, the Ten Commandments, written with the finger of God. "The Ark of the Covenant will pass before you," says Joshua. Whenever it leads into battle, the Israelites will conquer. Hittites and Hivites, Perizzites and Girgashites, Amorites and Jebusites will all be driven from their land.

Israel will take this land with the very words of God. Among those words is the terse command, "You shall not steal."

Our doorbell is ringing again.

I am perched on our back porch with the Saturday paper. The months have rolled by since the carriage house debacle. Fall and winter have passed, and spring flowers are in bloom.

Our attic is long since finished. Fresh paint and wall coverings hide every last trace of Thurston's great swaggering ineptness. Slowly, too, the sting of violation has released us from its grip. By contrast, we have tried our best over these months to strengthen the bonds of friendship with Alicia. Just recently she gave birth to a healthy baby boy. Late one afternoon, shortly after her arrival home from the hospital, we had appeared at her door with a baby gift, and Alicia had invited us in.

Immediately, she had begun to pump Donna with questions about the care of her baby, and Donna, a neonatal nurse practitioner, had cradled him in her arms as she answered every one. Esperanza, preparing dinner from the adjoining kitchen, had been attentive to the goings on, but she had not uttered a word. Julio, as usual, was nowhere to be seen. Their shame in our presence still seems to run deep. By this time, avoidance has taken on the character of necessity. This in part explains my shock as I spy three adult figures at the front door, one holding an infant. Before I can open the door, the doorbell sounds again, and this time our house sings out in vintage Westminster: "Mama mia!...the Garcias!"

As I open the door, Julio Garcia himself steps forward and places something in my hands: a flat rectangular object, gift wrapped in bright red tissue paper. I hesitate, then take it from him, my face betraying a great bewilderment. But immediately, Julio thrusts forward his hand and for the first time in months, we share a warm, firm handshake.

"Please come in!" I offer. I call for Donna and, waiting awkwardly for her arrival, I smile at the baby, his mother, and grandparents, all the while cradling the gift wrapped in red tissue paper as if it were a live, beating heart.

Donna arrives, Rachael toddling alongside her, and I hand over the Garcias' gift. She studies it, shakes it gently, weighs it in her hands. Then, a glimmer of recognition lights across her face. Somehow, she knows just what it is.

The baby gift, which earlier we had brought for Alicia, was a set of silver-plated picture frames, featuring the embossed shapes of balls, blocks, teddy bears, and the like. We knew she had recently purchased her first camera. Now she could display snapshots of her son with style.

The little niño's name, we have learned, is Salvador, after his great-grandfather. As is the way with names, this one speaks volumes. It tells a tale of a family's strength of character, of its determination to conquer adversity with grace. These are precious possessions that cannot be stolen. Here, they take the measure of a family's faith. Salvador, after all, means "savior."

And so my earlier concern about the child's future has been laid to rest: Salvador will be raised a Roman Catholic in the loving home of his grandparents. He will learn Spanish, eat corn flour tortillas, and sing the "Himno Nacional de México." He will belong. Now, as I watch his grandmother snatch little glances at him, I can almost hear her working it all out in her mind. Studying the lad myself, I perceive that in no way could this be an easy task for her — Salvador is the spitting image of his father, Thurston.

CAPITAL THEFT

Donna opens the gift. Taped in many places, the red tissue paper shreds and falls to the floor like confetti, adding to the celebrative meaning of the moment.

Donna holds in her arms a large picture frame made of rosewood. Etched into the frame at the top are what appear to be the spires of a church — three of them, each capped with a cross. At the bottom is a group of small human figures, positioned side by side. There are seven figures in all, the number of the Garcia family, counting Alicia's three brothers. But it is also the number of persons gathered just now in our home, the Garcias and Watkinses together. The figures are holding hands.

We smile our delight and our visitors smile back. Then

I notice on the bottom edge of the frame a label bearing the single word, Tamaulipas. The word is familiar. Indeed, I have just read it in a newspaper account covering the current national debate over the North American Free Trade Agreement, dubbed NAFTA. The Mexican state of Tamaulipas borders Texas near the city of Brownsville. This border region had figured prominently in the article.

From the Mexican side, much of the debate over NAFTA concerns the U.S.-owned manufacturing plants known as *maquiladoras,* which dot the free-trade zone along the Mexican-U.S. border. Proponents of NAFTA promise a dispersion of development away from the border, and with it a reduction in the pollution, poverty, and overpopulation long associated with these factories. They further predict a gradual increase in the standard of living across Mexico. The air will get cleaner, the water purer. Unemployment will drop dramatically.

Opponents, meanwhile, prophesy doom. Only the rich multinationals will see increased prosperity. The average Mexican will experience an accelerated race to the bottom in wages and living standards. The value of the peso will plummet. Thousands of small Mexican businesses will be forced out of operation by foreign competition. More than that, the very architecture of social democracy will be dismantled, all the way down to the revolutionary land redistribution program that will be amended to allow foreign acquisition of land for development. "Land for prosperity," some might call it. Others, I suspect, will dub it Robin Hood in reverse — Pancho Villa rolling over in his grave.

To listen to these harbingers of woe is to acknowledge the downside of laissez-faire capitalism: the necessity for winners and losers in every marketplace. While many U.S. critics identify the American worker as the likely loser in this deal, others insist the real casualties lie south of the border, already poor and destined to grow poorer.

The truth is that no one knows for sure what the final effects of NAFTA will be. But with Mexican unemployment and underemployment running as high as 60 percent, the pressure to find out is mounting. Those who already have money are convinced that there is more of it to be made. They are willing to bet the future of millions on it.

I hold ambivalent thoughts on the subject. I am a grateful American, continually relieved to be raising children here as opposed to the drought-stricken sub-Sahara or the war-torn Balkans. Yet I am sobered by the realization that my nation already consumes nearly one-third of the world's available resources. When this near-monopoly of means, power, and influence is described as "robbery," I am inclined to listen. Probably, if we were to go back far enough, we would discover that everything we have was initially acquired by force, that every possession has come to us by stealth in one way or another.

A GIFT BEYOND PRICE

The engraved picture frame from Tamaulipas, for all its charm, is not the real gift the Garcias have given us. Inside the frame is a large 6 x 10 inch photograph of a newborn child. He lies on a blanket, his deep-blue eyes staring up attentively at the camera. He looks happy, contented, the picture of peace. It is Salvador. This is the gift that has brought us such pleasure.

But Salvador's image means more. His hearty countenance brings to my mind a further theme of the NAFTA story I have been following. From *maquila* areas, including those near Brownsville, there is statistical evidence of abnormally high rates of neural tube birth defects, of babies born with small brains or no brains at all — robbed of their futures. Many believe this phenomenon is caused by unacceptably high levels of toxins in these industrialized border areas. Again, what will NAFTA bring: less contamination or more? Fewer ruined lives or an ever-greater number?

This ultimately is what all questions of greed and generosity, giving and taking boil down to: the well-being of real persons, especially the children who are, after all, tomorrow's hope.

Again, I regard Salvador, nestled tenderly in his grandmother's arms. He appears healthy, normal in every way. His future is bright, secure. Indeed, he is the future, a palpable source of a family's salvation.

Often over these last months I have wondered whether the Garcias are finally more sorry or glad that they have come here to Indiana to live. Now, it seems to me, there is little doubt of the answer. In a world greatly governed by need and greed, Julio and Esperanza have averted both. Their gamble for a better life is already vindicated in grace. We even have a photograph of it, framed and ready to hang on the wall.

The fallacy behind every act of robbery is the assumption of scarcity — the mind-set that there can never be enough stuff to go around. For us to have, we must take from others. Also false is its corollary: in order to keep, we are not free to share. Both ways, generosity loses out.

Only a faith in the plenitude of existence can teach us not to steal. Only a belief in the abundance of creation can convince us not to withhold what others need. At their most perceptive, the Hebrews interpreted the law against stealing as a call to right relationship, an invitation to mutual abundance and shared peace.

They were right. And so it remains.

You shall eat in plenty and be satisfied,
and praise the name of the Lord your God,
who has dealt wondrously with you.
And my people shall never again be put to shame.

— JOEL 2:26

9

TO TELL THE TRUTH

YOU SHALL NOT GIVE FALSE TESTIMONY
AGAINST YOUR NEIGHBOR

ON THE TRAIL OF TRUTH

The Hebrews' first concern in the wilderness is for their own well-being. Water, food, shelter, and safety lead the list. Slowly, these needs are satisfied. Israel gains a trust in manna to fall, in water to appear on the dry desert floor, and in God to deliver her from enemies (Exod. 16, 17). As Israel moves through the wilderness and into her Promised Land, life grows increasingly complex. A society blooms and, alongside it, a fresh hierarchy of needs emerges. High in the ranking is a new and exacting standard of truth: "You shall not give false testimony."

The law against perjury, like the commandments against stealing (8) and coveting (10), straddles the fence between the public and private spheres. On the one hand, the abode of lies is the privacy of the heart. Their goal is to remain hidden. Although many falsehoods eventually get exposed, others go to the grave with their perpetrators. God alone knows for sure.

Yet questions of truth and falsehood hold broad implications for public life as well. The original setting for the Ninth Commandment is the courtroom, where the stakes for truth telling are high and the penalties for crime are stiff. Hebrew law includes no fewer than thirty prohibitions that carry the penalty of death (see Exod. 21 and Lev. 20). Murder by various means, Sabbath defilement, sodomy, adultery, wizardry, blaspheming God's name, and cursing of parents by children are all capital crimes. Even with conscientious rules of corroboration (Deut. 17:6), the risks of false testimony are immense, and the consequences, fatal.

Questions of fairness, then, must be settled honorably, with veracity. If the truth about violations of the law cannot be established, then justice is thwarted and law loses its purpose. Public trust erodes; order succumbs to anarchy. In this way, truth telling emerges not as afterthought but as integral to societal good. As Israelites have learned to rely on Yahweh, so they must learn to trust one another. In the ancient world, absent of polygraphs and DNA analysis, justice demands truth: you must not give false testimony against your neighbor.

He will make your vindication shine like the light,
and the justice of your cause like the noonday.

— PSALM 37:6

It begins with an X, rendered with permanent marker on the wall of our entryway. The X, just below the light switch, is two 3-inch lines, crisscrossing near the middle of each. I notice it on a Saturday morning in mid-December, sometime between 9 and 10 o'clock. At 9:00, I had turned on the overhead light in our entryway. It is a brass chandelier with five cut-glass teardrop light shades. I installed it several years earlier as a stylish solution to inadequate sunlight and our dark Victorian decorating. Now, with the flick of the switch,

I get 300 watts of instant illumination. Any crack and crevice, any chink in old plaster, any aperture ever visited by a spider or mouse is exposed to light's blinding truth.

Each morning I flick on the light switch and square up to the hall mirror to comb my hair flat. It is a tedious exercise in hair strand placement. The slightest patch of bare scalp shines like a silver dollar in the sun. Painstakingly, I comb what hair I still have as evenly over my crown as possible before freezing it in place with a couple light bursts of hair spray. I have followed this practice for several years and may well continue it until, at last, the teeth of my comb glide silently over nothing but smooth skin. I am like a character in a melodrama who has been fatally wounded but won't die before one final soliloquy. I will go bald — but not gracefully.

My wife Donna has made my hair an object of ridicule. She suggests I cut it short, threatens to buy me baseball caps, skullcaps, and derbies. She says I'm fooling no one but myself. She has even offered to make an appointment for me with an old-fashioned barber who uses electric sheers. But I've largely ignored her. After all, she's never gone bald; she can't understand.

Given the strength of our entryway ceiling light, I could not possibly have missed the X had it been there at 9:00. Now, at half-past 10:00, the X still glistens like wet paint, as if it would smear if I touched it. The deed was done with a wide-tipped Magic Marker. Even against the plum-colored wall, the X stands out boldly. The marker was a deep shade of blue, possibly black. The two lines curve, suggesting they were made in haste.

These are my initial findings at the scene of the crime. As the domestic gumshoe on the case, I will pursue other leads. Law enforcement is not pleasant work, but a dedication to the truth is required in the just society of our household. Soon my interviews will begin. But just now, light radiates downward from our entryway ceiling without distinction, training truth equally upon an uninvited X and the crown of my fast-balding head.

NATURAL LIES

Now the serpent was more crafty than any other
wild animal the Lord God had made. He said to the
woman, "Did God say, 'You shall not eat from any
tree in the garden'?" The woman said to the serpent,
"...God said, 'You shall not eat of the fruit of the
tree that is in the middle of the garden...'" But the
serpent said to the woman, "You will not die..."

— GENESIS 3:1-3

Everything is propaganda.

— JACQUES DRIENCOURT

The natural world is brimming with deception. Flowers dress up like female insects in order to attract the male of the same insect species for pollination; spiders weave floral webs to coax other insects to their deaths; chameleons and walking sticks blend into their environment both to get a meal and to avoid becoming one. The more behavioral biologists look into such deception, the more intrinsic to nature it appears. Ironically, it was in part this widespread chicanery in nature that first revealed to Darwin the truth about natural selection and the origin of species.

Even in the biblical creation story, often deemed at odds

with evolutionary theory, the first creature we encounter, a serpent, introduces itself with a lie. "It will be okay to eat the forbidden fruit," it tells Eve. So she and Adam do. When later God seeks out the couple in the garden, they hide themselves — deception number two. By the time God gets to the bottom of it, Adam and Eve are prevaricating like there's no tomorrow. And human beings have been lying ever since.

Yet, there is something in humanity that does not like a lie. You may be an excellent liar, convincing in every way, but your own body will sell you down the river in a heartbeat. This, at least, is what the science of lie detection has long supposed. Polygraphs bank on basic physiology. When we lie, we generate an automatic electrical-hormonal response. Deep in the recesses of the brain, we betray ourselves.

The purpose of this internal lie detector is difficult to identify. Wouldn't the ability to lie with impunity be favored for selection? If this is true in the case of arachnids, then why not or humans? Maybe the enormous power of deceit in human language has simply overtaken biological evolution — the body cannot help but bristle at the wicked cunning of the mind. Or perhaps such bodily reactions are the evolutionary response to our human capacity for untruth — the soma, holding the psyche in check. Or could such responses be nothing more than the silent fingerprints of conscience, present even in the most hardened hearts? Might they simply answer to some larger moral design, to the still, small voice, to the hell within, or even to the primordial sound of God, still walking in the garden of our souls?

1, 2, 3, 4, 5, 6, 7, 8 — up the back staircase to the landing. It is a long, thirty-seven-stair trek to our attic. I am on a family fact-finding mission to my children's hideout for play, a place of lofty thinking where imaginations can run wild.

9, 10, 11, 12, 13, 14, 15, 16, 17, 18, 19, 20 — around the corner and up to the back hallway. The finished attic serves as a bedroom for my two younger daughters, but all four children consider it a place of daily escape, distant from the afflictions of life with two type-A parents. Now down the hall and left, through the laundry room, and to the base of the attic stairs.

21, 22, 23, 24, 25, 26 — I hear the animated voices of my children.

27, 28, 29 — stealth is what I need now.

30, 31, 32 — full stop. I can spy my brood from here, sitting crossed-legged on the carpet, huddled together for their game of choice: Truth or Dare.

Unable to help myself, I crouch down and listen in on a round, fascinated. Rachael, in a truth question, is just getting out of Rebecca that she thinks of a fourth-grader named Jake as her honest-to-goodness "boyfriend." I ponder just what this might mean in the fourth grade. From Rebecca's side, Jake has hardly been a well-guarded secret, but up until now no such open admission of a "relationship" has been forthcoming.

"Ooooo!" chant her siblings. "Jake and Rebecca sitting in a tree, K-I-S-S-I-N-G!" Rebecca, I can see, is blushing pleasantly, unmistakably pleased by the attention. "Puppy love!" I utter under my breath. "Harmless." This is surely the case, and yet I seem to need the confirmation of my own voice for reassurance.

I am surprised and heartened by Rebecca's own contentment with this fact on public parade. Private thoughts coaxed into the open do not always lead to smiles. Prickly truths can sting and embarrass, even deeply wound. Convenient obfuscation and courteous lies go down better. They can seem gentler, more soothing. This is part of a lie's allure.

Personally, I'd rather my children more often chose dare over truth in this game. If someone dares you to stand on your head, you might get a headache, but it'll soon go away. The revelation of an awful truth is not so easily shaken. Children's Tylenol won't kill the pain. But in this instance, truth suits my Rebecca admirably. The attention, not to mention the sheer giddiness of kiddy love, more than compensates for the sibling aggravation.

Next it is Seth's turn. He truth or dares Sarah, who also chooses truth. Now the question: "Sarah, what do you know that I'm getting for Christmas?"

From my perch on the stairs below, I let out an audible gasp. Four heads turn my way at once. I'm discovered. "Seth!" I cry up to him. "You can't ask that! That's not a fair question — Sarah, don't you dare answer it!"

"I want to, though!" she says.

"But why?"

"'Cause then he'll tell me — that's the way we're playing."

"Well, you can't play that way. And you can't ask that question, either!"

I say this, though I know better. The truth is my children can ask it and routinely do. Indeed, it has become a rarity in my home for a child's birthday to arrive without some prior knowledge of the gifts he or she will receive.

I often joke that this desire to swap secrets is a family trait on Donna's side. It is evident in her desire to give away movie plots before they resolve and punch lines of jokes before they are told. It plays out in her own irrepressible need to know ahead of time who in a fictional plot is good and who is bad, who lives and who dies, and who gets the girl or loses the boy. These obsessions are by turns endearing and maddening. Lately, they've grown as contagious in our household as the common cold.

It is equally tempting to attribute this quirk of personality to some puerile need for instant gratification, the "I want it all now" syndrome, but I have another idea. I have concluded that it answers instead to a visceral anxiety over not knowing that grows until it is too intense to stand. More than specific information on the secret contents of packages, it seeks relief from the fear of *un*knowing, the comfort of truth revealed. On one level or another, I suppose, we all crave this relief.

Rachael has been flashing me her fed-up look. "You were sitting there, spying on us?" she asks accusingly.

"Well..." I fumble, "I'm your dad! It's what dads do!"

33, 34, 35, 36, 37 — To reinforce the point, I climb to the top of the stairs, where I can tower parentally above their circle on the carpet. I also begin to scan the room for evidence, for open art boxes, uncapped markers, or any sign of dark blue ink. The tracks appear well covered. Then I have a brainstorm. "Can I play a round?" I ask them.

My children eye me suspiciously.

"Sure," Rachael agrees after an interval. "Sit down." I squeeze in between my eldest and youngest daughters.

"But it's still my turn!" Seth reminds us. Then, leaning toward me, "Dad, truth or dare?"

"Dare." I answer.

Seth hesitates. He was clearly hoping for "truth," but his recovery is quick. "Okay then, I *dare* you to tell the *truth:* Are you going bald?"

Giggling.

"Where did *that* come from?" I ask curtly. Still, I am not entirely opposed to the question, for it presumes that my baldness might indeed still be in doubt, even if only to someone under 4 feet tall.

The sensation is short-lived, drowned out by the ongoing sniggers of my eldest daughter. *"Going* bald?" she queries quietly.

"The *truth* is," I say, "that I am *balding,* little by little, just as we are all aging, day by day."

Rachael rolls her eyes. She starts, stops, then gives in: "But Dad, at this rate, you'll be dead soon!"

"Okay, my turn," I say, anxious to escape the subject. "And since I only have time for one round, I'll be democratic and ask all of you the same question at once."

"That would be cheating," Rachael says. "You can only ask a question to one person at a time."

"You're right," I say. "I'm cheating. Here goes: Rachael, Rebecca, Seth, and Sarah: Who put the pretty dark blue X down on our entryway wall?"

There is a long, almost conspiratorial silence. They eye each other but avoid my gaze. They are freezing me out, and who can blame them? I have turned their private game into a trial, their third-floor sanctuary into a court of law. I am the prosecuting attorney, judge, and jury; they are the defendants. They are playing their parts conscientiously, assuming the defiant posture of the wrongly accused.

I find myself unexpectedly moved by this display of restraint. My children do not always cover for one another. Generally, they read from the script of Adam and Eve: "He did! — She did!" Or, more often still, they adopt the passive response: "Not me!" and "Me neither!" But today they have formed a wall of solidarity. This does not make my detective work any easier, but it does elicit my grudging admiration.

At last, Rachael breaks the silence. "You forgot to say, 'truth or dare?' That's twice you've cheated. If you can't play by the rules, then you can't play."

And so the game ends.

WHODUNIT?

Having failed at an outright confession, I am forced to build a case on circumstantial evidence. Past experience points in three directions. Rebecca has a history of wall graffiti. Not long ago, all flat surfaces were at risk of becoming her next fresco. But months have elapsed since her last known rendering of noncommissioned wall art. Unless Rebecca has regressed, this is not her work.

On the other hand, art is Sarah's life obsession. She can sit for hours at a time creating elaborate drawings, paintings, and designs that she then fastens together into books. And Magic Markers are her tools of choice. Yet Sarah is a child of method, not prone to adventures off paper. I find it difficult to imagine her scrawling an X on a wall, like a cave dweller.

The best evidence points to our son. Seth had spent much of the summer and fall as an outdoor pirate, acting out elaborate scenarios around a tattered treasure map of our backyard. While crudely drawn, the map's placement of our sidewalks, trees, and gardens was surprisingly accurate. A skull and crossbones had been copied, I recall, from a Captain Crunch cereal box. Broken lines crisscrossed the map, leading always to its raison d'être: the X, marking the location of some priceless buried treasure — coins, trading cards, toys, and the like.

Often I would find the map lying around the house,

rolled up and secured with a rubber band. Each time I unfurled it, the X was in another spot. The yard itself was filled with crisscrossed sticks, corresponding to the X's most recent location on the map. Especially on lawn-mowing days, I would find the latest of these under a shrub or tree or even in the very middle of the yard above a bit of freshly turned soil. I mowed around them. Though I never unearthed Seth's treasure, secretly I reveled in its discovery, finding that it chased up to the surface some former thrill of the hunt, itself long buried.

Was it possible, now, with the onset of winter, that Seth had moved the game indoors? Might this X in our entryway be part of some elaborate marauder's ruse? The logic seems nearly irrefutable. Just why his sisters would even think to cover for him is still a mystery. But pirates and their mates are loath to divulge their secrets. No one is talking, and so I am left to puzzle.

COSTLY LIES

> Then Joshua son of Nun sent two men secretly
> from Shittim as spies, saying, "Go, view the land,
> especially Jericho." So they went, and entered the
> house of a prostitute whose name was Rahab, and
> spent the night there.
>
> — JOSHUA 2:1

Israel stands on the east bank of the Jordan River, bordering the land of Canaan. Joshua, Moses' successor, sends two spies across the stream to the city of Jericho. There they lodge in the home of a prostitute named Rahab, with whom they strike a bargain: Rahab will harbor them in secret if they will spare her family

when the Israelites take the city. It is a curious coalition. The
Israelite spies might ask, "How do we trust a harlot who would
sell her neighbors down the river?" Rahab could well wonder,
"How do I trust foreign spies?" Still, they deliver their futures
into each other's care.

Both parties keep their word. The spies escape safely back
to the Israelite encampment, and when Jericho falls, Rahab
and her family are spared (Josh. 6). The Israelites can thank
a self-serving prostitute for their passage into the land of
promise. Meanwhile, the populace of Jericho is slaughtered, an
eerie alliance of truth and falsehood having occasioned its
demise.

The modern mind bristles at such brazen destruction of life,
perpetrated in the name of God, yet it is hardly foreign to our
own experience. Contemporary examples of genocide or ethnic
cleansing betray an unremitting capacity for human cruelty.
They also point up a timeless human faculty for self-deception
— the kind required to label whole groups of people as evil and,
on that basis, to destroy them. People justify, rationalize, even
theologize on the most brutal course of action. Once truth and
God are in your camp, it is no difficult leap to cold-blooded
killing. How else can such heinous deeds be carried out with
unflinching conviction?

There are countless variations on this theme. Across time,
unsuspecting souls have been caught in its web like houseflies.
These include the falsely implicated, the unjustly accused, and
the wrongly condemned. Singled out for harm on spurious
grounds, they pay with their reputations, their livelihoods, their
very lives. In this way, falsehood itself has come to stand among
the greatest truths of history.

It is Monday evening, the last week of fall term. Donna gets off the phone with a mom whose children attend the same school as ours. She flashes me a grave look, then cocks her head toward our study, where I follow her, away from the eager eyes and ears of our brood.

"You are kidding!" are the words I had distinctly heard her exclaim on the phone. Soon I have repeated them verbatim. A middle-school English teacher has been accused of inappropriate sexual contact with an eighth-grade female student. The teacher, in his third year of instruction, is in his twenties and single. He has denied the charges but has been forced nonetheless to accept an indefinite leave of absence as an investigation ensues.

Meanwhile, the matter has quickly gone public. The story appears on the front page of the evening newspaper, including an evasive quote from the superintendent of public instruction to the effect that too little is yet known to warrant comment.

Soon, we learn that rumors of the incident have come home with Rachael as well, and quickly she has shared the middle schooler's insider perspective. "She lies, Dad!" Rachael tells me of the alleged victim. "All the time."

A friend of Rachael's, it seems, had been with the girl when she "told." It was at a Friday night slumber party where they had been playing, naturally, Truth or Dare. The subject of boys and kissing had come up, and the girls had to tell whether and with whom they had ever French kissed. The list of the girl in question had been long and had included the accused teacher. Their kiss had been long as well, she'd reported — and wet. No, there had been no other touching. Nothing but the kiss, and it had come only once, after English class when everyone else had already gone. Yes, he was a good kisser. Yes, she thought he was cute, but no, she didn't like him, because he was a teacher and he was too old.

All the girls had sworn themselves to secrecy — which had lasted until sometime between the end of the party on Saturday morning and Sunday evening, when the phones of parents had started to ring off the hook. First thing on Monday, the girl's mother and father and their attorney had arrived at the principal's office, demanding the teacher's dismissal. By noon he was already on a leave of absence. The girl's parents planned to press legal charges as well.

But a group of supportive parents was organizing to stand with the teacher and, if need be, aid in his defense. Two of them are lawyers. Donna and I do not know the girl involved and have hardly exchanged a word with the teacher. Still, I am inclined to believe my daughter. "She said other boys kissed her, too, Dad," Rachael adds. "Boys who I know would never kiss her. She makes things up. She's a liar!"

But Rachael goes further. "We like our teacher," she says. "He makes reading and writing fun! We're learning a lot about words and how to express ourselves."

If Rachael is right, and she usually is, there are words for this kind of thing, too — big, sad words: vituperative and slanderous come to mind; scurrilous and defamatory are not far behind. Donna and I decide to look into it and support the teacher if we can.

Meanwhile, a substitute instructor will fill out the remaining week of school before Christmas break, as the accused teacher sweats it out at home, cut off from students and faculty at a time normally reserved for end-of-the-year pageantry and celebration. Games like Truth or Dare can be instructive, imitating the choices of life. But sometimes, the games take on a life of their own, overtaking reality and shaping actual events for better or worse. The recent rash of reality game shows is only one current manifestation of this. As always with fantasy play, real people can get hurt. But rather than accepting this as a reasonable risk, these shows count on it. In our high speed, overprogrammed, interactive world, the line between truth and fantasy seems destined to grow increasingly blurred.

COSTLY TRUTH

> And Achan answered Joshua, "It is true. I am the
> one who sinned against the Lord God of Israel..."
> ...Then Joshua and all Israel with him took Achan
> son of Zerah, with the silver, the mantel and the
> bar of gold, with his sons and daughters, with his
> oxen, donkeys, and sheep, and his tent and all that
> he had; and they brought them up to the valley of
> Achor....And all Israel stoned him to death....
>
> — JOSHUA 7:20–25, PASSIM

Jihad is a matter of Israelite policy in the new land of Canaan. Everything, both living and nonliving, is to be dedicated to Yahweh. "Dedicated" is a religious term. Here, it is also euphemistic for words like "destroyed" and "eradicated."

But Achan, son of Zerah, would like to "dedicate" to his own use a few things from the plunder of Jericho — a robe and a little silver and gold. It is hardly stealing. Their owners are already dead. Who would miss them? And so Achan takes them, hides them, then goes about his business.

Yet as the story unfolds, Achan's deceit, his breech of commitment to total jihad, causes the formerly victorious Israelites to suffer their first defeat in battle, and "the hearts of the people melt and turn to water."

Later, after a ritual search for the culprit, Achan stands accused. "My son, give glory to the Lord God of Israel and make confession to him," Joshua adjures him. So Achan does, confessing openly all that he has taken. But purity is purity; jihad is jihad. As with the ancient victims of some dread disease, Achan and his family must be exterminated right along with the virus. Joshua and Israel stone them to oblivion. Achan's honesty as much as his falsehood has cost them their lives.

It is perhaps of some small comfort to recognize that Achan, as others in the biblical corpus, is being made into an example, that his story is an instructional case study for Israel. This presumably accounts for the tale's inclusion in the Hebrew Bible. We needn't suppose that such unmerciful punishment was commonplace. But what message is the reader to take away from this story? Is it that deceit wreaks havoc, or that honesty does you in?

Whatever the case, it's true that sometimes the price of honesty is stiff. No wonder lying remains such a popular pastime.

I call Rebecca in from the playroom where she is watching TV. In my hands I hold her last math assignment of the semester. "They're all correct," I inform her. She smiles, but looks away. I wish we could leave it there, but alas, we cannot. I have known it for some time: Rebecca and subtraction are not on speaking terms.

Indeed, they don't communicate well on paper, either, and this is the issue at hand. I have just been seated at the kitchen table, checking all her answers. I am stunned to find that they are all correct. Earlier, as I put up the outside

Christmas lights, Rebecca had been tackling the assignment from this same kitchen chair, but long before I was finished she had come out to join me. "Finished already?" I'd asked. "All done!" she'd said. And so she had helped me a while with the lights before we came in to warm up with hot chocolate.

Rebecca glances down, poker-faced, at her neat work on the math sheet. Her numbers are unusually tidy and regular. Even now I admire them. "Finally," I had thought just moments before, "she's got it down!" But then I had noticed it, sitting innocuously on the edge of the kitchen counter — the little pocket calculator we keep around for quick number crunching.

Glancing down again at the math sheet, I realized what was odd about the sums. Rebecca had not shown her work. No tens or hundreds crossed out, no ones carried over to the next column, just neat, two- and three-digit numbers below the line.

"Rebecca," I say, "did you do all this work by yourself?"

"Yes," she answers.

"You didn't *cheat?*" "Cheat" is not an apt term, I know. It fuels more anxiety than anguish, denial than contrition. The surest way to get a child who has just cheated to lie about it is to make an outright accusation of cheating. But before Rebecca can even answer, I continue: "You didn't use *this,* did you?" I say, waving the calculator under her nose.

"No!"

"You did your own work?"

"Yes!" she says defiantly.

"Then where *is* your work, Rebecca? Why didn't you *show* your work?"

Rebecca glances down at the math sheet once more. For

a moment, she seems to be preparing for her next rebuttal. Then, without warning, she bursts into tears.

The next several minutes are consumed with Rebecca's sobs, confessions, and explanations, as well as my own faltering words of comfort and mild recrimination. She used the calculator because it was there and it was easy and because subtraction "hurts my brain." I have to laugh at this, because many of us have experienced this arithmetic pain without knowing how to describe it.

I also admire most of Rebecca's innovative deceptions. Much greater than anything they conceal is what they reveal of her own inventive spirit. Deceit is an aptitude, a kind of art form unto itself, and while I don't wish to sanction it, I gladly give it its due. If my Rebecca can learn to devote half the creative energy of deception to the work of unraveling the mysteries all about us, she will make her mark.

But now what am I to do? Shall Rebecca be punished? Our rules are clear. Lying brings punishment, and she has lied, blatantly. If such rules carry weight, if they offer to her at least the comfort of a reliable, cause-effect universe, then am I not duty bound to enforce them?

And yet — though at my prodding — Rebecca has confessed. This makes a difference to me. I want her not only to tell the truth but to believe in truth telling, to trust that while deceit typically delivers harm, honesty most generally leads to good things. I wish for Rebecca always to be more afraid not to tell the truth than to tell it. And so in the end I simply hug her, then set her down for a fresh crack at subtraction — longhand!

But I put the pocket calculator in my pocket, just in case.

FAITH WITHOUT SIGHT

For now we see in a mirror, dimly,
but then we will see face-to-face.

— 1 CORINTHIANS 13:12A

It was as a young child that I first suspected the heavens themselves are fond of a good lie. Sitting on our front porch in a thunderstorm, I watched lightning flash silently across the sky. Moments later there followed the roll of thunder in the darkness. Each time it was the same: lightning with no sound, followed by thunder with no flash. I knew instinctively that this sight and sound represented the same event, yet clearly one or the other of them was lying about it. At least, I thought, they were carrying off the deception with a great measure of consistency.

My conclusions, although more intuitive than reasoned, were still disconcerting. If the heavens themselves could not be trusted, how could I have ultimate faith in anything or anyone? Further, if all such realities were divine creations as I had been taught, then how was I even to trust God?

I did not know at the time that such phenomena reveal more about human sense perception than about reality itself. Yet does this matter? Is reality truly knowable if it can be encountered only through such limited means as eyes and ears and human touch?

For all its immense gains in knowledge, modern science has only solidified this intuition into the relativity of truth and fact. The more we learn, the greater grows our reliance upon variables — location, perspective, point of view, and the like. This is so in all matters of truth. Paul the Apostle said it best: "Now we see through a mirror, dimly..." Two thousand years have passed, and the mirror remains.

I have located a map! It is the Wednesday after I first spied the X in the entryway, and we have been busy cleaning the house in preparation for holiday guests. Emptying the trash, I lay eyes on a roll of paper stuffed in the waste can. Along the roll lengthwise are printed the words "Top Secrit!"

I unroll the paper and, to my delight, discover there a map of our house. It is an impressive piece of work, laid out like a blueprint, with first and second floors. Rooms are neatly labeled. Proportions, while not exact, are reasonably accurate. The two staircases also are included. Even large pieces of furniture have been penciled into place.

But quickly my eyes are drawn to the map's most prominent features, tied to its apparent purpose. Scattered about the floor plan, small but dark and with bold letters beneath them, are four Xs. I examine the simple words beneath each X and immediately their meaning sinks in. "MOM" and "DAD," they read, and in two locations, "US." These Xs seem to mark the locations of hidden treasure. I know this without a doubt because of the telltale location of the largest X of all.

For years we have hidden Christmas presents in a blank space off the back staircase, accessed by way of a removable panel, held in place by screws. When our children are not around, I remove it and place bags with Christmas purchases inside. The blank space lies along the north side of the house. When Donna and I speak of the "North Pole," this is the spot we have in mind. On Christmas Eve, when our children lie fast asleep, we remove the gifts stashed here, wrapping some and setting up the rest on behalf of Santa. Though we have tried to be discreet, our children have long known about the secret space behind the stairway panel. As

Christmas approaches, they can be observed pausing at the staircase landing, gawking at the panel fixedly, as if through X-ray vision or telepathy they will decipher its contents.

Beneath this X on the map is the word, "US." The other "US" lies beneath a smaller X at the location of our master bedroom closet. Here we sometimes place boxes and bags before hiding them behind the stairway panel. It comes as a surprise to me that my children know of this habit as well. Not a great surprise, however.

This leaves the Xs marked "MOM" and "DAD." One of these, marked "DAD," is in the front entryway in the exact spot where Magic Marker still mars an interior wall and my own peace of mind. The other is in the corner of the back upstairs hallway, where it turns left into a laundry room.

I rush upstairs to the back hallway and there it is, just beneath a window pane, a dark X that might be easily missed against the brightness of sunlight streaming in through the window above it. But today these late morning rays do me a favor. Where they strike the floor at a soft angle is a furnace grate, and in the grate something shimmers in the light. Down on all fours, I discover there what appears to be shiny wrapping paper and a bow. A Christmas present is buried in our floor heating duct. An X on the map marks the spot.

Now it begins to become clear. These clues do not point to Seth's designs alone. The discarded map is part of an attempted cover-up. I begin to smell a blessed conspiracy — a holiday plot of concealment. I run downstairs to the entryway, where I find the story is the same: a floor duct is home to a pretty package with a tag marked, "Merry Xmas, To Dad!"

Here is a lesson for the Watkins annals of truth. Things,

even those close to home, are often not what they seem. Maybe the X was for Xmas all along.

DECEIT UNRAVELED

Woe to those who call evil good and good evil,
who put darkness for light and light for darkness,
who put bitter for sweet and sweet for bitter!

— ISAIAH 5:20

We do not talk to say something,
but to gain a certain effect.

— JOSEPH GOEBBELS

In the eighth century B.C.E., Israel is divided north and south. Isaiah prophesies in Jerusalem, seat of the southern kingdom, Judah. His message is a biting indictment of the rich who amass wealth and property at the expense of the poor. The righteousness of God will not tolerate it forever, he warns. Judah is in jeopardy.

Hand in glove with this system of dishonest gain is a corrupt legal process, the system long charged with safeguarding the well-being of common people. The very existence of prophets like Isaiah points up the failure of law to deliver justice. "Ah, you who make iniquitous decrees, who write oppressive statutes, to turn aside the needy from justice and to rob the poor of my people of their right, that widows may be your spoil, and that you may make the orphans your prey!" (Isa. 10:1–2).

Here is cruel genius: the sanctioning of harm and death dealing by the very institutions that exist to prevent them. Lying has become codified. Only a voice trumpeting from beyond the system holds any hope of shattering it. In this way, the prophets "speak truth to power" — the kind of speech that

even today can send the brave to an early grave. According to
tradition, Isaiah was executed for his fearless rhetoric. It is said
he was sawed in two.

The news comes on the Thursday evening before Christmas
break. We and several others have just arrived at the home
of two of the parents to discuss the situation of the accused
English teacher when it is announced: the eighth-grade
female student at Rachael's middle school has recanted her
story. She now claims there was never any physical contact
with the accused teacher. He just looked at her funny, she
says, looked at her long and hard, like he had wanted to kiss
her, so that she had wondered what it would be like. But
then she had left the classroom, still just imagining.

The parents have refused to drop the charges, maintaining their case of sexual harassment, but the attorneys in our
group believe it will never stand. One of them has just
spoken to the superintendent, who has stated off the record
his hope that the English teacher might be reinstated early
in the coming term. There are cheers around the room, as
well as sighs of real relief.

These may be premature. Many parents have lined up
on the other side of the issue and will not likely back away
easily. By now, after only three short days, the local media
are running nonstop coverage of the story. Our young
English teacher is fast becoming a household name. Not surprisingly, the teacher has been greatly traumatized by the
whole business. It is doubtful, some say, he will teach in this
school system again, or anywhere else.

But at least in this instance the truth will prevail. It will
take time, but his good name will be restored. Over the year

1692, the testimony of frightened children in the Salem witch trials sent twenty accused witches to their deaths. Under the Khmer Rouge, children were assigned the task of judging the loyalty of Cambodians in the killing fields, leading to the arbitrary deaths of countless innocents. Totalitarian regimes the world over thrive on perjurious testimony against adversaries who are then easily eliminated. Any time false testimony is exposed by truth's light in time to avert lasting harm, there is cause for great rejoicing.

COMBS AND BASEBALL CAPS

On the day after Christmas I am back in the attic, sitting with my children in a tight circle on the floor. Atop my uncombed crown is a new blue baseball cap. It had appeared under the Christmas tree in a brightly decorated package between 9 and 10 A.M. on Christmas Eve. I know this because the light of truth in our entryway illuminated that same shiny paper down beneath the floor grate at 9:00, as I combed my balding head, but by 10:00 the duct was empty. On Christmas morning I unwrapped it to find the cap, and I have been wearing it ever since.

The game is Truth or Dare, and it is Rachael's turn.

"Truth, dare, double dare, promise, or repeat?" she asks. The game has grown more nuanced. Its options are now five. But I am undeterred from my renewed interest in veracity:

"Double truth!" I answer.

"OK," she says, "The truth: How do you like your hat?"

"Love it!" I say. "Isn't it obvious? Now, my turn — Rachael: Truth, dare, double dare, promise, or repeat?"

"Truth," she follows suit.

"Rachael, did your mother know about the baseball cap?"

Rachael smiles, cackling after her fashion, then hesitates for effect. "She *bought* it!" Rachael says. "It was *her* idea!"

"Thought so," I say. "My sweet Delilah!"

But I don't mind. Indeed, I have already been toying with the idea of surrender, of visiting the barber with the electric sheers. Perhaps, I've been thinking, all honesty, all truth telling has its brutal side, involves by definition some degree of sacrifice and pain. Get used to it. Maybe someday soon I'll stop lying to myself about the roof over my head. But until that day, it's combs and baseball caps for me.

The X on the entryway wall will stay awhile as well. Seth has now confessed, gleefully, that it was his work all along. "You know how he goes overboard," Rachael explains. But none of this any longer matters. The X is now my X, too. It will stand as a reminder that the truth is often elusive, and the overzealous pursuit of it can put us at cross-purposes with goodness

10

A DAY AT THE MALL

YOU SHALL NOT COVET

Out of the ground the Lord God made to grow
every tree that is pleasant to the sight and good for
food, the tree of life also in the midst of the garden,
and the tree of the knowledge of good and evil.

— GENESIS 2:9

Evil and good stand thick around
In the fields of evil and sin
Where we shall lead our harvest in.

— EDWIN MUIR

A WORLD OF DESIRE

*Eden is a place not only of great bounty but of immense beauty.
God goes to pains to make its fruits "pleasant" to the eye (nehmad
in the Hebrew) as well as satisfying to the stomach. This divine
virtuosity in creation is a blessing in what might otherwise have
been a very bleak cosmos. It is often argued, in fact, that the loveliness of creation is ultimately what makes life worth living.*

God fills the world with things of beauty. And where there is

269

no beauty, there is majesty, or charm, and where neither of those, then at least interest. Human beings, meanwhile, are given the five senses to distinguish between these wonders. We know a butterfly from a bumblebee and a growl from a grunt. We can tell poison ivy from Virginia creeper by sight, poison hemlock from parsley by scent. Red bands next to yellow on a snake's skin mean the deadly poison of a coral snake, red against black rings, a harmless milk snake.

The variety is endless, far more than any one person could take in over a lifetime. No wonder that, although Adam was given the privilege of naming every living thing (Gen. 2:19, 20), the human race has been working to finish the job ever since. There is no end in sight.

To covet (hamad *in the Hebrew) is to want what is pleasant* (nehmad). *Indeed, the words,* hamad *and* nehmad *are closely related.*[1] *However, desire for what is pleasing is not itself bad; it is as natural as breathing. The world is a veritable smorgasbord of pleasantness. At issue in the Tenth Commandment is whether and how we nurture and act upon our desires. "Do not covet" means "Do not crave that which is inappropriate to one's relations with God and neighbor." Just what "inappropriate" might mean, of course, remains hidden until desires produce action: Cain commits murder after coveting Abel's blessing (Gen. 4); David commits adultery after coveting Bathsheba's beauty (2 Sam. 11); Absalom steals the hearts of the men of Israel after coveting his father David's throne (2 Sam. 15). Unchecked desire is the seedbed from which other violations of the law arise. Evil deeds plunder the world; covetousness plunders the heart.*

---

1 See J. Gerald Janzen, *Exodus* (Louisville, Ky.: Westminster John Knox Press, 1997), p. 156.

Without going out-of-doors,
one may know the whole world.

— OLD CHINESE PROVERB

It happens the very moment they cross the threshold. It is
reflexive, as involuntary as a blink at the sound of a pounding hammer. Four pairs of them pop open wide on the
prowl. They are hazel and bright blue and deep brown. They
are young and eager. They are the eyes of my own dear children, ogling about the aisles of a toy store.

It is the last Saturday of summer break, a day that
seemed to hold the very promise of heaven — mild air, a
gentle breeze, a sky of ambient blue. "Where should we go,
kids?" I had earlier asked my brood. "To the zoo, maybe, on
a long bike ride, for a romp in the woods?"

There had followed a brief silence, broken by my daughter Rachael. "The mall!" she had said. "Definitely the mall."

"Yeah!" her siblings had chimed in. "Let's go to the
mall!"

It had come out so clearly, so unequivocally, so devoid of
interpretive wiggle room.

"What do you mean, 'the mall'?" I'd asked stupidly. "We
don't want to be inside on a day like today! How about a trip
to Holiday Park, a picnic in Brown County, paddleboat
rides on the canal?"

"Mall!" Rachael had repeated. Then she had spelled it
out like a Valley Girl. "We want to *g-o* to the *m-a-l-l!*"

"Yeah!" followed the sibling chorus, "The mall!"

I'd cast one helpless glance at my wife Donna, who
had simply shrugged, saying nothing. Grim inevitability had
closed in around me. "But it's a perfect day outside!" I'd
pleaded. "One day in a hundred!"

"The weather's *always* perfect at the mall!" Rachael countered.

"Yeah, the mall! The mall!"

And so we had loaded up and headed downtown.

EYES

So, when the woman saw that the tree was good
for food and that is was a delight to the eyes, and
that the tree was to be desired to make one wise,
she took of its fruit and ate; and she also gave some
to her husband, who was with her, and he ate.
Then the eyes of both were opened,
and they knew that they were naked.

— GENESIS 3:6–7A

He takes what he covets,
and he covets what he sees.

— FROM SILENCE OF THE LAMB

The tree of knowledge sits in the very middle of the garden. It is like all the others, pleasant to look upon and good for food. But it is different as well. God has set it off-limits, has forbidden the garden guests to draw near. They shall eat of its fruit only at the forfeit of their lives. The question we have about this story is always "Why?" Why put it there in plain view, where it can haunt us and taunt us and drive us insane?

The answer has little to do with acquiring knowledge — which God presumably wouldn't begrudge us (Exod. 31:1–3; Num. 24:15, 16; and others). It has more to do with the manner in which such knowledge is gained. In the world God made, there are things we can see that we must not seize. To keep at arm's length from the tree is really to embrace our own limits, to accept the parameters proper to being human. It is also to leave some room for blessing, to believe that, with due patience, goodness will come as a grace, without grasping.

Meanwhile, there sits the tree. Adam and Eve cannot take their eyes off it. Indeed, coveting is all about eyes. Long before the fruit touches Adam's and Eve's lips, they have already devoured it visually. This in turn has stimulated the back of the brain, which has signaled the heart to race with longing. Desire soon runs through every blood vessel to every corpuscle in every far-flung recess of their beings. Adam and Eve have not yet eaten, but already the fruit has swallowed them whole — all because of a pair of staring eyes. This is how coveting works.

It is a cruel affair, and we all know it. For the tree lives in the middle of our lives as well, and we have tasted its fruit many times. In this way, at least, we are all the offspring of Adam and Eve.

The Circle Center Mall is an ingeniously designed complex of new construction and renovation, knit together into two city blocks of seamless shopping and fine dining. The mall boasts several renowned hub stores and level after level of specialty shops. These are accessed via escalators that traverse its cavernous corridors, rising past glistening fountains, fluted columns, and marble floors. Video screens sit atop pillars like street lamps to light the way. These dance with explicit images of pop culture to fire the heart. Banners twirl in the perfumed air announcing the advent of happiness, excitement, love — all that we crave: "The Diamond That

Will Capture Her Heart," "A Scent to Enslave the One You Love," "The Bra That Will Never Let You Down"...

Each visit here, I am coaxed into the grandeur of it all. This is no mere shopping experience; it is religious ritual, this grand edifice of marble and metal less a mall than a temple devoted to the god and goddess of gratification. The entrance to every shop is like the access to a holy shrine, where alms may be left in exchange for a token of blessing or two.

My children hurry us past the jewelry and body-and-bath shops and the store of unmentionables with the poster of the bra that does not let you down. There is so little to the bra that I slow up to consider whether this might be false advertising, but Donna grabs me firmly by the arm and ushers me along. We pause at the convenient and irresistible pretzel shop and order six for lunch, then move on to an ice cream and yogurt emporium and buy four smoothies to wash them down, and finally visit an espresso bar, where Donna and I treat ourselves to lattes, "grande." Then, it's on past the kitchen store and a serious collectors' emporium and up to the third mezzanine, where a 20-foot teddy bear stands sentry at our destination.

The toy store is world famous. As if to underscore the point, flags from many countries are displayed, strung like clothes on a clothesline above the entrance. By motorized conveyance, the flags revolve around a stationary store logo. We are at the very center of the toy universe.

Just inside, one encounters an enormous artificial tree with a humanlike face. As shoppers approach, its big eyes blink and a toy store anthem sounds from within its trunk, drawing children like the Pied Piper. The tree also talks. Its lips move, telling a tale of the wonders that await children down every aisle. Everything is mentioned but the price. It is not the first tree, I am thinking, to speak with forked tongue.

Of course our children, as Adam and Eve before them, are hardly innocent victims in this charade. They possess their own calculating reasons for having chosen the mall over a stroll in the park. Donna and I, too, bear responsibility. We have fallen into the dubious end-of-summer habit of purchasing each child a back-to-school gift. Originally these were to be practical, school-related items — a new book bag, an electronic calculator, an art set with carrying case. But we were increasingly lobbied to widen the options: a Sony Walkman for the school bus, a Barbie "back-to-school" doll, a hand-held, three-in-one telescope, microscope, flashlight. Soon the scholastic intent had lost out entirely, but the tradition survived, shepherded along by underage audacity.

In truth, Donna and I live in a state of love-hate with the habit. We enjoy being generous to our children beyond the obligatory birthday and Christmas routines. And yet it seems that our children, like others in their generation, deem such generosity more an entitlement than a privilege. What are such practices more likely to engender — spirits of gratitude or patterns of acquisitiveness? What is the final legacy of Eden? we might as well ask — gratitude or greed?

> You shall not covet . . . anything that belongs
> to your neighbor.
>
> — EXODUS 20:17

Just now, the son of Adam — my son, Seth, that is — appears to be zeroing in on his heart's desire. As I look on, he sizes up the chief contenders for the honor: the Dynotronic Tyrannosaur; Tekno the Robotic Puppy, who sings, dances, and does card tricks, all with "real-time emotions and moods"; and the GI Joe Friendship VII Capsule, of Project Mercury fame, which must have fallen back to earth with a thud because it is on clearance. In the world-famous toy store, these are moderately priced items. I am thankful Seth has missed the motorized Ferrari on the top back shelf. But even such toys as these are too upmarket for me. Indeed, nothing he has touched yet except the Friendship VII will ever leave the store under his arms. He should know how this works by now, but desire courts its own logic.

For this reason, among others, I would have preferred to take my children to an old shopping mall on the city's east side. Long in decline, it lost its hubs of Sears and JC Penney years before and is now home to factory liquidation outlets and low-end merchandising stores. Its very existence hangs by a thread, which makes it everything a mall was never meant to be: lonely, peaceful, almost holy. If you stand with your eyes closed in its single long corridor, you can nearly imagine yourself in the nave of a great cathedral, where the slightest sound reverberates around you as from the world beyond. Senior citizens come to this mall to walk because there is never any foot traffic to contend with. I'm not yet a senior, but this is my kind of mall.

The old eastside mall has one run-down toy store, a Mecca for bargain hunters. The selection is quite limited, and the merchandise rather shoddy. Few of the trendy toys are stocked. Customers find no high-tech pets or collectors' Barbies in glass display cases, and they are greeted by no flags of the world or talking trees. Virtually none of the merchandise at this toy store would make the cut at the world-famous toy store. But if you are fortunate enough to find what you seek, the price is guaranteed to fall within your budget. Today, though, we are at the downtown mall, where such mundane matters as price tend to vanish in all the razzle-dazzle.

Now Seth has located the source of his craving. The Commandobot is the ultimate remote fighting machine. It launches up to ten weapons, is fully ambulatory, and obeys commands from a distance of seventy-five feet. The key word is "obeys." The Commandobot is every boy's dream: someone other than the family dog who will lick his boots and never talk back. It lists for $158 and to Seth is worth every penny.

He has already begun to frame his ill-fated rationale for our purchase of this weapons-cache-on-wheels. He spins it as a prudent investment. With its purchase, he will never again be any trouble for us at all; he will always make his bed; he will give up his allowance for a year.

"One year?" I think. "At a dollar a week it would take him at least three to pay this off!" And long before then, the Commandobot will be buried deep in the city landfill. I know — I was there once with a toy of my own, a remote-controlled auto racer. As a lesson in personal finance, my parents agreed to float me an interest-free loan for it against my 25¢ weekly allowance. Other than our home, it is the only thing I have ever bought on time. At $12.99 plus tax, it took a solid year to pay my parents back — no bubble gum or baseball cards for twelve months of my childhood. The racer itself had broken for good after only four.

But Seth's last offer is his most creative: if we buy the Commandobot, a wealthy schoolmate of his will no longer be bored when he comes to our house to play. He can bring *his* Commandobot so they will each have one, "'cause Kyle's even a worse sharer than *I* am!" Seth adds reflectively.

It's all true. In fact, it was through Kyle-who-has-everything that Seth first encountered the Commandobot. Donna and I have only ourselves to blame. As parents, we knew the risks of allowing our children to play with kids from "the other side of the tracks" — kids with stock/mutual fund portfolios, cell phones, and the model Ferrari that sits on the top back shelf of the world-famous toy store. But things have already gone too far. Seth has seen the fruit, and now he longs to taste it.

It is more than the money. I fear my children may be tempted to feel disgrace over what they do not have — to be ashamed. Shame was once thought the proper emotional response for possessing too much of something — hoarding the best toys or hogging all the cookies in the cookie jar. These days, shame is increasingly associated with the experience of having less of what others tell us to value. When pangs of conscience come to be reserved for what we lack that others have, rather than what we have that others lack, then we have lost touch with the real and dire needs of the world.

None of us is immune to this tendency of our time. We are bombarded with images of the rich and famous, of the overprivileged few, and this has a corrosive effect on our hearts. We are so titillated by the desire to share their rare good fortune, or at least to live it vicariously, that we lose the capacity for empathy. This squabbling of the haves over the earth's spoils is salt poured in the gaping wound of the true have-nots.

Once or twice I have resorted to shaming my children back from the brink of envy by contrasting their life situation with that of the child we are sponsoring through an international development fund. Irma is from a large family living in a single-room dwelling in the Mexican state of Puebla. Subsistence farmers, they earn approximately $1,375 annually. Even Irma is well off, however, by the standards of many of the world's poor. Drought, pestilence, natural disaster, and civil unrest make life for much of the world's population a daily struggle, if not a perpetual misery. I remind my children of this from time to time when they complain about eating green vegetables, but they cannot really understand it. I can scarcely understand it myself. Our stomachs are always full; the bloated salaries of athletes, pop stars, and CEOs are a source of constant consternation; the downtown mall looms near. There is little attention left for the plight of poor souls we will never meet.

Besides, such abstract comparisons rarely work. Covetousness is conquered not through guilt but through gratitude, less out of compunction than compassion. Although Jesus railed against the predators of society's most vulnerable, it is his parables of the Prodigal Son and Good Samaritan that have been the moral compass of Christian history. By experiencing life as trustworthy and good, children learn generosity. There is no substitute for the human encounter with grace.

But now I must bring my son back to reality: he cannot have the Commandobot. I march him back to the GI Joe Friendship VII Capsule. It is one of the only GI Joe toys on the market to meet Donna's criterion for allowable combat dolls: "No guns!" "Little wonder it's on clearance," I think.

But aloud I remind Seth that briefly, before seeing the Commandobot, he had looked upon it favorably. I could go on, of course, could confess that the Commandobot costs more than we can afford, could suggest that it will too easily break, could propose that Kyle-who-has-everything has probably grown bored with it by now anyway. But Seth would accept none of this. Instead, I make it plain. "You can have the Friendship VII. You cannot have the Commandobot. It's the Friendship VII, or nothing at all!"

Seth is a smart if stubborn child. He selects a Friendship VII from the clearance stack. So sizable is the box, it is all he can do just to carry it. "At least it's *big*," I hear him thinking.

LANDFILL OF THE SOUL

> Once when Jacob was cooking a stew, Esau came in from the field.... Esau said to Jacob, "Let me eat some of that red stuff, for I am famished!"...Jacob said, "First sell me your birthright." Esau said, "I am about to die; of what use is a birthright to me?" ...So he...sold his birthright to Jacob.
>
> — GENESIS 25:29–33

> I got plenty o' nothin', and nothin's plenty for me.
>
> — FROM PORGY AND BESS

Not far away, Rebecca's appetite has been more easily satisfied. Appetite is the right word. She has a natural craving for sugar and spice. Our children's culinary cravings cover the spectrum, but Rebecca possesses the broadest palate by far. She even enjoys sautéed mushrooms, and asparagus with cheese. Just now she is flirting with a popular item, stacked in quantity at the juncture of two aisles: a cotton candy machine.

With her accustomed audacity, Rebecca is describing it as a back-to-school item. She has picked up somewhere that sugar is instant brain power. Cotton candy will help her think. This is true, of course — the same way my morning coffee is liquid IQ.

"But what does this have to do with school?" I ask.

"Breakfast," she says.

This is vintage Rebecca. More than even sugar, our middle child craves to know she is special. She longs to stand out. Nothing feeds the need like food does. While her siblings chomp on Cheerios or Cream of Wheat, Rebecca will be cotton candy queen at the Indiana State Fair. "You can make it in pink, blue, and green," she educates me.

"All right," I tell her. "An *after*-school snack, just for now and then."

"I love you, Dad," she says. She is beaming.

This is the way I most like our Rebecca, her face scribed in exuberance. Of course, those same muscles can easily flex the other way, and often do. Rebecca feels nothing casually. Rapture, distress, and everything in between come to her with rare intensity.

All of our children have highly individual styles of complaint. Seth's is a transparent whine, performed in pathetic rhythm like the whistle of the Little Engine That Couldn't. Sarah makes a faint whimper, punctuated by the ping of her pouting lower lip. Rachael, my eldest, rarely dissolves into tears at all. Instead, she quietly retires to her room and journalizes. In a flurry of ink, the offending party is tried, convicted, then mercifully pardoned. When Rachael again emerges, she is back to her cheery self.

But no one weeps like my Rebecca. Hers is a lament of existential gravity, echoing from the deepest recesses of her soul. When Rebecca weeps, the world must weep along with her. She is either the best actress on planet Earth or the epitome of pitiable youth.

Only days before, I recall, her pathetic side had been on vivid display. The circumstances were undeniably tragic: Rebecca had mistakenly traded away her Barbie travel trailer to Rachael in exchange for a milk crate. When she told me, I could barely absorb the truth. The previous Christmas, Santa had flown his sleigh a good five thousand miles to hand deliver the travel trailer to our fireplace hearth, just beneath Rebecca's stocking. It became a treasured possession. But then Rachael converted a simple milk crate into an elaborate Barbie house. She had lined its outer walls with strips of fabric to simulate wallpaper and had divided the inside into separate rooms. These she had furnished with her own Barbie accessories. It was all quite ingenious and, more to the point, new and exciting. Novelty is always the draw — that, and clever packaging. Like the cheapest toy money can buy dressed up in a fancy package, the crate took Rebecca in completely.

Rebecca traded her Barbie travel trailer for the alluring milk crate. But once Rachael emptied it of all its charming Barbie paraphernalia, which was not part of the deal — its table and chairs, armoire, shoe rack, entertainment center, tea set, chest of drawers, and vanity — regret and remorse had paid Rebecca a visit. In no time she was pleading with her sister to cancel the trade. "You always do that!" Rachael had told her. "But this time, you can't have it."

Into Rachael's room had come the travel trailer, where she stored it high on a closet shelf. Several times a day Rebecca had sneaked into her sister's room to glimpse it there, appearing so sad and neglected. The more she spied it, the greater grew Rebecca's desire to reclaim it. Unable to resist, she began to renew her pleas to Rachael to reconsider, cranking up the pathos, weakening her opponent bit by bit.

Rachael is as hard-nosed as eleven-year-olds come. But because when our Rebecca weeps, the world weeps along, not even Rachael could hold out forever. She had dumped the trailer unceremoniously in Rebecca's lap and stormed away, firing off some choice invective as she went. "You are not even my sister!" had been the last of it, and this had lodged like an assassin's bullet.

Soon afterward I had heard the sob, the wail I could pick out of a crowd of mourners. Rebecca was descending the back staircase, one pain-racked tread at a time. As she turned the corner at the landing, I beheld her wretched, blotchy-eyed countenance. It was the unmistakable look of one who has regained a travel trailer but lost a sister.

"Was it a good trade?" I had asked.

Rebecca had to think. "No," she had said at last. "I want my sister back!"

Here was a great truth about desire. There is nothing we covet more than that which we have lost, whether travel trailers or sisters. Yet *what* to desire is equally as urgent a judgment as *how* or *why*. We can desire things or we can desire people, dead stuff or living souls.

"Where's Rachael now?" I had asked.

"In her room," Rebecca answered, "with the door shut."

She was no doubt journalizing her sister into purgatory.

I had eyed my daughter with equal shares of worry and whimsy. Rebecca's tribulations were not life threatening. Still, there was much I might have said to her — about cultivating love and trust, and the way to a person's heart, and grading the value of things. But I cut to the chase instead.

"Give it back. Write your sister a note and tell her you're sorry and leave it with the trailer by her door."

Rebecca's eyes had welled up once more with tears that washed down her puffy cheeks. "No, Daddy!" she had whined. But then she had done it anyway.

That had been only days before. Now, in the toy store,

her face is bright and fair. She has spun sugar on her mind. For what, down the road, will she trade away her cotton candy maker? A stick of gum, maybe? A Snickers bar? Like Esau's birthright, will it ultimately matter? Cotton candy vanishes anyway, the very moment you touch it to your tongue. Here lies the final irony of covetousness: all possessions are ephemeral.

But from deep within Rebecca, something is rising of lasting consequence. Rebecca is sprouting seeds of self-love — a love that will diminish her need for proof that she is special, for she will know her own worth. Her self-love will allow her to stop striving to shore up her sense of significance, for her significance will be as settled as the sweetness of sugar. Then she will put away her covetousness. She will smile, and the whole world will smile along.

Rachael gave the trailer back to Rebecca. She ripped a blank page from her journal and wrote, "Thanks, Rebecca, but you can have it back. I guess I'm outgrowing Barbies anyway." The "thanks" meant more to Rebecca than the "you can have it back." A sister's love is more precious than travel trailers.

MOURNING IN AMERICA

My son better is to die than to be poor;
for now Money is the world's god.

— HENRY PEACHAM

I pay MasterCard with Visa.

— CAR BUMPER STICKER

America is awash in consumer household debt — $6.5 trillion nationally in the year 2000. Meanwhile, the national savings rate has dropped to a historic low, from 13.6 percent in the 1940s to near zero in the 1990s.

Many factors fuel these trends. Some point a finger at 1970s inflation, to a basic shift in the consumer logic in the face of steadily rising prices.[2] Once inflation became a fact of life, it no longer made "cents" to save and pay cash for a new car or an automatic dishwasher. By the time you had earned enough, the argument goes, the purchase price would have increased right out of your range. "Buy now!" became the new mantra, installment debt, the symbol of progress. Ben Franklin's admonition, "A penny saved is a penny earned," joined the junk heap of history along with the layaway plan. After that, it took only a dash of deregulation and a touch of high-tech innovation to birth the brave new world of revolving credit. Suddenly it was possible to have your heart's desire, however large or small, years before you had to pay for it — if indeed you ever paid for it at all. In the blink of an eye, the entire Puritan ethos of thrift and savings came to an ignominious end. But society was too enamored with the new possibilities of purchasing power to notice.

This great "democratization of credit" promised more prosperous living for everyone. The young could join the ranks of the middle class before ever graduating from college. The newly unemployed could maintain accustomed levels of consumption right through an economic downturn. Even the poor could live rich by leveraging an endless future. While appearing foolhardy on its face, in the popular imagination such a view seemed justified. It was, as one of our presidents eloquently put it, "morning in America."

---

2 Robert D. Manning makes a strong case for this view in his book *Credit Card Nation: The Consequences of America's Addiction to Credit.* (New York: Basic Books, 2000).

Naturally, it could not last. The democratization of credit has been exposed as a myth. While the convenience of credit comes free for those who can pay off credit card debt in full each month, for the poor it can be astronomically expensive. Interest rates on credit debt run as high as 34 percent. The financially desperate scrape the bottom of the financial barrel, which is identified with payday loan companies, check-cashing offices, and pawnshops. In these settings, credit charges annualize to many times the initial value of a loan. Meanwhile, the personal bankruptcy rate has grown in recent years to the highest in history, even though unemployment dropped over the same period to historic lows. Morning has turned to "mourning" for millions of Americans.

Worst of all, perhaps, is the coming-of-age of a generation for whom revolving credit is the sole model of financial conduct and the temptations of predatory lending are a fact of life. Such expectations only fuel our already strong inclinations to covet, to desire to have and have now, heedless of the consequences.

There is something to be said, of course, for faith in a bright economic future. Even as I write, the U.S. economy has slid into recession and, reluctantly, consumer confidence along with it. The highly touted "irrational exuberance" of the 1990s was the last hope for a sluggish economy. As a few have known all along, emotional optimism is the real engine of long-term prosperity. But emotions are volatile. If euphoria can sail a ship, fear can sink it. The real test of optimism is what happens when the lake dries up.

The Bible reminds us that, by faith, Abraham defied the odds against survival in the land of Canaan. Moses and the Israelites practiced that same faith in the desert, as did the judges, prophets, and the occasional king in the land of promise. The question today is, Faith in what?

Abraham's faith lay not in the promise of short-term advantage, or narrow escape, or miraculous deliverance, or economic ease. His was faith in God's reliable and reassuring presence. Abraham trusted God's love. All else is ephemeral.

Our trip to the mall is half over. Two children have their minds made up. Rachael and Sarah, however, have so far failed to settle on anything. For Rachael, the problem is puberty. With its onset, she has begun to straddle the disparate worlds of childhood and adulthood. One moment, her thoughts are with her grown-up future, with college and career and romance. The next, her desires revert to former things, to dolls and pretend play and fits of sophomoric giggling. She is riding a hormonal roller coaster.

Today she is all teenager, and the toy store is bland and boring. One item only has captured her attention — a password journal. It is voice activated and programmable to open only to the command of her voice. "Keep your secrets safe!" the box urges, because after all, "Girl Tech knows girls!"

"It even has a built-in night-light!" Rachael explains.

"Great!" we say, but Rachael is uncertain. She puts it back, choosing to hold out for something more.

Sarah is a curiosity. Unlike her twin brother, Sarah has simple, straightforward tastes. She alone among our children finds the world-famous toy store overwhelming. "She'd do much better at the run-down mall," I tell Donna. "Fewer choices!" Sarah looks tired to me, so I scoop her up into my arms as I queue up to pay, Seth and Rebecca beside me, bearing their boxes.

"What would happen to cotton candy in outer space?" Rebecca asks, shifting her eyes from Seth's Friendship VII to her cotton candy maker.

"I don't know," I answer, but there is ample time to contemplate such a thing. Three or four customers are ahead of us. At the world-famous toy store there is always a line. At the run-down mall there is never a wait.

At last we arrive at the counter and present our merchandise. "Credit or debit?" asks the clerk, not even looking up. I have yet to even open my wallet. I would probably have reached for plastic anyway, just as the clerk has anticipated, but somehow her assumption to that effect has rubbed me the wrong way.

"Neither," I announce brashly. "Cash." I crack my billfold and peer inside. At once the previous hour at the mall flashes through my mind: the hot sourdough pretzels, the smoothies for the kids, the lattes for Donna and me. These indulgences have caught me up short. Cash seems increasingly insufficient for even the simplest of shopping ventures.

"Make that debit," I tell the clerk, hoping to hide my chagrin. She swipes the card, but it doesn't read. She tries again, then a third time. I look on as she runs it through the grid quickly, then slowly, from the right side, then the left. She hems and haws, then prepares to punch the numbers manually, but they are so faint she can hardly make them out.

"Would you happen to have another card?" she asks, almost politely.

"Sorry, I don't," I reply. "Only the debit."

She studies me as if I just fell from the sky in the Friendship VII. A woman behind me shakes her head fretfully. I feel myself begin to slink down, to assume the humiliated posture of a shopping pariah, a pimple on the face of mercantile etiquette, fit only for some shabby liquidation sale.

Just then Donna comes to the rescue, pulling out her debit card, which reads on the first try. "Sale approved." I breathe a sigh of relief. But the sting of embarrassment lingers. As we leave the store, I can sense every eye watching me in cold judgment.

Now the answer to Rebecca's question comes to me: in outer space, cotton candy would freeze in a millisecond, then vaporize into nothingness — a lot like credit in a Chapter 7 personal bankruptcy.

SEDUCTION

If you've got it, flaunt it, girl!

— APPAREL ADVERTISEMENT

We exit the world-famous toy store and maneuver through the mall. Rachael again is leading the way, back past the serious collectors' emporium, snaring customers with displays of the Cinderella Suite of Dreams and the official vinyl portrait doll of Rose, heroine of *Titanic* fame. My children know to envy here with one eye closed because such extravagances are not of our world.

Next, we reach a trendy girls' apparel store, which draws Rachael like a magnet. She stops in front of a large sale poster. At the center of the giant picture is a perfect belly with the button showing, and a good deal below it, too. It is an advertisement for hip huggers and belly shirts.

"There it is!" Donna smirks. "What every little teenage girl in the place was wearing." The place was the coliseum, and the event was a concert by a trendy all-male pop group. They had been in town for one night only. That evening had been passing peacefully when, at 8:30, a friend of Rachael's called from outside the coliseum with two extra tickets. "Sorry," I had told her. "Rachael won't be able to make it."

Among all her school friends, Rachael alone, it seemed, had never attended a pop music concert. This was as I wished it. She was too young and unsuspecting to smell a hoax, and what passed for a musical event was, in my view, little more than vulgar entertainment, a two-hour infomercial for overpriced CDs and pop group paraphernalia. I had already told her as much in different words, just as my father had told me back when vinyl was still the thing. "When you're older, you're free to do as you please — with your own money," I had said, echoing her grandpa almost verbatim.

On this occasion, though, the tickets were free. All that was left to stand on was naked principle. I was prepared to hang up the phone when Donna, who had been listening, shined a light into my darkened understanding: "If you don't let her go she'll resent you for it, and she'll just crave it all the more."

I knew this argument — the forbidden fruit scenario: Eve in the garden, staring at the tree, was unable to resist. But if my Rachael really saw, really tasted, wouldn't she desire all the more? How could I be certain?

In parenting, there are no certainties. But Rachael's resentment appeared all but inevitable. I could see her already, holed up with her journal, writing me out of her confidence for good. In the end, I agreed with Donna that we should let Rachael attend the concert, with her mother as chaperone.

Naturally, Rachael got swept off her feet by the great to-do of it all. She arrived home in a trance. "It was so amazing!" she had said. But Donna had a different take on it. "Twenty-thousand girls screaming in unison, "Take me!" — every one with her belly showing. High-wire acts, high jinks, and grown men strutting the stage like peacocks." Just to hear about it was enough to make the musician in me cringe.

Back at the mall, we all stare at the apparel shop poster. "Kawabunga!" hoots Seth.

"Jean envy," the caption reads. I know a double entendre when I see one. All bellies are not created equal; beautiful bellies are in the "genes." And yet at this brief fashion moment, all girls are led to believe that the secret to a beautiful belly lies not in the genes but in the jeans — specifically, hip huggers or hot pants worn with belly shirts. The sultans of vogue have ruled. All underage bellies shall be exposed — fat, skinny, and in between. Rachael's belly is the in-between kind. She is due for a growth spurt. Still, she eyes her mother hopefully, a sale table just inches from her grasp.

"Don't even think about it," Donna says.

"All items 40 percent off!" declares the sale sign. "If you've got it, flaunt it, girl!"

"Got what?" I wonder, "the money or the belly?"

"Kawabunga!"

DESIRING GOD

As the deer longs for flowing streams,
so my soul longs for you, O God.
My soul thirsts for God, for the living God
When shall I come and behold the face of God?

— PSALM 42:1-2

With the Tenth Commandment's prohibition of coveting, the commands come full circle. They have progressed from God to neighbor and back again. As murder, stealing, and adultery each originate with the impulse to covet, so coveting itself arises from desire turned askance from God.

Yet, as the Psalmist understood, thirst for God is more than a craving; like physical thirst, it is a requirement for life. To deny it is to shrivel. But to turn in faith to God means to live without fear in the presence of people, things, and earthly desire. It is to know, as the deer does, the source of living water. In the wilderness, the child Israel named that source Yahweh, and she followed it, though falteringly, into adulthood.

We, meanwhile, continue to clutch at meaning and fulfillment in a close-fisted, cynical culture. Into this predicament is made an astonishing claim, old as Israel and older: however far afield we wander, God is there to greet us and fill our deepest longing. More than we desire God, God desires us. Yahweh's steadfast love, ground of the universe, refuses to abandon us, but prods us gently, relentlessly, back to itself.

We arrive at the mall's premier CD and video mart. I want nothing more than to see Rachael pass right on by, but it would be easier for her to do back flips down the escalator. Somehow, she and I have both known all along that this journey through the mall would land her here, still shy a purchase and short on time.

In the store window are several large posters of a teenage boy with bleach-blond hair and a baby face. He is kid brother to a member of one of the pop bands Rachael and her friends have been fawning over, and his solo debut album has just been released to new heights of promotional hype. Overnight he has gone from an average Joey to a pop superstar, even though he plays no instrument and by some accounts can just barely sing. Copies of his CD line the racks at the store's entrance, leaving the impression that this might be the sole item for sale here.

A special store display with a dedicated CD player and headphones entices listeners to sample the CD right on the spot. *"Now, now, now, now, now, now!"* reads the sign above it — six wavy "nows," grinning out at us like the jagged teeth of a jack-o'-lantern. A long line of listeners waits beneath it, anxious to be swallowed in sound. I feel a sudden urge to grab a CD of a Mahler symphony, go to the back of the line and, when it's my turn, listen to all four movements from beneath the sign, while the line stretches all the way out to the parking lot. But I scowl quietly instead, as the current victim gyrates to the beat like a puppet on a string.

Rachael has been watching me. She picks up a copy of the CD, plastered with the face of the pubescent teen who wouldn't recognize a treble clef if it bit him in his boxer shorts. She gapes at his image, her eyes wide with longing, waiting for me to cringe. It is a short wait.

"Dad," she says, "are you . . . *jealous?*"

"What?" I ask, taken aback.

Rachael grins. "You are, aren't you?"

"Stop it!" I tell her. But her words are like a mirror into which I am constrained to peer: me, jealous of a thirteen-year-old poster child for pop culture, a pawn in a sophisticated corporate chess game, the unwitting bedfellow of an incestuous industry on perpetual prowl for the next big score?

Of course I'm jealous! We are all jealous of the success of those we regard as undeserving. It is human nature. Yet I also feel ashamed. I'd like to think I am above such things, a mere advocate of quality and depth and the notion that success and recognition follow from excellence and hard work. But the truth is that I am not sure. Perhaps I am standing on firm principle. Or maybe it's a case of covetousness, pure and simple. Either way, the outcome is the same: music of and for the unschooled masses, and the questioning few shall be put to shame.

"Well," Rachael says, "Can I *have* it?"

I knew this was coming. "No!" I say sharply, but only to myself. Something holds me back from utterance. I want to raise children who are not only discerning but also tolerant. How will I manage this if I am not so myself? How can I be their trustworthy arbiter of truth if my own desires are narrowly fixed on self-centered aims? How will they find God, if their desires become framed as mere choices between gods?

The real choice is between one of two covets, hers or mine, or neither. In the end, it is no choice at all. There will be other opportunities to influence a daughter's judgment.

"You can have the CD, Rachael," I force it out, "if you want it." Rachael stares at me in surprise. She had no more expected me to give in on this than for her brother Seth to be schlepping around the mall his very own Commandobot. But already she is keeping her own counsel, which is the only choice I've left her. Rachael must make her own determinations about such matters — delineating needs versus wants, distinguishing between sources of pleasure, weighing desires, cultivating tastes. She alone can determine the relative worth of things. These will involve decisions, big and small, rare and routine, mutually exclusive and compatible. Together, they will forge a pattern of conduct, Rachael's moral habit of being. In this way, she'll leave her mark on the world for better or worse. I'm putting my money on better.

Rachael turns the CD over in her hand once, twice more, and finally puts it back on the rack. "No, I guess not," she says. As usual, my eldest daughter delivers the last surprise.

In the end, Rachael marches us back to the world-famous toy store, back to an electronic password journal with voice-activated access and built-in night-light. Knowing Rachael, she'll hole up in her room the moment we get home and journal for better than an hour. She'll put to paper every detail of our end-of-summer sojourn at the downtown mall. She'll record what happened here, then interpret what it means. I can't help but wonder if, perchance, she'll include some favorable word about a dad who stood with his daughter at a small crossroads and let her choose the path for herself.

AFTERTHOUGHT

You made us for yourself, and our hearts find no
peace until they rest in you.

—— AUGUSTINE

Now only Sarah has yet to chose a back-to-school prize. She is so aloof and self-possessed at times that it would be easy to leave her out of today's exercises entirely. But now she has yanked on her mother's arm with her free hand, while the other clasps a shiny plastic box, soon revealed to be the case of a videocassette. Its title: *The Book of Pooh*.

Donna responds to the tug, staring down into her daughter's confident smile while Sarah holds up the box for her mother's perusal. But Donna barely notices it, so taken is she with this specter of alluring innocence. The real tug here is on the heartstrings. Not a word is exchanged. None is required.

We arrive once again at the counter of the world-famous toy store. Donna's purse is open as the clerk scans the password journal and then picks up the Pooh video. Now her face assumes another frown.

"This is not from our store," she says.

We look it over, then turn to Sarah. She shrugs sweetly, her eyes round and mischievous. "Where did you get this, Sarah?" we ask. Again not speaking, she points down the long corridor of the mall.

"I think she means the CD store," says Rachael, Sarah's official interpreter. Sarah nods her head. She had picked it up there and casually followed us right out of the store, her face firmly fixed on the cover. In our haste, we had not even noticed. Why an alarm didn't sound as we exited the store we'll never know. It was probably disarmed by her confident smile.

"Yes, every life of crime starts innocently!" I intone somberly. "The coveting, the taking, the slippery slope to self-destruction . . ." But I am joking. Sarah is as pure as wild mountain honey; she is a creature of Christopher Robin's Hundred-Acre Wood; she still lives with one foot in the Garden of Eden.

We traverse the mall once more, past the serious collectors' emporium and the apparel stores and the jewelry shops, down the great nave of the good ship *Mercantile,* back again to the CD and video mart and into line at the checkout counter. We charge the Pooh video and I place it into Sarah's outstretched arms. She holds it tightly, a chunk of rectangular plastic, like a favorite rag doll. She is contented.

But not forever. In time, her eyes will angle wide, her

tastes will complicate, her desires will augment. She will wander east of Eden, as sooner or later everyone does. My Sarah will join the great wilderness search for fulfillment that occupies all earthly days. Like the child Israel, she will seek a faithful framework for experiencing and sharing life's goodness. But she will not find it; it will not appear on a wall or roll off a tongue in a well-crafted speech. Instead, it will bubble to consciousness like an early memory — a clear recognition of what she has always known: that life is grace, and living it in cherished relation to God and neighbor is the only paradise. And Donna and I will have taught her these things, and she will have discovered them on her own, and they will have been the simple gift of God.

Today we have covered only a tiny corner of the downtown mall, a mere swatch of the pleasure-filled world of desire. But the lessons of this day are universal. All human life is like a shopping spree for meaning. Creation itself is busy seeking its beginning and end, its source and final purpose. It is a search fraught with turmoil, distraction, and heartache.

Yet, like the Hebrews, the original children of the wilderness, we carry with us a guide to conscience, a pattern for gracious relations within the world of others. It is a treasury of aspirations, hopeful words by which to live — Ten Words that ultimately are one: "I am the Lord your God. You shall have no other gods before me."

INDEX

T. WYATT WATKINS holds a master of divinity from Christian Theological Seminary (Indianapolis) and a bachelor of music in violin performance from Indiana University. In addition to writing, Wyatt has held various ministerial posts in Protestant churches in Indiana. He is a first violinist with the Indianapolis Chamber Orchestra. Wyatt has contributed to works on ethics for the Baptist Center for Ethics and has published two previous books, *Gospel, Grits, and Grace: Encountering the Holy in the Ridiculous, Sublime, and Unexpected* (Judson Press, 1999) and *How Sweet the Sound: Stories Inspired by the Hymns We Love* (Judson Press, 2001). He lives in Indianapolis with his wife and four children. In addition to writing, Wyatt Watkins enjoys a ministry of speaking.

If you would like more information, you can write to him at: 593 Woodruff Place West Drive, Indianapolis, Indiana 46201; or contact him via e-mail at watkinsdt@aol.com.

New World Library is dedicated to
publishing books and cassettes that inspire
and challenge us to improve the quality
of our lives and our world.
Our books and cassettes are available
at bookstores everywhere.
For a complete catalog, contact:

New World Library
14 Pamaron Way
Novato, California 94949

Phone: (415) 884-2100
Fax: (415) 884-2199
Or call toll free: (800) 972-6657
Catalog requests: Ext. 50
Ordering: Ext. 52

E-mail: escort@nwlib.com
www.newworldlibrary.com